DIGGING UP TR

DIGGING UP TROUBLE

THE ENVIRONMENT, PROTEST AND OPENCAST COAL MINING

HUW BEYNON, ANDREW COX AND RAY HUDSON

Rivers Oram Press
London, New York and Sydney

First published in 2000 by
Rivers Oram Press Limited
144 Hemingford Road, London N1 1DE

Distributed in the USA by
New York University Press
838 Broadway, New York, NY 10003-4812

Distributed in Australia by
UNIReps
University of New South Wales
Sydney, NSW 2052

Set in Baskerville by NJ Design Associates, Romsey, Hants
and printed in Great Britain by TJ (International) Ltd, Padstow, Cornwall

British Library Cataloguing in Publication Data
A catalogue record for this book is available from the British Library

ISBN (cloth) 1 85489 112 X
ISBN (paper) 1 85489 113 8

CONTENTS

GLOSSARY OF TERMS AND ABBREVIATIONS

ARA	Amsterdam Rotterdam Antwerp (ports)
BCC	British Coal Corporation
BCO	British Coal Opencast
BR	British Rail
CC	County Council
CCC	Coalfield Communities Campaign
CCGTs	Combined Cycle Gas Turbines
CHP	Combined Heat and Power
CEGB	Central Electricity Generating Board
CENE	Commission on Energy and the Environment
CICS	Coal Information and Consultancy Services Ltd
CPRE	Council for the Protection of Rural England
CO2	Carbon Dioxide
DoE	Department of the Environment
DETR	Department of the Environment, Transport and the Regions
DTI	Department of Trade and Industry
FGD	Flue Gas Desulphurisation
FoE	Friends of the Earth
GHGs	Greenhouse Gases
GJ	Gigajoule
HMSO	Her Majesty's Stationary Office (now called the Stationary Office)
LAAJMARG	Local Authorities Association Joint Minerals and Reclamation Group
MGR	Merry-Go-Round (train)
MAFF	Ministry of Agriculture, Fisheries and Food
MPA	Mineral Planning Authority

MPG	Mineral Planning Guidance
mt	million tonnes
MW	Megawatts
NCB	National Coal Board
NO$_x$	Nitrogen oxides
NUM	National Union of Mineworkers
OE	Opencast Executive
OFFER	Office of Electricity Regulation
PPG	Planning Policy Guidance
TGWU	Transport and General Workers' Union
UDM	Union of Democratic Mineworkers
UN	United Nations
UNECE	United Nations Economic Commission for Europe

LIST OF ILLUSTRATIONS

PREFACE

This book began as a piece of research funded by the ESRC (the UK Economic and Social Research Council) in 1988 to examine the growth and impact of opencast coal mining on local communities. During the 1980s each of us, in somewhat different ways, had been involved in research projects which touched upon the political economy of coal mining. Beynon had been funded by the ESRC to examine the political organisation and economic restructuring of the Durham coal-mining industry.[1] Hudson had been involved in similar researches[2] and in 1985 they worked together on part of the ESRC's research initiative into the Changing Urban and Regional System.[3] At that time Cox was involved in his PhD research at the Department of Chemical and Process Engineering at the University of Newcastle upon Tyne[4] which involved a consideration of opencast coal mining.

Throughout that decade coal mining seemed to be at the centre of major economic, social and political upheavals in the UK, most notably during the miners' strike which lasted a year from March 1984. During these twelve months, the opencast sites continued to work and this served to bring increased attention upon a form of mining which had a questionable impact upon the environment and upon people's lives. Public inquiries became more frequent and local councils and mineral planning authorities in the North East of England were increasingly concerned to obtain advice from 'experts' with a knowledge of the industry. In 1985 and 1986, for example Beynon gave evidence at five public inquiries. Subsequently, Andrew Cox, as consultant and editor of *UK Coal Review* has given evidence at over twenty such inquiries throughout the UK.

This book represents a genuinely interdisciplinary approach to the study of opencast mining. It is based upon detailed empirical researches including in-depth interviews with MPs and civil servants, local planners and county councillors, managers of opencast companies, members and officials of trade unions and of local protest groups. It also draws upon our own direct experiences of these events as (sometimes reluctant) participants in what has been the hurly burly of coal field politics.

It has taken us ten years to complete this text. In the politics of university research this is a terribly long time, spreading over three research assessment exercises! Over the period of our research the politics of coal 'on the ground' have changed, in their details, with alarming rapidity. Much of our time has been spent on 'keeping up' with the changes, interpreting them and digesting their meaning. Sometimes, good research takes time and it doesn't fit neatly into the cycles of RAEs. We hope you think that this book has been worth the wait and that even after ten years something worthwhile can be produced!

A final point about our sources. We have, of course drawn upon the academic literature and a range of secondary sources. In addition (and perhaps more importantly), our involvement in the 'day to day' details of the industry (made most clear in Cox's role as an editor) has given us access to materials which rarely appear as a published resource. These materials (press releases, planning decisions, public inquiry evidence and decisions, local council plans and reports, trade union and corporation policy documents) have become known as 'grey literature' and we have relied upon it heavily. This grey literature is an invaluable resource and provides the kinds of detailed access to the discourses and thinking process of participants rarely revealed in other forms of writing. It does, however, present a problem to the researcher in knowing how best to reference it. For example, these texts rarely acknowledge a publisher and often do not have a date of publication. We have chosen a form of footnoting which provides as much details as possible to the reader who might wish to track down any particular item.

Many people helped us for funding the research in many ways in the research. We need to thank the ESRC and our secretaries in Durham and Manchester, Joan Dresser and Anne Morrow who have kept us on the straight and narrow. Arthur Corner and his colleagues in the Cartography Section of the Durham Geography Department provided maps and diagrams. Ian Simmons also kindly and constructively commented upon the manuscript. What follows is a list of the others who are almost too many to mention: Eric Lee, Andrew James, the Rev. Jon Hale, Viv Hancock, Peter Carmichael, Pitch Wilson and the other members of the North East Opencast Action Group; Bill Etherington MP; Richard Bate (Green Balance); Bob Peck, Susan and Keiran Lee (SNAG); Michael Rainsbury and Adrian Walker; Valerie Gillespie (Notts CPRE); Brian and Angela Chamberlain; Alan Whiston (Brown Edge Opencast Action Group); Tim Sander and Elaine Gilligan (FoE); Andrew Towlerton and Chris Mallander (Rotherham MBC); Roger Kojan, Chris Brooking, Martin Seddon and Martin Clay (Wakefield MBC); Gordon Halliday, Chris Offord and Mary Campbell (Northumberland CC); Richard Simons and Miles Walker (Gateshead MBC); Graham Garnham (Blyth Valley BC); Richard Hurd and Stuart Provan (Durham CC); John Geldard (Lancashire CC); Andrew Farrow (Cheshire CC); Dennis McBride (Wigan MBC); Paul Wilcox and Jeff Rhodes (Staffordshire CC); Peter Kendall (Carmarthenshire CC); Joan Dixon and Dave Parry (CCC National Secretariat); Brian Parkin; Geoff Deeley, Cyrus Heppenstall and the members of the Tinsley Park Action Group; Peter Stringer (Tir Dafydd Action Group); Dr Mark Temple (Gwent Health Authority); Dr T. Pless-Mulloli, Maxine Craven and Professor Bhopal (University of Newcastle Medical School, Department of Epidemiology); Jacqui Tait; Lesley Rutherford and Derek Peart; Howard Armstrong (University of Durham); Jean Roberts (former postgraduate ICCET); Bill Fischer, Jenny Whysall, Mike Prior and Adam Simmons; Eric Wade and Andrew Trigg (Open University); Mark Hurst (Coal Services International); many members of the Bar and legal profession—including: Eric

Owens, John Barratt, Frances Patterson QC, Martin Kingston QC, Tina Douglas and Mark Heywood; and finally, Brent King and Hazel Cox. Ray Hudson would also like to acknowledge the generous award of a Sir Derman Christopherson Foundation Fellowship by the University of Durham for 1998–99 that allowed him time to complete work on the book.

INTRODUCTION

Over the last twenty years British society has changed dramatically. Basic industries have closed down and new ones opened up. More people go out to work but more are also unemployed. Those in work feel insecure about their future. In reflecting on these changes, sociologists have come to see contemporary society as a 'risk society'; one in which previous certainties have been eroded and where life now involves unpredictability and risk.[1] People marry knowing that the risk of divorce is high; they move to a new job, recognising the possibility that they will be made redundant; they take out a loan and worry that it may not be repaid. People worry about their health, about the available standard of medical care and the effects it will have on them and their children. Major decisions (especially financial ones) are weighed in the balance and cover is offered by private insurance policies. But some things cannot be insured against—most especially the risk of negative equity, the risk that house values drop below the level of the loan. This can happen for many reasons. Housing markets fluctuate with the financial and economic cycle; they are also affected by changes in local circumstances—the proximate routing of a new motorway, or an opencast coal site developed in the locality. For these and other reasons, 'the environment' has begun to figure more and more strongly as an issue of significant concern for people.

As the perceived certainties of the past have been weakened so too have questions been raised about the new world offered through the expansion of markets and private property. At one level there have been renewed worries over the capacity of expansionist industrial societies to put the future of the planet at risk. Worries about global warming increased and exacerbated by the apparent inability of scientists to agree on the level of danger involved, or of politicians to come up with a solution. In popular culture Hollywood contributed to these worries through films like *West World* in the 1970s through to *Blade Runner* and *Mad Max* and then *Terminator* and *Waterworld*, all of which emphasised the fallibility and unknown consequences of modern technological processes. At the more mundane level people experienced their daily lives blighted by traffic jams and new urban pollutants; they worried as asthma cases reached epidemic proportions. More generally, the worries that had once been fiercely expressed over the atom bomb seemingly became displaced towards nuclear energy and toxic wastes. People (especially women) worried and eventually protested, over the effects of these processes upon the health of those who lived near to atomic power stations or waste plants.

By the end of the 1980s, the environment had emerged as a major political issue. Opinion polls indicated that 75 per cent of voters in the UK perceived the government as not being sufficiently concerned about the environment. More significant perhaps was the finding by MORI that a substantial proportion of the population—about one-fifth—had their consciousness of environmental issues raised permanently in a way that had changed their lives. MORI's standard unprompted questions: 'What is the most important issue facing Britain today?' and 'What do you see as other important issues?', began to record changes in the late 1980s. In 1988 responses which mentioned 'the environment' peaked, with 30 per cent seeing this as the most important issue. At this time, only 14 per cent of people were involved in five or more 'green' activities (MORI's definition of a 'green activist'); in 1991 this peaked at 31 per cent. In the view of the *Independent's* columnist (10 September 1991):

> The changes made by these 'green activists' may not appear profound. They may have joined a pressure group, begun recycling bottles, cans and newspapers, switched to lead-free petrol. But they are starting to take the environment into

account in everyday choices and decisions. Green issues will affect what they buy, where they holiday, and how they vote— even if it's not for the Green Party. The activists tend to be younger, better educated and more affluent than average.

In reflecting upon these developments, social scientists began to write of a new 'environmental consciousness' and a changing relationship between individuals and their locality.[2]

In the 1980s opencast mining also took on a new significance within the British coal mining industry. Unlike deep mining, opencast (or 'strip' mining as it is known elsewhere) involves the removal of the earth that covers the coal seams and is, as a result, much more invasive of the countryside. The National Coal Board's Opencast Executive (building on its achievements under the Labour governments of the 1970s) entered a new and planned expansionist phase. This expansion was linked with the rise of a significant group of private coal companies, eager to develop coal extraction for profit. It took place at a time when the deep-mine sector of the industry was engulfed in a major crisis; one which precipitated a year-long strike by its miners, the closure of most of its capacity, and the privatisation of that which remained.

The ways in which these changes combined with people's emerging sensitivities to issues of the environment and the countryside is an interesting story that we tell in this book. At this point we should simply note that the Council for the Protection of Rural England (CPRE) has described opencast mining as: 'one of the most environmentally destructive processes being carried out in the UK'.[3] It shared this view with the Coalfield Communities Campaign. The CCC was a formalised group of local authorities established in the wake of the closure of the deep mines with the view to establishing a common policy on the future economic and social development of the coal districts. It claimed that opencast mining had become:

one of the most damaging forms of land use [having] a major detrimental impact on the quality of life in surrounding settlements.[4]

This view was presented in *The Opencast Charter* which aimed at establishing 'an acceptable framework for opencast coal mining'. In arguing this case it pointed to the ways in which the statutory planning system needed to adapt to cope with the changes that were taking place in the coal industry and the environments of the coal districts.

This book is about the social, legal and environmental context and impacts of the UK coal mining industry. It focuses on the ways in which opencast mining has become more significant and how local communities and politicians have become antagonistic to it. We demonstrate how the processes of decline, privatisation and diversification are linked, and how these relationships have affected the perceptions of local people and the manner in which they have protested against them. As such the book focuses attention upon a number of broader and large-scale processes at work in contemporary society. For example:

■ Coal is a valuable mineral; the total reserves lodged in seams near the surface are finite and limited. Are short-term market forces (the fact that the mineral can be sold for a profit) the best ways of determining the use of this resource?

■ The contemporary state has been concerned to privatise state-owned assets and to cease operating as an economic agent. However it still seeks to regulate and control social and economic behaviour. These controls are conducted through detailed administrative apparatuses which respond to and are influenced by the context within which they operate. In the case of the opencast industry regulation has historically involved two national ministries (Energy and the Environment), a National Planning Inspectorate and a variety of Mineral Planning Authorities (MPAs) run by different political parties. The ways in which these forces come together to deal with particular local issues is of considerable interest; the ways in which they relate to something which might be termed a national policy is even more so.

■ The right to dissent has been viewed as one of the defining characteristics of British society. The question of dissent also invites questions of protest, organisation and mobilisation. How, in the context of unwelcome developments, do people register their dissent? How do people move from apathy and acceptance toward dissent and protest? In this process, access to knowledge has become increasingly important. With it come questions as to how people obtain the knowledge that will allow them to contest decisions that have been taken within a complex planning system, often involving public inquiries calling upon the views of 'experts'.

It was made very clear to us, in the public inquiries we attended, that there was little basis for consensus in relation to planning permission for opencast sites. Disagreement existed at almost every level. Even the most elementary questions relating to coal output, coal sales and the types of coals mined (points which you might think would be easily resolved via 'official statistics') were vigorously disputed. Our observations here, and our involvement in a variety of different meetings, convinced us that the issues involved in these disputes were symptomatic of broader changes. Certainly there were (as there always have been) conflicting interests involved, but since the late 1980s it seemed that these conflicts were being organised within different parameters, with new and unusual alliances being formed. In places where opencast mines had previously worked without protest, residents become recalcitrant and opposed to new schemes. In new areas, the experience of other neighbourhoods was sought and discussed.

A number of processes were at work in producing these changes. The move from state-owned to private industry can easily be presented as a clear-cut change from state bureaucratic monopolies to innovative entrepreneurs. However in presenting change in this way, it shouldn't be forgotten that many state-owned industries worked hand in glove with private capital. This is particularly the case with regard to the opencast sector of coal mining where the state (as owner of the coal) was involved in its extraction through the operations of private contractors. In this context, new coal companies emerged, and local hauliers and contractors benefitted considerably. Local people observed these developments and, as 'the market' has become more pervasive and self interest more openly disclosed, many of them have questioned their past tolerance and asked 'What about me? What about my interests?' These people, with no direct interests as producers or consumers of coal (and thereby excluded from the market), discovered an alternative language based on the rights of people as 'citizens' and upon people's responsibilities to each other and to the environment.

For generations, people in these areas have lived amongst the grime of industrial production, accepting the need for environmental pollution as a necessary part of economic activity. Yet in the wake of the closures of collieries and steel mills a different kind of language emerged. Ex-miners and steel workers talked of the 'human environment' and the future of their families in a world without mining and heavy industry. In this context the arguments which were used to justify the closure of these industries are turned back upon developments which attempt to resuscitate them in new forms. While older people may look back upon their past with some fondness, they are clear that it can't be repeated and that their children and grandchildren need something else; something different. These perceptions and sensibilities are often shared (but not always, as we shall see) by local planners and developers. In the heart of Durham, for example, the Derwentside Industrial Development Agency was charged with the task of repairing the damage done to the local economy as a result of the closure of the steel works at Consett. On occasions this organisation supported planners and local people in their opposition to opencast mining, arguing that new economic developments in the district would be hampered by the presence of such mines. In their turn, the opencast contractors have argued that the sites could be developed as significant tourist attractions.

The economic and social structures of the old coal districts changed dramatically in the 1980s. Where areas such as these were once dominated by manual, 'blue collar' workers, increasing numbers (and now the great majority) are employed in new jobs ('white collar' or, more accurately, 'blue blouse' jobs) in the new manufacturing and service sectors. Commuting has accompanied these developments, and the old coal districts formed the sites for many homes for first-time buyers, as well as the often substantial properties of a new managerial class. They were also attractive locations for 'telecommuters': professionals, 'working from home' with the aid of a computer. In short, many of these places went through a form of gentrification involving a mixture of retired manual workers, employees in the new industries (often occupying two-income households) and members of the professional and managerial middle classes. In addition to any attachment these people may have to the place in which they live and its local environment, they also, as house owners, have a financial interest in resisting the encroachment of opencast sites. It has been to this interest (with promises of land restoration and the construction of golf courses and other kinds of local amenities) that the mining companies have addressed themselves. These promises and developments, however, have often failed to offset people's fears.

These issues involving questions relating to the mobilisation of protest, the nature of 'single issue politics' and questions of political legitimacy are critical ones for our society. A study such as this can therefore be read in two ways: narrowly, it can be seen as a helpful guide to the issues and questions being raised throughout the exposed coalfield areas of the UK, and as a kind of 'handbook' for people involved in tackling these issues. Generally, it can be seen as more broadly applicable and understood as a story of our time.

1. Opencast at work

I
TWO INDUSTRIES IN ONE
OPENCAST AND DEEP MINING

In the postwar period, the coal industry became equated, in the public mind, with nationalisation. However, the sale of the British Coal Corporation in 1993 made clear that a significant private coal industry already existed in Britain. While BCC had the monopoly of deep-coal mines, private capital flourished through the production of coal from small-scale, shallow drift mines and surface or opencast mines (referred to as sites). The growth of this sector and of a powerful group of independent coal producers is one of the more interesting aspects of postwar industrial history.

HISTORICAL ORIGINS

Opencast mining is found in those portions of the UK coalfields where the coal seams either reach the surface (outcrop) or exist at relatively shallow depths (see p.11). Unlike deep mining, which reaches the coal through underground workings, opencast sites mine the coal from the surface (see p.12). For this reason, the deep miners in the UK came to refer to the opencast workers as 'sunshine miners'. The difference in mining techniques produced different kinds of mine organisations and cultures. This was exacerbated in the UK by financial and legal processes which are complicated and have been subjected to a variety of significant changes. The issues derive from the fact that coal is a mineral, embedded in seams in the ground. Since the mid 1930s, this mineral has been owned by the state, and for most of this period it has been a part of the monopoly of the National Coal Board and its successor British Coal.

However the owners of the coal have not been directly involved in opencast mining operations. These have been conducted by private civil engineering and coal concerns either under licence or sub-contract to the coal owners.

Prior to the Second World War only limited opencast activity took place, normally as an adjunct to the quarrying of clay or other minerals. Coal output was probably less than 1 mt per year, but this increased during the coal shortages of the war years. Under a temporary emergency measure in 1941 wartime authorised contractors were paid for each ton of coal produced.

Initial surveys in the latter half of 1941 indicated that sufficient reserves existed to make such a scheme feasible. Potential sites were identified and an eleven point action plan was drawn up. The first two 'official' sites started in the autumn of 1941. Within seven months 40 contractors were working 22 sites and a further 63 sites had been identified.

Surface mining involved the state taking powers in relation to the possession of the land, and the restriction of access to it while it was being worked. These arrangements were initially handled through the Defence of the Realm Act (1939), supported in 1942 by Defence Regulation 51A which dealt specifically with opencasting, and regularised through the Ministry of Fuel and Power. Then, in a way which was to prefigure much of the industry's future, responsibility was shifted to a newly formed Directorate of Opencast Coal Production within the Ministry of Works and Planning. Under these arrangements, all coal produced was purchased by the Ministry of Fuel and Power. The task of organising and supervising opencast mining did, in fact, return to this Ministry in 1945. This complex arrangement, established in a time of emergency, was to provide the basic framework for the future development of the industry. It would accompany the industry into nationalisation.

The Coal Industry Nationalisation Act (1946) confirmed that the ownership of the coal and the coal industry would be vested with the NCB. The Board (as it became generally known in the coalfields) owned the mineral rights to almost all coal, at all depths.[1] The Act confirmed that opencast mining would continue to be conducted by the privately owned civil engineering

FIGURE 1
The exposed coalfield

Areas of shallow
deposits of coal

FIGURE 2

Opencast and deep mining compared

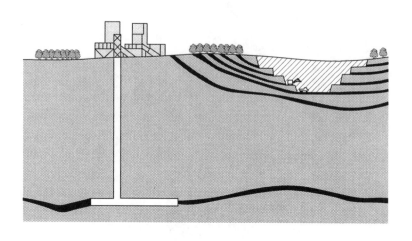

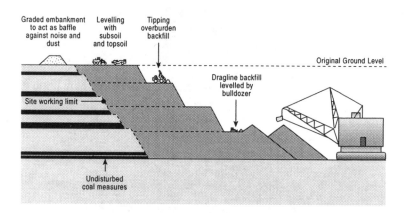

industry. It also established the distinction between opencast sites run by contractors to produce coal for the NCB, and 'private licenced' sites, which would be allowed to mine and sell 'nationalised' coal on the open market with payment of a licence fee to the Board. While there was no size limitation placed on the former, the Act restricted the size of the private licenced sites to 25,000 tonnes. At the time, most sites were under 10,000 tonnes so this figure was not seen as a restraint on the development of this sector. Neither was it seen as contentious.

In 1946, it was agreed that the coal industry would be dominated and organised by the state owned corporation and the Ministry of Fuel and Power. This was reinforced in 1952 when the Ministry transferred the control of its opencast sites to the NCB's newly formed Opencast Executive. The OE had its own budget and was responsible for the effective organisation of opencast production. It says much for the continuity of these times that this transfer did not affect established organisational procedures in the industry. Nor did it serve to raise questions about the aberrant legal position of the opencast sector in the mining industry.

Under the OE, the NCB continued to use contractors for site operations rather than develop its own large-scale site workforce. During these early days the quality of coal produced on opencast sites was often very poor and restoration was frequently of a low standard. Some of these 'restored' sites are still eyesores today. Consequently, the opencast sector developed a bad image and was most usually seen as marginal to the 'real' coal industry and dominated by the activities of 'cowboy' contractors. Nevertheless, the sector continued to produce additional revenues for the Board, and there seemed little for it to gain by involving itself directly in mining operations in which it had little expertise. The OE was to concentrate on prospecting, acquiring land and organising sites prior to development. It subsequently developed a series of coal disposal sites where site contractors delivered the coal they had extracted. For its part, the National Union of Mineworkers (NUM) made no attempt to organise opencast workers into the union. As 'sunshine miners' they were seen to be 'in' but not 'of' the industry. Will Paynter was President of the South Wales area in this period, and it was clear, in discussions with him, that these workers were seen as a temporary adjunct to the industry and entirely marginal to the operation of the deep mines which were the fulcrum of the newly created NCB. His view was a general one.

Thus at the fringes of the NCB, a private, but dependent, system of production was established as a part of the state-owned industry. These arrangements were consolidated in a separate act of parliament (The Opencast Coal Act (1958)) which formalised many of the industry's established practices and confirmed that opencast had a permanent place within the affairs of the coal-mining industry. However, it was badly affected during the coal crisis of the late 1950s and 1960s. At a time when half the deep mines were being closed, the activities of the OE were restricted to a few large contract sites and a number of smaller ones producing scarce special coals such as anthracite. However, under the leadership of Alf Robens, Chairman of the NCB, the sector was reorganised and as the markets for coal strengthened opencast output increased rapidly: 6.17mt in 1967 to 10mt in 1973. Thus, on the eve of *Plan for Coal*, the OE of the NCB felt in a strong position to argue for an increase in opencast tonnage. By this time it was pushing at an open door.[2]

THE *PLAN FOR COAL*

The 1974 *Plan For Coal* was a blithely optimistic document, which argued (from little evidence) that market demand for coal would increase as part of a general and continuing movement away from oil in an expanding energy market. Output was planned accordingly to increase from 110 to 135m tons by 1985 and to 200m tons by the end of the century. Although new deep mines (notably the complex at Selby in North Yorkshire) were to be sunk, there was apprehension over the possibility of the existing mines increasing output sufficiently in the short term.

Opencast mining, being more quickly adaptable, was to make up any shortfall. But this was no more than a general feeling. The specific figures (involving 15 million tons of opencast coal each year) came from an *ad hoc* arrangement within the tripartite committee that produced the *Plan* and many analysts now see it as little more than a 'back of an envelope' calculation. It was a calculation which was nonetheless to become significant. It was one which was based upon a growing strength and confidence within the OE, and which came at a time when civil engineering companies were geared up to the task of earning profits in coal mining. In this sense the *Plan for Coal's* assessment of the supply potential of the private sector (back of the envelope or not) was correct. It was potentially the most accurate part of the whole *Plan*.

Perhaps this was the most surprising feature of the implementation of the *Plan for Coal*. Despite clear signs that the underlying market assumptions were badly flawed, no attempt was made to scale down the planned output of 15mt from opencast sites. This growing output was allowed to contribute to an increasing surplus of coal supply. In this the OE was aided by (often Labour controlled) local authorities, sympathetic to the idea of a national plan, but clearly uninformed about the changed market situation. As such, detailed regional targets, deriving from the *Plan for Coal*, were used by the OE to justify the opening of new sites. Local planners found such targets compelling and gave these requests a sympathetic hearing. For their part, the contractors with investment tied up in physical plant were pressing for expansion to be maintained.

Consequently, opencast output reached the 15mt target in 1980—roughly five years ahead of schedule. It maintained this level of production through the 1980s and then proceeded to exceed it (see Table 1). As a result it increased its share of UK coal production—both absolutely and relatively. In 1980 opencast production represented 12 per cent of the total UK coal output. By 1988 this had increased to over 17 per cent of total output (17.9mt), most of which supplied the power station market.

THE EXPANSION OF OPENCAST PRODUCTION

During the 1960s the opencast sector had gone through a period of major reconstruction. Systematic research commenced into improving restoration techniques and site operations, and new production techniques were developed. Previously the technical limitations of war surplus earth moving equipment had restricted sites to shallow depths of excavation, removing only the coal seams immediately below the surface. However with the introduction of larger custom-built equipment, the cost of moving the covering top soil and sub-strata ('the overburden') decreased dramatically. As a result the economic exploitation of deeper seams, with depths of up to 150 metres, became possible and with it the expansion of the opencast sector. For its part, the OE, with the support of the NCB's Chairman Alf Robens, became better managed and organised to secure such an expansion.

A key indicator of the changes in the working pattern of the opencast sector was the increasing overburden ratio— the ratio of coal extracted to overburden excavated on a site. In the 1940s the ratio was typically 1:6 (one tonne of coal to six tonnes of overburden). This increased over the next 30 years to overburden ratios of up to 1:30. Eventually the barrier to higher ratios worked on sites was the saleable value of the coal rather than the technical capacity of the machinery. Consequently, the production process associated with opencast mining has had to be a pragmatic one influenced by the price of coal and the geological structure of the site. As the OE put it:

> The selection of equipment for the opencast mining operation is a complex decision in which many factors have to be taken into account. The area and depth of the site are foremost amongst these factors together with the contract tonnage and working life of the site. Total volumes and rates of extraction of overburden can then be related to the type of overburden to be removed, the dip and strike of the strata

TABLE 1

NCB/BCC Deep-mine and opencast output (mt) 1971–94

Financial Year	Deep-Mines	Opencast
1971/72	135.5	8.1
1975/76	114.5	10.4
1980/81	110.3	15.3
1985/86	88.4	14.1
1990/91	72.3	17.0
1993/94*	42.7	13.5

* last full year prior to privatisation
SOURCE: NCB/BCC *Annual Reports and Accounts*

and seam, the extent of geological faulting and the thickness of the strata between seams.[3]

In spite of these necessary variabilities, it is possible to outline the processes generally involved in the mining of an opencast site. These methods remained remarkably consistent throughout the 1960s and 1970s. Initially, the overburden masking the first coal seam is removed through the use of electric rope shovels. These involved scraping the surface with a large steel bucket. The operation which followed has been well described by Hancock:

> the typical scheme involves a series of parallel cuts which progress across the site. The first cut (known as the box cut) is usually the widest and also the shallowest. The reason for starting at the shallow end is that until coal is extracted the operation is intensely cash negative…the shallowest coal is the cheapest to mine so the two activities quickly balance each other out.[4]

This first cut excavates coal, seam by seam, using hydraulic shovels which dig out the coal and the overburden, transferring both to dump trucks which transport them to the surface. Given the depth of the hole, ramps are constructed along which the trucks travel. Once the second cut is excavated, a step is formed between it and the box cut. Large multi-seam sites are therefore characterised by a series of downward steps, each seam or series of seams being worked at the level of each step (see Figure 2). These steps also facilitate the movement of the dump trucks and the use of drag lines. A drag line essentially combines the function of the shovel and the dump truck. A huge, bucket-like construction with a serrated edge is attached to a chain and a jib. It is dragged along the surface of the coal seam, and once filled it is swung out of the hole and on to the stock pile:

> A drag line can be introduced into the operation once the second cut is excavated and a step is formed between cuts one and two....The benefit of drag lines is that they reduce the requirements for other plant, especially dump trucks. The alternative to the drag line is at least two shovels and six dump trucks.[5]

Clearly decisions on whether to use a drag line are related to scale. Until privatisation in 1994, they were mainly associated with the sites organised by the OE which, as a result, took on a different appearance and method of organisation to the smaller licenced sites.

Such was the financial return on opencast mining that the major plant and equipment producing companies rapidly extended and developed their machinery. This had a major impact upon the organisation of production on opencast sites in the UK. In the words of the OE, the 1980s was a decade:

> during which time the excavating and haulage equipment being selected by opencast mining contractors has changed significantly to meet the challenge of an increasingly competitive market.[6]

Two major changes illustrate the trend. To begin with, the number of drag lines in operation declined significantly from

TABLE 2
Drag lines in operation on UK opencast sites 1980–89

Size of bucket m³	1980	1989
10>	73	23
10–25	9	11
<25	2	3
Total	84	37

SOURCE: *Mine and Quarry*, January/February 1991

84 in 1980 to 37 in 1989. Most of this reduction related to those with buckets sized under 10 cubic metres (see Table 2). BCC replaced its aging stock of Bacyrus Erie 1150B drag lines with new Bacyrus 1260Ws and the huge Ransom and Rapier W2000 with a bucket size of 27.5 cubic metres. In 1989 the largest drag line in operation was employed at the Butterwell site in Northumberland, operated by Taylor Woodrow Construction Ltd. Known as 'Big Geordie':

the machine weighs 2,900 tonnes and has a bucket capacity of 50m³ which is equivalent to the largest capacity dump truck used in the British Isles. Given the cycle time for a bucket pass in the hands of an experienced operator is in the region of one minute, the economies of the operation over the use of the shovel and truck are enormous.[7]

By 1995 'Big Geordie' had been overtaken by the 'Ace of Spades' on the Stobswood site in Northumberland as the country's biggest drag line, testament to the fact that these developments were ongoing and enduring.

The intensification of drag line activity was but one aspect of change. Perhaps the biggest change in opencast production related to the development of new diesel hydraulic shovels by three German companies (O&K, Demag and Liebherr) with huge shovels and increasing stability and maneouverability. As the number of drag lines decreased the number of shovels

TABLE 3

Rigid dump trucks in operation on opencast sites 1980–90

Capacity	1980	1990
50 tonnes	409	138
85 tonnes	113	431
over 100 tonnes	–	45

SOURCE: *Mine and Quarry*, January/February 1991

increased (from 64 to 132 in 1989) with a significant expansion in their average bucket capacity. The giant Demag H485 with a bucket capacity of 25 cubic metres contrasted remarkably with the machine that had dominated the industry in the 1970s and 1980s, the Caterpillar 245, with a bucket capacity of just 3.8 cubic metres. As a consequence of this development in shovel technology the size of dump trucks also increased.

In 1980, opencast sites were dominated by dump trucks of 50 tonne capacity, and the Terex R50 was the most likely vehicle to catch your eye. Ten years later production had been revolutionised with large 85 tonne capacity trucks dominating alongside Caterpillar 785 and 789 trucks with a capacity of 135 tonnes and 170 tonnes, respectively (see Table 3).

A similar process applied to the stock of electric rope shovels. By the end of the decade, the industry had consolidated around large- and medium-sized buckets. The Lima 2400B and the Manitowoc 4600, both with 5.4 cubic metre buckets, were increasingly scrapped and replaced with more powerful machines.

These changes reflected, in part, the strong concern by BCC to have aging machinery replaced by 'long life, high cost items of plant'. In pursuit of this end, it entered into a policy of purchasing these items and supplying them to contractors on particular sites. In justifying this development it argued that:

> this policy applies in particular to drag lines as contractors are unable to purchase machines of this size given the short

life of a single site with no guarantee of continuity. The decision to invest in drag lines is based on the return of the investment obtained by contractors tendering competitive prices based on the lower operating costs of drag lines.[8]

The precise rules governing these arrangements were obscure, and reflected a general tendency for the OE to enter into financial arrangements with opencast contractors which can best be described as 'flexible'. In this particular instance it indicated the way in which BCC (as the owner and purchaser of the coal) purposively became involved in restructuring the productive process by encouraging and financially subsidising the purchase of new machinery. In the view of the financial director of the OE at the time:

> With drag lines of 'Big Geordie's' ilk costing up to £18m, and given the relatively short life of a single site with no guarantee of continuity, contractors are not always willing to purchase. In order to overcome this and to ensure the cheapest method of operation the Corporation identifies a series of two or three sites for which a drag line will be required, purchases the appropriate machine and builds the use of that machine into the tender documents for the contracts in question.

He added:

> improvement in productivity has been forced upon the civil engineering industry as much by the general slackness in the areas of major road and building contracts as the instinct to increase profits. This has been evidenced by the fact that several contractors have been the subject of takeovers.[9]

Therefore at a time when all public attention was directed towards the deep mines, major changes were taking place in the other part of the coal industry which were to assume critical importance. By 1989 the opencast sector was much more capital intensive, with much heavier and more reliable machinery; it was also poised to make a major leap forward.

**2. Baffle banks at the end of the garden —
living with opencast**

Productivity had increased sharply with larger amounts of coal
and overburden being discharged more quickly and with fewer
workers. These changes were seen most dramatically in the
decade which straddled the coal miners' strike of 1984/5.
Between financial year 1978/79 and financial year 1987/88,
output from OE sites increased from 13.8 to 15.1mt, while average manpower fell from 6267 to 4507. This represented an
increase in output per manshift from 9.6 tonnes to 14.6 tonnes.
Profit per tonne had stood at £5.73 in 1976/77; it had
increased to £16.71 in 1987/88. These changes emphasised
the attractiveness of opencast operations to BCC and also
served to place further pressure for productivity increases upon
workers in the deep mines.

CHANGING PARAMETERS

In the wake of the strike that had hit the deep mines in 1984
and 1985 the newly named British Coal Corporation (BCC)
adopted a radically different approach to the business of producing coal. Termed the *New Strategy For Coal*, it made clear that

costs were to be the dominant criterion for determining future coal production. In this new context it indicated that production from opencast sites was highly advantageous. It was its stated view that the Corporation needed to 'maximise output in our low cost collieries and opencast sites as a means of reducing average costs'.

In 1986 BCC introduced a new method of measuring cost of production—basing it not on cost per tonne but cost per unit of energy. On the basis of this measure (cost per gigajoule) the Corporation estimated that the average cost of producing opencast coal was £1.09/GJ with about one-fifth of the tonnage below £0.52/GJ. The operating profit from these mines was £28.84 per tonne.[10] In its evidence to the Energy Select Committee, it stated:

> In view of the economic, strategic, and marketing advantages, the Board plan at least to maintain the present level of output and to increase it where additional low cost output becomes available.[11]

This view was reiterated and strengthened in its subsequent statement *Opencast Coal—A National Assessment*[12] in which it suggested a production target of 18mt per annum for the OE. At this time it made it clear that it felt that the main obstacle to achieving this target lay in the planning system.

Profits from its opencast operations had always been important for the nationalised coal corporation. In the years before 1971/2:

> deep mining produced only about half of the NCB's accumulated operating profit of £450m, whereas £138m came from the far smaller opencast sector. From 1972 the contrast in profits in favour of opencast was enormous.[13]

In 1978, when the NCB's deep mines made an operating loss of £13.2m, the OE produced a profit of £88m. By 1986, there was an operating profit of £41m from the deep mines and one of £224m from opencasting. Interest charges had risen to

£386m and as such these opencast profits became increasingly important as the Government intensified the financial constraints under which BCC operated. In 1987 the requirement to break-even on operating costs, as a prelude to privatisation, represented a distinct tightening of the financial screw. As Prior and McCloskey noted:

> A large and increasing volume of opencast coal profits is essential if BCC is to have any chance of meeting the Government aim of breaking even in 1988/89 after interest payments and whilst financing all investment from internally generated funds. There is simply no way to increase deep mine profitability in such a short time.[14]

Whilst success was by no means guaranteed, increasing opencast profits represented BCC's only hope of meeting the financial targets set by the Government.

Not only were BCC's opencast operations very profitable—'the OE is currently one of the most profitable mining operations in the world'[15]—but the profits were very easily come by. The system established in wartime continued. Contractors would bid to the OE for extraction contracts for each site. If successful, they would be paid a fixed fee per tonne produced and delivered to BCC, which took a slice of the profit. On the small licensed sites contractors paid a 'royalty' per tonne extracted (about £14 per tonne in 1988) and were allowed to sell the coal on the market, BCC retaining the payment as a form of tithe which contributed to its overall balance sheet.[16] In all of this, BCC reaped a revenue which derived from its formal ownership of the coal, from very little financial outlay as it was not directly involved in the mining of the coal. Its opencast operations provided profit from a minimal investment on its part. It was an economic rent. Any risks involved were passed on to the private contractors. As Peter Cotgrove put it:

> I know contractors' profit margins aren't very good, but that's

their problem. We aren't forcing them to tender and from what I can see they're still eager for work.[17]

Given these arrangements, it was not surprising that BCC argued that opencast coal was cheaper to produce and more profitable to market than deep-mined coal.

A NEW PRIVATE SECTOR

The expansion of BCC's opencast profits related to the activities of the private companies that dug out the coal on opencast sites. Historically, these had been off-shoot activities of large civil engineering companies like Taylor Woodrow, Wimpey and French Kier. In the 1980s these companies still dominated production on the BCC sites. However, they were facing intense competition in the tendering process from a number of specialised private coal companies. Sometimes referred to as the 'second division', smaller operators, like H.J. Banks, Coal Contractors, and R.&A. Young, became a critical source of dynamism in the sector, often outbidding their 'first division' competitors for BCC sites whilst continuing to expand in the 'licensed' sector.

The small licensed sector, operating alongside the BCC sites, had spanned a large number of small operators, often related to the road haulage industry. Over time, and with the financial benefits becoming clearer, these firms became larger and developed licensed mining in ways which some had anticipated. Whilst the greatest tonnages continued to be produced in OE sites, output on these grew by only 5 per cent between 1983/84 and 1987/88 whilst on licensed sites it grew by 90 per cent. Whereas output from licensed sites represented 6.5 per cent of saleable opencast output in 1983/84, by 1987/88 it had risen to 11.3 per cent. This pattern of increases in the level of licensed site output and its relative share of opencast production was general in all regions except the Central West. This pattern continued into the 1990s, and was maintained in spite of the continued limitation on the size of these licensed sites. Within its general pattern of expansion, however, it remained heavily concentrated in the North East of England and in Scotland, where in 1990 it contributed 33 per cent and 20 per cent, respectively, of total opencast production.

In the North East, a number of small, dynamic companies had emerged, determined to retain and expand their place in the coal sector. They worked within the local political parameters, challenging them when they were seen to be interfering with their incremental growth. In 1980 they were active in forming the National Association of Licence Opencast Operators which subsequently acted as a highly effective lobbying group for the private sector. Theirs was a determinedly neo-liberal agenda which was encouraged by the rhetoric of the newly elected Conservative government. In this context, companies such as H.J. Banks & Co., the Young Group and A. J. Budge thrived. In doing so they gained great publicity for themselves and for their views favouring the privatisation of the industry and the expansion of opencast mining. Other companies (most notably John Mowlem and Ryan International) were attracted into the industry and others such as Christian Hotson encouraged to the view that the private sector was on an upward trend.[18] However, there were some upsets along the way. The Young Group suffered a crisis in 1989 and the company was taken over by RJB Mining in 1993. This transaction brought Richard Budge to centre stage in the unfolding drama of coal privatisation.

Budge had been involved in opencast mining since it was awarded its first contract by the NCB in 1974. It continued as a contractor for the OE and only commenced mining under licence in 1982. This signalled a general expansion of the A. F. Budge Group in the coal mining sector. It was involved in a number of major applications for opencast mining, including the OE site at Tinsley Park. In 1991 the company produced 15 per cent of British Coal's opencast output, a share exceeded only by Ryan International. The 'second division' had taken over. The extent of Budge's growth was made clear by the purchase of Blenkinsopp Colliery in 1990. At that time, Young was also expanding his interests in private drift mines, and in this way these two private coal companies were positioning themselves for the possible purchase of BCC's mines as they became available.

In February 1992, Richard Budge led a management buy-out of the coal-mining activities and related plant business of the A. F. Budge Group and established RJB Mining as a dedicated coal company. The collapse of the R.&A. Young Group allowed Budge to capitalise on the experience of both companies and promote his ambitions for RJB. Commenting at the time Budge said he was:

> delighted to have made this acquisition which increased our long term supply to the power generators and provides substantial new coal reserves. The businesses have a complementary fit with our own and we are confident that their performance will improve significantly as part of the RJB Group.[19]

Its share-offer document of the following year described the company's development in the following way:

> RJB was floated on the London Stock Exchange in May 1993 and has expanded to become one of the largest private sector coal companies operating in the UK. The private mining business of Young's was acquired in December 1993 which provided RJB with additional supply contracts with National Power. Subsequently the group acquired Monkton, a manufacturer of smokeless fuel for the industrial and domestic markets. The Group's expansion into deep mining operations has continued with the lease and licence of three former British Coal collieries at Clipstone, Rossington and Calverton in the last year. These collieries had been closed by British Coal.[20]

These words were written at the time of privatisation, and convey the importance attached by RJB to the company's dynamic development as a private operator in a coal industry dominated by the state-owned corporation. It also makes clear the salience which market contracts had come to have in the coal industry. This was not going to go away.

AN INDUSTRY TRANSFORMED

The rise of RJB was not accidental. As with the rise of the private sector in general, it was a highly politicised development. In an interview we conducted with him in 1995 Budge reflected on how the process of lobbying and government decision-making had operated in a way which was mutually reinforcing.

> This company has been gearing itself up for the privatisation of BCC for nearly seven years. Ever since Parkinson's speech mentioning the 'ultimate privatisation'. That is when we started working toward this. It was behind every step we have taken.[21]

For Budge, and the other private companies, these steps involved a reassessment of established divisions between the private and the public sectors, with the ultimate aim of transcending them. In the context of the Conservative Government's avowed intention to privatise the state-owned industry, this was a real possibility and the private companies were the most persistent advocate for such a change.

Privatisation was a complex and long drawn out process (see p.32). The Coal Industry Act (1994)[22] involved the transfer of the ownership of the coal reserves to a new regulatory body, the Coal Authority, which would be the main licensing body for all coal mining activities in deep mines and on opencast sites. The mining activities of BCC (deep-mined and opencast) would be sold off as five regional mining businesses. A 'pre-qualification process' to assess the capacity and fitness of potential bidders was established. This took place during the early summer of 1994, and was followed by a round of bidding from successful candidates.

Malcolm Edwards, once Marketing Director for the NCB and BCC, was one of the hopeful bidders. In the run-up to privatisation Edwards had already leased four of the mines closed by BCC, through Coal Investments plc. In the words of his 'profile' writer, he was 'The man who would be King Coal'.[23] However it was not to be. The industry was to be sold to a man with no direct connections with BCC; a man who had made his money in the opencast sector of the industry—Richard Budge.

During the privatisation period Richard Budge had taken a high political profile. For example, on 10 September 1993, he landed by helicopter—RJB Mining logo clearly visible—in the centre of Doncaster Racecourse in the middle of the race meeting. He was accompanied by Lord Wakeham, Tory Leader in the House of Lords and a Cabinet Minister. According to a statement by Stephen Byers MP, reported in *Hansard*:

> Budge met the Minister for Industry and Energy, who is responsible for coal privatisation, to discuss matters relating to that privatisation. Those meetings were all held at important and strategic times: 17 June 1992, 29 June 1992, 1 March 1993, 26 March 1993, 15 April 1993, 15 June 1993 and 7 July 1994. [24]

On 12 October 1994, RJB Mining was named by the government as the preferred bidder for what remained of the English coalfield.[25]

The unsuccessful bidders were openly disappointed and angry at the decision. In late 1994 the media and technical press carried a series of stories either attacking Richard Budge himself or the logic and economic viability of RJB Mining's bid for the English industry. However, despite these continuing attacks, RJB Mining managed to raise the £400m in bank loans and also raise a further £400m in a major share placing. In the words of *The Times*:

> Richard Budge, chief executive of RJB Mining has pulled it off. Instead of being cold shouldered by the City, he has won support for his £400m share issue.[26]

RJB had won the auction for the English mines by offering significantly more than its rivals—£900m subsequently reduced to £815m following negotiations with the DTI. The company claimed that its financial projections for future revenues were realistic although based upon more favourable assumptions than many people thought reasonable. Much of the disagreement related to the assumed productivity of the mines and the long-term stability of the coal market. After closing many of its high-cost mines BCC managed to increase productivity from about 700 to over 2,000 tonnes per man/year. In its share prospectus RJB Mining provided projections for productivity at the mines acquired from BCC. Productivity was forecast to increase to over 3,300 tonnes per man/year in FY 1999/2000. Certainly, if RJB could achieve such levels of productivity gain then it could well maintain its market share in the face of other competition. At the time it seemed reasonable, however, to agree with the conclusion of *The Times*:

> There is no doubt that the company's future is open to interpretation. Its future revenue flows vary according to the assumptions used. Mr Budge claims that he used conservative assumptions while his critics claim that the assumptions are optimistic. The truth will emerge in about five-years' time.[27]

What was indisputable, in the new dawn of privatisation, was the fact that the coal industry was going to remain a difficult industry in which to survive. Enormous competitive pressures (from major international corporations and from different fuel sources) would have an effect upon both the new private companies and the older ones which had been expanding profitably in the opencast sector. In the view of one analyst:

RJB's experience in opencasting will provide it with an economic benchmark against which it will judge the performance of its new deep mines.... The nineteen collieries (plus eight leased to other companies) is significantly more than most commentators predicted for the industry back in 1992. The number can only be maintained by lower rates of production (as has been witnessed in Coal Investment's pits). In the long term RJB should be looking to maximise production at the cheapest pits and reduce the portfolio where markets cannot support it.[28]

The emergence of RJB Mining as the new 'King Coal' raised questions within the opencast sector. Would Budge continue with the OE's practice of establishing sites and inviting tenders? One view in 1995 was that:

It is probable that RJB will decide to retain the services of the competitive contract to spread the workload and, in some respects, the risk.[29]

And this seems to have been borne out by the facts. In 1995, RJB Mining produced 38mt of coal, 80 per cent from its deep mines and 20 per cent from surface mines. Richard Budge seemed content with this balance.

Nevertheless, the privatisation of BCC and the ascendance of RJB Mining and the Coal Authority seemed to have achieved a weakening of the independent coal sector in England. In Scotland and Wales the new privatised coal companies—Mining Scotland and Celtic Energy—were also opencast companies that were to dominate the industry. In this new context firms like the Ryan Group (a bidder for the Welsh coal contract in 1994), found themselves squeezed.

Oddly, BCC had supported the independent sector through encouraging an unrealistically large number of competing companies to tender for its opencast site contracts, and by buying coal from private opencast operators. The new coal owners discontinued these practices and it became clear that there were too many companies operating in the opencast sector. A series of takeovers commenced as the larger companies which had

FIGURE 3

Privatisation of the BCC: Chronology of key dates

1991 (May)	Announcement of the government's intention to privatise the mining interests of BCC
1992 (Mar)	General Election
1992 (Oct)	Announcement of establishment of the Coal Review
1993 (Mar)	Publication of the Coal Review White Paper
1993 (Sept)	Announcement of the structure of the privatisation of BCC's mining businesses
1994 (Apr)	Issue of Preliminary Information Memorandum
1994 (June)	Completion of pre-qualification process
1994 (July)	Coal Industry Act
1994 (July)	Revised Mineral Planning Guidance Note No. 3 (*MPG3*) published
1994 (Sept)	Bids for BCC mining companies received
1994 (Oct)	Preferred bidders announced
1994 (Oct–Dec)	Due diligence process
1994 (Dec)	Sale of companies completed and transferred to new owners

SOURCE: National Audit Office, DTI: *Sale of the Mining Operations of the BCC Corporation*, HC 360, HMSO, 1996

been successful in obtaining coal supply contracts with the electricity generators and other coal consumers acquired their
weaker competitors. Thus NSM bought the South Wales mining interests of the Ryan Group, Rackwood Minerals bought
DS Supplies and the Wimpey Group sold its mining subsidiary
to Miller Mining. As the three main producers, RJB Mining,
Scottish Coal and Celtic Energy, began to develop new sites
themselves rather than through outside mining contractors this
process accelerated, and coal companies began to go to the
wall.

Anglo United had built up a significant business in the coal
trade. This included a successful takeover of the Derbyshire-
based Coalite fuel group. During the speculative financial
boom of the 1980s Anglo acquired other fuel businesses, with
the stated ambition of achieving market dominance in the solid
fuel sector. However, the company was burdened by debts
which became unsustainable as the coal market declined. The
company's bankers initiated a coup, installing their own chairman and senior management, selling off many of the
businesses. Similarly NSM plc went into administration at the
beginning of 1997. In addition to the Ryan Group, NSM had
several subsidiaries involved in waste disposal and opencast
mining (including Fitzwise and Coal Contractors), together
with coal interests in the USA. It was the level of losses
incurred by the US subsidiary in 1996 which led to adminis-
trators being called in to sell off the group. In 1999, Rackwood
Minerals was also forced into administration by heavy losses.

In the new market environment, the coal companies were
finding that they missed many of the advantages of the state-
organised system. In particular they felt threatened by their new
vulnerability to public protest and opposition within the planning system. When we talked with Malcolm Edwards in 1995
he made it clear that he considered these protests to be a major
obstacle to the industry's growth.

If you are a serious opencast producer, with up to ten to
twelve sites on the go, then there could be a lot of difficulties when the sites need renewing. I think there is going to

be a lot of difficulty with opencast [and]…it is unrealistic to assume that there won't be….Down in West Yorkshire and other areas they will fight it tooth and nail. With opencast there is a limit to what you can sensibly plan. I think there will be increasing difficulties in getting replacement opencast sites. If there is a change of government this view will be even stronger…it will be more difficult under a Labour Government.[30]

In a speech in 1995 Budge also addressed the issue of opencast mining and added that:

We appreciate that coal is an emotive subject and, as an industry we realise that we have to continue educating and understanding the objectors' points of view. However, RJB Mining can offer them the assurance that we will not be expanding our opencast operations at the expense of our deep-mine production. In fact, quite the opposite. We at RJB want to increase the amount of underground production and require opencast to augment our deep mines, to satisfy both quality and market requirement.

He alluded to the problems encountered in the planning system by RJB and the other coal operators brought together under the umbrella organisation CoalPro.

With regard to planning issues we have to assist the local authorities while co-operating with the plan led system, and in conjunction with other CoalPro members, already started exploratory talks with the DoE and representatives of local authorities. The aim would be to develop better understanding on both sides—of the intentions and strategies of the industry, and of the priorities and concerns of local authorities—so that the industry can focus its development programmes in the locations which will cause the least environmental or ecological impact. Such action would hopefully reduce some of the conflict and consequently reduce costs associated with expensive public inquiries to both applicants and tax payers alike.

He concluded his comments on opencast coal by adding:

> But opencast objectors should remember it must be better
> to buy British coal rather than imported, with the obvious
> employment implications.[31]

This is yet another of the paradoxes which have accompanied
the privatisation of coal. To unravel it we need to look in some
detail at the relationship between the coal industry and the state
planning system.

2
REGULATING OPENCAST

In order for an opencast site to operate today, it needs to have been granted planning permission by the relevant Mineral Planning Authority (MPA). In making its decision, the MPA evaluates the site in the context of planning legislation and guidelines issued by the government department concerned. Should permission be refused, the applicant has the right to appeal; such appeals often end in public inquiries chaired by an inspector from the Planning Inspectorate. As such, in the state regulation of opencast mining, a variety of different issues and interest groups are brought together. Decisions on site applications need to balance the market need for coal and the effects upon the environment of the new site: the rights of the coal operators and the rights of local inhabitants. The local impact needs to be assessed in the context of national planning guidance as well as any local unitary/structure and mineral plans. These relationships have altered greatly as the industry has evolved and as issues of the environment have become of greater political concern.

For many years, the industry was allowed to expand in a rather unregulated way, often at odds with the developing Town and Country Planning legislation. The Town and Country Planning Act (1947) had introduced a national system of planning control over the development of land. This was defined to include opencast coal working and meant that the NCB and privately licensed sites required planning permission. However control over NCB sites remained with central government, through the Minister of Fuel and Power. The Opencast Coal Act (1958) regularised these arrangements, but confirmed the exceptional status of these sites. In effect the 1958 Act[1] confirmed the distinctive legal position of the sector. While it introduced an obligation on the opencast industry to have regard to the environment, decisions on applications continued to be taken by the Minister of Fuel and Power. The Act did give affected local authorities an opportunity to be consulted on applications, and in cases of severe disagreement this could lead to a public inquiry. However, the ultimate decision on authorization and planning permission remained with the Ministry which (under its other hat) was responsible for supporting the NCB in its coal extraction strategies. These arrangements remained unchanged for twenty years. Increasingly, however, people found this situation unsatisfactory.

THE COMMISSION ON ENERGY AND THE ENVIRONMENT

The Commission on Energy and the Environment (CENE) was set up by a Labour Government in 1978, and its final report *Coal and the Environment*, published in 1981,[2] can be seen as a defining moment in the history of opencast mine regulation. In the early 1980s this report was usually described as 'The Flowers' Report' (after its Chairman, Professor Brian Flowers). It was frequently referred to in our discussions with local planners as 'The Bible'. The report contained by far the most authoritative investigation conducted into the relationship between energy production and the environment that had taken place since nationalisation. In considering the coal industry, the report aimed at examining:

> the longer term environmental implications of future coal production, supply and use in the UK, looking to the period around and beyond the end of the century. (Para. 1.4)

In this it took a particularly hard look at the expansion of opencast production and strongly recommended that all decisions on site applications should be placed in the hands of the MPAs with responsibility resting with the Secretary of State for the Environment rather than Energy. The Commission recognised that there was a balance to be struck between the need for coal and amenity interests, but:

> even if the greatest care is taken in both extraction of open-cast coal and the subsequent restoration of the land ...opencast mining has a severe impact on the environment in both the short and long term. (Para. 11.66)

In relation to the future development of the coal industry it recommended that:

> as older, more unprofitable and less environmentally accept-able deep mines are closed and more efficient and profitable operations take their place, the volume of opencast mining should be allowed to decline. In the meantime, there should be no increase in the present target of 15 million tonnes per year. The uniquely sensitive character of the British countryside and the high population density in much of the country would not be able to accommodate, without unwarrantable damage, a target in excess of that level. (Para. 11.82)

The CENE set out guidelines which could be used when considering potential opencast sites. It regarded these as a 'broad sieve' which included issues such as proven need for the coal; the likelihood that the coal would otherwise be sterilised; the potential for restoration (Para.11.84)

The Tory Government's initial reaction was one of support. Just before the 1983 General Election it published a White Paper[3] that was generally understood as a positive endorsement of Flowers' approach. However, while making clear that the Government was committed to strengthening the framework of environmental control over opencast mining, it also asserted the economic advantages of opencast, arguing that they needed to be set against the important environmental considerations. The detailed provisions of the White Paper and the subsequent administrative changes emphasised this dilemma.

The White Paper accepted the recommendation that NCB opencast applications should be dealt with under the normal planning system as defined by the Town and Country Planning (Minerals) Act (1981). Departmental circulars[4] (pending legislation) transferred decision-making on opencast applications to the MPAs. This was widely welcomed. In their evidence to the Commission local authority associations could point to the successful operation of planning controls over other forms of mineral development. A degree of involvement already existed in relation to the NCB's proposals for authorization, the MPAs had jointly agreed a Code of Practice in 1980; and, in some counties, had agreed long-term working programmes with the Board.

However there were to be no production targets for opencast mining, and certainly no nationally agreed rundown. Rather:

> ...The Government see no case for continuing to endorse a target for opencast output. Each project should therefore be considered in terms of the market requirement for its planned output (taking into account the alternative sources of supply, including deep-mine coal) as well as the environmental, agricultural, and other planning consideration. (Para. 15)

These changes placed the MPAs in a position in which they were required (as part of the planning process) to adjudicate on issues relating to energy markets which, in no small degree, were shaped by policy decisions of national governments. Few planners had either the experience or the expertise to deal competently with this situation, and they had hoped for some nationally agreed production target (like the 15 mt under the *Plan For Coal*) which could easily be assimilated into the planning system. Reading the markets and the variety of issues involved in assessing supply and demand and the 'need' for coal was an entirely different matter. Without additional resources and with the increasing financial constraints facing local authorities, they would need to seek independent advice on these issues if the determination of planning applications was to be a credible process.

This problem took on an added dimension in April 1986 with the abolition of the Metropolitan County Councils. The powers of these authorities were devolved to new unitary Metropolitan District/Borough Councils which became the MPAs. Mineral applications in some of these urban areas had been comparatively rare, specialist mineral teams had not been established, and the newly created MPAs were palpably deficient in the specialist skills necessary properly to assess opencast applications. With the more aggressive spirit that surrounded the emerging market-led approach to opencasting, moreover, many of these authorities found themselves facing numerous applications for opencast mining. Many felt that they were out of their depth. As a consequence they were forced to seek assistance, relying upon the specialist advice of hired consultants and support from personal contacts with other MPAs.

There were aspects of the new policy which exacerbated their difficulties. In line with the recommendations of the White Paper, *Circular 3/84* established a set of specific guidelines. However these differed in important respects from those set out by the Commission. Most notably they were to fall far short of 'a broad sieve' for all planning applications as the CENE had proposed. While it picked up on several of the recommendations (on sterilisation, environmental improvement and the like) it added up to a far less intrusive system.[5] (Para.16)

The most notable absence was any reference to the restriction of opencast working to environmentally acceptable sites. Rather than offer a set of clear guidelines built around unambiguous principles the *Circular* presented a set of parameters around which there was almost infinite room for disagreement and negotiation. It was this that was most regretted in the local authorities. Certainly the mineral planning officers we interviewed at this time were hoping to receive a comprehensive checklist of criteria which they could bring to bear objectively on each application. Instead, they felt that they would be working in shifting sand and (to mix metaphors) on a terrain with which they were unfamiliar and on which they were uncertain of their competence. However, the *Circular* did specifically direct the authorities to consider coal from deep-mine sources as an alternative to opencast, and this, as an apparently clear, materially identifiable directive, was seen to be important. Frequently, however, it proved to be a more complex matter, and one which was often difficult to reconcile with other aspects of the *Circular*.

Circular 3/84 emphasised that the 'need' for the coal should be an essential element in any consideration of an opencast application. In language reminiscent of the CENE, it argued that:

> the application…will be supported by such details as the mineral planning authority would normally require of any mineral application. These would include the need for the coal…(Para. 5)

It was this paragraph which was criticised most vigorously by the opencast industry which saw it as an avenue through which its opponents could stall and delay its development. Indeed, the idea of 'need' was the one concept made available by *Circular 3/84* which provided support for environmentally sensitive arguments. As a result evidence relating to need became an essential part of the debate at public inquiries into opencast proposals. For their part, BCC and the private operators sought to side-step this issue, relying upon paragraph 15 of *Circular 3/84*—which stated that: 'each project should be considered in terms of the market requirement for its planned output'. In this way issues of 'need' could simply be collapsed into the establishment of market requirement; 'need' was therefore a matter of supply and demand. Increasingly demand became equated with disposability, and 'need' with the presence of a potential buyer. Objectors, in turn, argued that this interpretation was far too permissive and that 'need' could only be proven if there was no readily available alternative supply, and if the buyer was involved in a production process which required the specific type of coal available in the site. This issue of coal type and the operation of specialised markets became a dominant theme in these discussions.

Regularly, public inquiries involved detailed evidence on the supply and demand of specific grades of coal. Often these discussions were unproductive. For example, coal seams in West Durham contain supplies of scarce high grade coking coal known as rank 301b. This coal has excellent properties which had seen it dominate the British steel and foundry industries for over a century. The closure and reorganisation of these industries led to the closure of the deep mines in the area.[6] In the mid-1980s, large numbers of planning applications were submitted to mine these reserves from the surface.

Objectors frequently questioned the wisdom of mining this scarce resource for inappropriate uses. They demanded to know the amounts of these coals in the chosen sites and the details of their final market uses. The coal companies would often evade such questioning. At one public inquiry in Witton-le-Wear, the operator, was cross-examined in relation to these specialised coals and the adequacy of the information provided in the application. In reply, it was argued that the information was not available, and that it was unreasonable to ask for it, as the company did not have the resources of the NCB to undertake the amount of drilling necessary to establish the proportions of each rank/grade of coal in the site. Furthermore it was argued that the information was unnecessary and entirely irrelevant as they were assured that they could dispose of all and any coal from the site through coal factors. When pressed, the coal companies often claimed that commercial confidentiality prevented them from providing the information requested. Frequently they complained that it was not the business of the MPA to inquire into their affairs. In its statement to the public inquiry into the Jobs Hill site near Crook in Co. Durham, H.J. Banks & Co. maintained that:

> what the local authority might later say about national need and their talks with the National Coal Board are of no concern to this Inquiry...what matters is that *the appellant* is able to establish the need for the coal from the site...There can be no merit in the Council's laboured evidence about national need and local targets.

There are many people employed within local authorities

with no responsibilities other than Town Planning. They do not see time being lost on appeals which should be more beneficially utilised within a business. The outcome of appeal decisions does not concern them. They can afford to be irresponsible and incompetent and they have no idea of their cost to industry and the economy.[7]

The discussion of *Circular 3/84* and problems associated with its implementation was the first clear indication that opinion was beginning to polarise around opencast mining. The Town and Country Planning Association (TCPA) had strongly endorsed the conclusion of the report and expressed the view that:

in agricultural terms, all the evidence shows that opencast mining can only be regarded as a form of creeping land erosion.[8]

The organisation was extremely unhappy with the ways things developed under *Circular 3/84*. So too was the Council for the Protection of Rural England (CPRE). In its view:

the recommendations of the Flowers' Committee have been turned against the environment and the concept of balance and environmental control appear to (us) quite simply to have been discarded.[9]

In its publications it highlighted opencast mining as one of the most serious threats to the countryside.

For their part, the OE and the private operators felt increasingly frustrated by the growing amount of detailed information required for successful opencast applications in certain areas. They were also unhappy about each other; the OE was criticised for acting too much like 'Big Brother' while it felt that the smaller licenced operators were giving the industry a bad name at a particularly sensitive time.

Furthermore, the first year of operation of *Circular 3/84* virtually coincided with the divisive miners' strike and the scenes of tremendous hardship within mining communities were reinforced by continued opencast production. It was at this time that the NUM became fully alerted to the significance of the opencast sector. Striking coal miners picketed opencast sites and, amid scenes of confrontation, many of them were arrested. The situation became more heated as opencast operators took out writs against the trade union. Strong pressures were brought to bear upon local councillors in these mining districts, many of whom had worked in the deep mines. This made life even more difficult for local planners. They were not helped by the Conservative Government's response to the EEC directive on environmental impact assessment which made it clear that such assessments would only be required for the largest opencast coal proposals in the UK. Such a requirement would have greatly strengthened the arm of the MPAs in their dealings with the industry.

AN ATTEMPT AT COMPROMISE

No one was happy, and there would have to be change. In the first instance the initiative came from the local authorities and it was constructed in a spirit of compromise.

In an attempt to clarify these questions of 'need' and 'demand' local MPAs sought to amend the *Code of Practice* formally agreed in 1980. After protracted negotiations a comprehensive revised *Code* emerged in 1986. This required BCC to engage in a series of quite detailed discussions with the MPAs. As part of this, BCC would produce both a national and a regional assessment of its opencast working plans; it would attend regular consultations to discuss these assessments in the light of Structure and Local Plan policies and land reclamation programmes; it would disclose all prospecting results (indicating type of coal and extent of reserves) to the local authority; it would come to an agreement on a rolling programme of sites which would be updated every two years; full information would be submitted with all planning applications; and there would be cooperation over breaches of planning control. For their part, the local authorities were prepared to agree to an uncontested number of site applications for coal output established within the rolling programme. In addition they would involve the OE in early discussions on any possible planning conditions.

This new arrangement seemed to have a good chance of success. In a way it represented an attempt to integrate the new requirements into the kinds of mechanisms established previously in some areas under the *Plan For Coal*. MPAs such as Durham and Northumberland with an extensive experience of opencast mining took a lead. Northumberland sought to extend the limited guidelines of the Circular into a comprehensive and publicly available checklist of criteria to be used in the appraisal of opencast applications. Durham, in contrast, took a unique approach in submitting a *Structure Plan Alteration* dealing solely with opencast policy. As part of this new approach it attempted to provide additional protection for specialist coking coals by only approving such applications if there was a proven demand for them. Gateshead followed with a similar policy in its local plan. The new approach contained two flaws which were to be its undoing, however.

To begin with it was constructed without the private operators. This was not an oversight. The OE was, at this time, the dominant producer with its position firmly established in law as having sole right to establish large opencast sites. The MPAs felt that they could easily establish a coherent planning system with one large operator, while it would be difficult if the many smaller operators were involved. They were much more at ease with the OE; and didn't properly understand the rising number of independent operators, and at root they appeared not to trust them. For their part, the operators felt excluded and became determined to utilise their national lobby to gain a more secure foothold in the industsry.

The second problem related to BCC and its newly emerging approach to coal production which included a *National Assessment* of the market requirements for opencast. This *Assessment* was to be discussed with the Local Authorities' Association with a view to their endorsing it and commending it to individual authorities. The first of these was submitted by the OE in September 1986, and it proceeded to discuss the national requirement for opencast coal under three headings. Each of these was written in an assertive manner and contained very little in the way of supporting evidence or justification. Opencast coal was seen as an undisputable:

- source of low-cost coal. This was seen to be of great benefit to British industry and a considerable help to higher cost deep-mine production;

- contributor to the provision of special market needs, specifically for anthracite, blending and coking. No specific totals were given for each of these markets;

- substitute for imports. Here it was argued that the current levels of opencast production could either not be produced in the deep-mines or produced there only at costs which would render it quite uneconomic. If any significant part of the current 14–15m tonnes output was lost, the likely effect would be an equivalent acceleration in the reduction in deep-mine output. This claim (by far the most expansive and having profound implications) was not supported by evidence and the OE made no attempt to explain or justify it.[10]

On this basis, the *Assessment* concluded that BCC needed to maintain opencast at a minimum of 14m tonnes per annum, with possible expansion up to 18m tonnes and beyond. In this scheme of things private opencast output would be between 1.3m and 1.5m tonnes per annum.

Needless to say the private operators found this arrangement to be restrictive and high-handed. It was viewed with near disbelief by the MPAs. Through the Local Authorities Association Joint Minerals and Reclamation Group they argued that it contained no acknowledgement of BCC's statutory obligation to have regard to environmental and amenity issues (confirmed in the Housing and Planning Act (1986))[11] and, in pressing for ever more opencast production, it ignored the reduced demand for coal in the UK. In brief the MPAs found BCC's response to the *Code of Practice* unacceptable and the compromise was visibly coming apart. *The Code of Practice* had served only to displace conflict from one arena to another.

In this context, planning agreements in relation to opencast mining became increasingly conflictual. Co. Durham is an illustrative case. Prior to 1984 the County Council agreed a long-term working programme with the NCB, specifying an annual opencast production of 900,000 tonnes as its contribution to the national target of 15m tonnes. But when the MPA sought to renegotiate its contribution to a lower level, BCC's response was to submit planning applications for five major sites in 1985. Not surprisingly, perhaps, all were refused and appeals lodged. Four of the five sites were subsequently rejected following public inquiries. The consensus had clearly broken down. A mood of acrimony and conflict prevailed in the coal districts. BCC complained that 'the major limitation on opencast development is now the operation of the planning system'.[12] The House of Commons Select Committee on Energy, while sympathetic to the environmental objections to opencasting, concluded that:

> it is clear from the evidence presented to us that the concept of 'national need' for opencast coal is too ill-defined to be of use to MPAs when making finely balanced judgements about environmental costs and economic benefits…The government should set about clarifying and defining the guidelines on which planning authorities should generally proceed. We recommend that the government urgently consider how to meet this need to disentangle the confusion which currently surrounds planning procedures for opencast development.[13]

A MARKET-LED APPROACH

At this point, the Conservative government intervened, developing new planning guidances to replace *Circular 3/84*. The most notable of these was *Minerals Planning Guidance Note 3* (*MPG3* as it became known).[14] *MPG3* laid out a full and comprehensive statement on opencast coal mining. It revealed in the clearest possible way that the principles which had informed the work of the CENE had been replaced by those of *Lifting the Burden*[15] (the Government's White Paper on the need for reducing controls and regulations in the interests of promoting enterprise). As one local planner put it to us: 'Flowers is dead.' As he said this he offered us his copy of the Commission's final report which he thought might be of interest to students at the university. His exasperation contrasted with the enthusiasm of BCC's senior managers for whom *MPG3* represented 'an attempt to redress an unforeseen balance favouring local environmental factors at the expense of the nation's low fuel costs'.[16]

In doing so, *MPG3* refashioned the rules in a revolutionary way. It was built around a series of guidelines which dealt with national policy considerations, handling specific development proposals, restoration and aftercare, and accelerating the planning process. The national policy considerations were particularly important. They set out, ostensibly, to strike a balance between opencast coal mining and environmental protection in a way that would not cause undue damage to the environment. *MPG3* departed from *Circular 3/84* in paying less attention to the 'need' for coal from a site. Instead the approach was built around the view that: 'the overall level of opencast production is determined by the market'. It regarded 'the low resource cost of the coal' as a positive benefit. This view was expressed most powerfully in paragraph 2:

> Opencast coal is an important national resource. The Government recognises this and also recognises that proposals for opencast operations need to be considered with full regard to their potential environmental effects....It is therefore essential to strike the right balance between the nation's interests in exploiting this mineral resource and that of protecting the environment. The planning guidelines seek to provide local authorities with advice to help them resolve the conflicting interests which inevitably arise in considering particular development proposals.

In cases where there were 'clear planning objections to a particular proposal', *MPG3* required the planning authority to consider the economic arguments advanced in support of the application.

> The applicant may wish to advance, and the mineral planning authority should consider any material arguments which might outweigh these objections....The greater these benefits are the stronger the environmental objections would need to deny permission. (Para.10)

It went on to argue that:

> the greater the environmental objections to a particular site, the more material will be the possibility of supplying the market from less damaging alternative sites or secure sources of supply. Although a factor to be considered here is whether the coal could be supplied at a similar delivered cost. However, the existence of an alternative site or source of supply is not normally a sufficient reason for refusing planning permission if the development is acceptable in planning terms. It is not the function of the planning system to seek to regulate an industry's own commercial judgements on how best to meet the demands of the market e.g. through the appropriate mix of deep-mined and opencast coal or the balance of opencast output between coalfields. Reasons for refusal must always be based on sound environmental considerations or on other planning grounds. (Para.11)

As a general view the *Guidance* argued that 'there is a strong case in the national interest for allowing these resources to be developed unless there are *overriding environmental considerations*'. (Para.6, our emphasis) Generally, it argued that opencasting involved little more than ' a temporary use of the land which generally lasts no more than a few years', and that 'sites can be restored to a high standard which can produce landscape improvements...particularly in the clearance of derelict or despoiled land'. (Para.6)

The goalposts had been moved. Under *MPG3* the rules increasingly favoured the operators. This further emphasised the aim to speed up the planning process. Although it conceded that the issues involved were often complex and contentious, it insisted that MPAs consider applications expeditiously and that:

> If an authority needs additional information from an applicant every effort should be made to ensure that the applicant is not repeatedly approached with different questions.[17]

This was supported by changes in the rules relating to public inquiries in 1988 which were also introduced as a means of increasing the speed with which appeals were dealt.[18]

These changes led many of the people involved to think that 'planning' as a technical activity had become subordinated to political and economic forces. While the planning arrangements had moved from the Department responsible for energy, there is no doubt that its officials continued to 'make our view known', and that occasionally this view was pushed very strongly. This was especially true during the mid 1980s and in the period which led up to *MPG3*. At this time we had numerous discussions with staff at the Department of Energy and some MPs involved in the Select Committee on Energy. There is no doubt that the planning procedure and its effects upon opencast planning applications were the source of real irritation and that *MPG3* marked a significant attempt by coal interests to intervene in the planning process.

These developments left some local planners feeling that they were becoming a political football. George Hardy, for example, while approving of attempts to restrict the length of public inquiries, was unhappy about the role being played by British Coal. Chris Offord and Gordon Halliday in Northumberland felt that while *MPG3* demonstrated the Government's 'generally favourable attitude toward opencast coal expansion', it also highlighted the environmental implications. However, they were not 'totally disheartened', and felt that:

> *MPG3* highlights the importance of forward programmes

and pre-application discussions between the Opencast Executive and Mineral Planning Authorities.

They were also clear in their view that:

> Despite British Coal's claim to the contrary, the County Planning Officers Society Statistics clearly demonstrate that nationally the opencast industry is receiving sufficient provisions to maintain production levels....In our view mineral planning authorities already recognise the need to strike an appropriate balance between opencast production and environmental protection.

What everyone accepted however was that the relationship between the industry and the planning process had become a fluid and, economically, a contentious one.

In late 1991 the DoE initiated a detailed monitoring exercise to investigate how the guidelines were working. This revealed that *MPG3* was widely viewed as having been written in conjunction with the opencast industry, and that it had created a bias in favour of production and profit as against other concerns such as those for the environment. The paragraph which extolled the virtues of opencast production—adding that it was 'in the national interest'—was frequently mentioned in this context. It was illustrative of the kinds of problems planners and local action groups faced in relation to sustaining a reasoned objection to a site application. What was resented most was the way in which this paragraph greatly assisted the expansion of private licensed sites, which were seen by MPAs to be more difficult to regulate, monitor and control.

Our own researches supported these findings. It was clear to us that *MPG3*, once tried, did not carry the support of most of the people involved in operating its rules. A serious campaign developed throughout the country to replace it with a fairer *Guidance* note. The CCC played an important role in this. It brought together statistics[19] which compared the five years after the introduction of *MPG3* (1988–93) with the five years which preceded its introduction (1983–88). This comparison revealed that the acreage approved for opencasting in England and Wales was 33 per cent higher in the second period. More telling was the fact that at appeal the success rate of the opencast operators (as measured by land area) rose from 37 per cent before *MPG3* to 65 per cent after the change. As a result, it had become common practice for the opencast operators to go to appeal in the firm hope that the public inquiry would overturn the recommendation of the MPA. There is no doubt that planning officers felt that the local planning system was being seriously undermined. On 15 July 1992, in the aftermath of the General Election, the DoE announced that it was the Government's intention to revise *MPG3*.

THE INTERIM GUIDANCE

Immediately following the publication of the Government's *Coal Review* White Paper[20] the Secretary of State for the Environment, Michael Howard, published interim planning arrangements for handling planning applications for opencast coal.[21] *The Interim Guidance* was initially published in an answer to a written Parliamentary Question from Angela Knight (MP for Erewash) on 25 March 1993. It outlined three broad principles upon which the forthcoming draft guidelines would be based and made reference to 'wider environmental objectives' and the 'principles of sustainable development'. Mr Howard thought that further advice was necessary 'to ensure a consistent approach between the White Paper and the Guidelines' and, in the interim, paragraphs 5 and 6 of *MPG3* would be withdrawn. Their replacements, while continuing to assert the absence of a national target and the benefits of opencast mining, also made reference to the fact that:

> The Government is firmly committed to the protection of the environment and wishes to ensure that the right balance is struck between development of opencast coal resources and proper protection of the environment and local amenity.

And the need for proposals to be:

determined in accordance with the development plan unless material considerations indicate otherwise, as required by Section 54A of the Town and Country Act (1990).

Several months after its publication a public inquiry was held in Wakefield Town Hall, West Yorkshire, to hear the appeal by Miller Mining Ltd against the refusal of planning permission for its Cutsyke Road opencast site, located near North Featherstone.[22] Under the previous *MPG3* the result of an appeal of this type *could* have been something of a foregone conclusion. During 1993 Wakefield's planning officers had recommended that the site be granted planning permission. However, the Councillors decided to take a different stance and rejected the application. The public inquiry was held over a four-day period during mid-January 1994 and much to everyone's surprise, the inspector's report rejected Miller Mining's appeal, concluding that:

> It is common ground between the parties that the *Interim Guidance* on opencast coal has created a new context, particularly with regard to the removal of the statement on maximisation being in the national interest. (Para. 24.1)
>
> Having regard to the *Interim Guidance* and the Draft *MPG3* [described below] it seems to me that the shift in emphasis towards greater protection for the environment is clear…(Para. 24.2)

The report generally highlighted the environmental impact of the proposed site and the final conclusions removed any doubts on the matter:

> My overall conclusion is that the appeal proposals would be contrary to national policy and to the *Development Plan* since the particular environmental harm attributable to the proposals outweigh any local benefits or special market need. (Para. 27.1)
>
> The appeal site is sensitive greenfield land whose disruption would not be compensated for by any substantial local or national benefit. (Para. 27.2)

This decision (endorsed by the Secretary of State) was viewed across the planning system as extremely significant and the Conservative Government had signalled a change of policy on opencast mining. However, given the political significance of the industry this signalling needed to be deeply coded and what emerged was a gradual change in tone, rather than a U-turn. This remained the situation until the Government decided that it had to press ahead with the revision of *MPG3*.

THE REVISION OF *MPG3*

A newly revised *MPG3* would accompany the industry into privatisation, and it was eagerly awaited. At the time, there was concern amongst planning officers and environmental groups that, without radical reform, the *Guidance* notes would create a situation of 'open house' in the coalfields. Once the OE had been removed from the scene there was a fear that the new expansionist private coal companies would have a devastating impact upon local amenities. For their part, the private operators considered that they had improved their act. Their determination to present themselves in a sophisticated way was facilitated by their recruitment of senior management from local government and their use of public relations firms and expensive barristers. They had been extremely pleased with *MPG3* and were lobbying hard to retain most of its favourable clauses.

On 14 December 1993 the DoE issued a consultation draft of a revised *MPG3*.[23] In a press release the Environment Minister, Tony Baldry, expressed the view that:

> The guidance builds on the changes to the planning framework governing coal extraction that we have made over the last five years…I believe this will set a clear planning framework for the industry which balances the protection of the environment with the importance of this indigenous resource.

The draft made some concessions to the critics of *MPG3*, but retained many of the offending paragraphs including the reference to the 'national interest'. The document portrayed opencast sites as sources of temporary nuisance which needed to be recognised but which was not significant enough to interfere with the legitimate interests of business. The opencast operators were conveyed as benign forces whose knowledge could be used to assist local authorities in their plans.

In planning offices and in local communities this was seen to fly in the face of daily experience. A national campaign developed aimed at a comprehensive reform of the *Guidance*. In all, the DoE received 237 responses to the consultation document. Eighteen were from consultants, mining companies and employers organisations. A large number of responses came from local authorities and local authority associations (74 in all) from as far afield as Avon, Wigan, Easington and the Wrekin. All of these made critical points based upon their direct experience. So too did those of the 13 environmental organisations, 9 professional institutes and associations, plus 22 local action groups. In addition there were letters and submissions from 101 individuals, who mainly wrote complaining about the effects of opencast mining and the need for *Guidance Notes* which related to the real damage being inflicted upon the environment as well as the problems being experienced by people living in close proximity to opencast sites.

On 21 July 1994 the *Revised MPG3*[24] was published in its final form. It had been considerably amended. The reference to the 'national interest' was removed. The DoE had issued a statement on 28 June 1994 announcing that in this revision it had been forced to bow to pressure. In an answer to a written Parliamentary Question from John Greenway (MP for Ryedale), the Environment Minister, David Curry, commented that:

> To avoid any misunderstanding, we have decided to delete the statement in the draft guidance that '...it would be against the national interest to refuse permission for coal extraction...' It is clear from the responses to consultation that the reference to 'the national interest' in paragraph 15

of the draft guidance has been wrongly interpreted as giving an extra presumption in favour of coal mining development.

Generally, these changes were welcomed. Richard Bate of Green Balance Planning Consultancy put it this way:

> Prospective developers will no longer be able to hide behind this fig leaf from Whitehall, but will have to make out their own positive case for coal mining at the local level. Boosting public confidence locally in coal mining activities could become more of a priority for the companies involved.[25]

The DoE had therefore produced a document which went some way towards creating a framework within which all parties could sensibly discuss opencast applications. However it had its problems.

The Department remained committed to planning arrangements for opencast mining which were consistent with the Government's overall policies:

> The Government's energy policy is to ensure secure, diverse and sustainable supplies of energy in the forms that people and businesses want, and at competitive prices consistent with wider economic policies, the promotion of energy efficiency, and the full and proper protection of the environment. It believes this can best be achieved through the operation of competitive and open markets. (Para.5)
>
> It is for the operators to determine the level of output they wish to aim for in the light of market conditions. (Para.6)
>
> Applicants do not normally have to prove the need for the proposed development, or discuss the merits of alternative sites. (Para.62)

However, it recognised that opencast extraction can have a 'significant environmental impact' and that it 'often take(s) place in areas of attractive countryside'. In building a bridge to the requirements of environmental planning, the revised *MPG3* contained two important sections covering sustainable development and development plans.

The notion of 'sustainable development' is an environmental one which was given a significant push by the Earth Summit in Rio de Janeiro. It had been used in previous DoE documents, which reflected the Government's declared policy in *Sustainable Development: The UK Strategy*.[26] All this was influenced by the strong feelings being expressed throughout the UK on the effects that mineral extraction was having upon the lived environment. In the words of the new *MPG3* 'it is becoming increasingly difficult to find sites that can be worked without damaging the environment to an extent that people find unacceptable'. (Para.7) In the following paragraph it attempted to operationalise these ideas, by outlining five objectives for mineral planning. These were:

- to conserve minerals as far as possible, whilst ensuring an adequate supply to meet the needs of society for minerals;

- to minimise the production of waste and to encourage efficient use of materials, including appropriate use of high quality materials, and recycling of wastes;

- to encourage sensitive working practices during mineral extraction and to preserve or enhance the overall quality of the environment once extraction has ceased;

- to protect areas of designated landscape or nature conservation from development, other than in exceptional circumstances where it has been demonstrated that development is in the public interest;

- to minimise impacts from the transport of minerals.

The revised *MPG3* drew attention to the job-creating features of opencast mining, as well as its role in improving derelict sites. However, it also recognised the disruptive effects which opencast mining could have on local communities. As such:

In applying the principles of sustainable development to coal extraction it is relevant that, whilst coal is a finite resource, mineral working is not a permanent use of land and sites can be restored to a beneficial use of value to the community once operations cease. Consideration should therefore be given to the duration of the intended development and the proposals for restoration and to the extent to which the proposal provides national, regional or local benefits to the community which outweigh the disturbance occasioned during development. (Para. 9)

In this way therefore the view of free and open markets has related to another contrasting principle of sustainable development. On the one hand:

the Government wishes to see the largest economically viable coal industry for the longer term within its broad objectives of encouraging competition, promoting economic growth and assisting in the creation and maintenance of employment.

On the other:

this must be consistent with land use planning criteria.

In considering how this circle might be squared the Government came forward with the second new initiative which linked the consideration of opencast mining applications to that of the local development plan:

the best way of striking the balance between the economic importance of this indigenous energy resource and the protection of the environment is through the careful consideration of individual applications within the framework of the development plan led system. (Para. 10)

Under the Town and Country Planning Act (1990), MPAs were required to draw up plans for the extraction of all minerals across their areas. The revised *MPG3* gave added impetus to these plans indicating that 'the Government expects there to be substantial coverage of these plans by 1996'. (Para.13) Furthermore:

the Government believes that a plan-led approach to the supply of land for coal extraction and colliery spoil disposal will provide more certainty for the industry and for the communities in those areas where coal reserves exist. (Para. 14)

The plans would be required to set out criteria against which individual proposals would be assessed. These included the effects on employment, local agriculture, landscape and amenity, hydrology, the need to avoid piecemeal development and any environmental improvements that might occur. In addition, plans should indicate, where possible, areas in which opencast mining would be acceptable in principle, and those in which its acceptance would be unlikely. It added that 'the Secretary of State will expect MPAs to take a balanced approach in implementing the approach set out above'. (Para.15)

The development plan therefore was to be both a constraint on business *and* a facilitator of business expansion. The problem of balancing the market with the environment was displaced to the mineral planning officers. *They* would need to make the judgements which reconciled potentially irreconcilable approaches. It was *their* task to ensure that 'policies and proposals in the development plan should be consistent with national policies and strategic and regional planning guidance'. (Para.19) In this however, they could expect more support from the industry itself. Hitherto, many planning officers had complained of being kept in the dark with regard to reserves known to the industry and the plans of the private companies. They had therefore viewed privatisation with enormous apprehension. Paragraph 20 indicates that:

The industry has an important role to play in making available to MPAs information on the extent of known reserves and their forward plans and discussing and cooperating in the production of outline forward programmes of sites.

The revised *Guidance* created the prospect of a much closer working relationship between the industry and the local planning system. While accepting the scepticism of Richard Bate ('we still have to wait to see what effect the change makes to the way the Government uses its default powers of intervention in local mineral plans and decisions') the document represented a remarkable *volte face* by the DoE, and contrasted significantly in tone and content with the draft revision which was published seven months earlier. For example the draft had indicated that:

> opencast voids can also provide opportunities for the disposal of colliery spoil.

The final version recognised that 'the capacity of voids created though opencast mining is usually rather limited'.

The DoE had also proven open to persuasion on the vexed question of 'need'. The draft had made it clear that:

> in drawing up policies for coal extraction, mineral planning authorities should have regard for the fact that there is no general requirement on an applicant to demonstrate a need for the proposed development. (Para. 26)

To many, this statement seemed to be at odds with the proposed idea of sustainability. In the view of Durham County Council:

> The concepts of sustainability and the need to conserve non-renewable resources should be applied more credibly and consistently through this *Guidance*.[27]

While Wakefield MDC had focused explicitly on 'need':

> Much greater consideration should be given to the need for opencast coal if the principles of sustainability are to be applied, and if the Government's priority of the 'best use of mineral resources' is to be applied.[28]

In this, Wakefield MDC was making reference to Government policy as spelled out in the document *This Common Inheritance*.[29] There were, it felt, real tensions between the principles outlined here and in the draft of *MPG3*. Generally, it was thought that:

> The introduction to draft *MPG3* makes some very contradictory points and fails to set the scene for a rational appraisal of the 'need' for opencast coal....This is especially the case when the UK deep-mined coal industry is being reduced in size but the opencast sector is maintaining production and even expanding in certain areas.[30]

The final version of the revised *MPG3* made some concessions to these views. In doing so it drew upon the fact that coal companies had often argued in their case for planning approval that certain types of coal were needed for blending purposes with other coals, or that a buyer particularly needed coal of a certain quality. The coal companies had been inclined to voice these arguments in cases where there were strong planning objections to the proposed site. In these cases the revised *MPG3* instructed that in future:

> Where the major argument advanced in support of an application is that the need for the development outweighs the planning disadvantage inherent in it, it may be necessary or permissible to have regards to the possibility of meeting that need from alternative sites or sources of supply. Generally, the greater the planning objections to a particular site, and the greater the reliance on need to overcome those objections, the more material will be the possibility of supplying the market from less damaging alternative sites or sources of supply. (Para. 63)

The issue of 'need' had resonated, in a clear way, with issues of sustainability in relation to the mining and use of specialised coals. There had been a growing concern over this issue in a number of MPAs, and this had been mentioned in the consultation period. Earlier (in 1989) we had interviewed Robin Mabey, Head of the Minerals Division of the DoE. He had been remarkably sanguine about both the environmental problems raised by opencast mining and the issues raised about 'strategic reserves':

> It is not the role of government to establish the detailed nature of the resource. We do carry out resource studies where we think that there may be a problem such as the sterilisation of a scarce resource but this problem has not yet occurred with coal and we don't envisage it in the near future. Resource studies are very expensive and we don't use them unless we really have to.

We pressed him on this issue, pointing out that our researches were revealing that this was a recurring problem in planning inquiries. He remained steadfast in the view that such an issue was 'not a necessary part of land use planning'. He supported this with the claim that:

> A clear-cut issue, involving specialist coals has not come before the DoE ministers as part of an application.

In the revised *MPG3*, however, Para. 73 pointed to the fact that:

> There are a number of differing views about the supply and demand for coals of special quality and whether opencast coal has particularly advantageous characteristics. The Government intends to commission research on these issues.[31]

The revisions to the draft guidelines were a clear indication of the strength of feeling that had been building up, in a complex way, through different social groups and institutions in the late 1980s and early 1990s. This was represented in the national campaign. It also surfaced in other public documents. The Countryside Commission's Advisory booklet, *Opencast Coal Mining: Advice on Landscape and Countryside Issues*[32] had highlighted potential problems for the countryside (and corresponding challenges for the mining industry) as opencast mining increasingly focused on greenfield sites. The Select Committee on Trade and Industry[33] had considered carefully the arguments relating to opencast coal production and had recommended that it not expand. The Welsh Affairs Committee[34] had also expressed concern over the future of opencast mining in the Principality. In 1994, the DoE adjusted its approach to the opencast mining industry in a way which brought it more in line with a growing body of feeling and opinion. As a consequence, the pattern of decisions made at appeal returned to that which had existed before the introduction of *MPG3* in 1988. The appeal decisions issued between July 1994 (when the revision of *MPG3* was announced) and July 1998 reveals that 21 of the first 30 appeals were dismissed.[35]

3
OPENCAST MINING
THE CHALLENGE

Judged in conventional economic terms the history of the opencast sector of the British coal industry over the past fifty years can be seen as one of significant achievement. It has increased output and productivity; its product has competed successfully with imported coals. Moreover, the industry has proved itself adept in developing new technologies and working practices. It has also been the source of considerable entrepreneurship and the basis for a number of highly successful new medium-sized companies. One of these companies RJB Mining proved strong enough in 1994 to win out in the bidding for BCC.

A similar story in almost any other branch of British industry would have been heralded as a major success story. With coal the interpretation has been different. Mostly this relates to the fact that the industry is based upon *extraction*. Extractive industries work directly upon nature; they have tended to be short term, moving on when the natural resources have been exhausted; they have also drawn to themselves the epithet 'rapacious'. After nationalisation, the state-owned deep mines managed to escape this negative image, fostering the idea of community and permanence. But it was not to last. The short-termism of shallow surface mining represents the worst side of this character in its destructive transformation of the environment. That is why the industry, at the height of its economic achievements, attracted the greatest opprobrium.

THE OPENCAST ENVIRONMENTALISTS

Faced with this growing criticism, the coal industry and the

Government (through the Department of Energy and then the DTI) vigorously attempted to create a favourable image of opencast mining in the late 1980s and early 1990s. This discursive concern with 'image' had very material consequences, as it was perceived to have a crucial impact within the planning process. The continuation of opencast coal mining as a highly successful economic activity was related to the public perception of the industry and the likelihood that the affected public would happily accept (or at least unhappily endure) the expansion of this activity. This representational reconstruction of the industry *in the mind of the public* was seen as an essential aspect of the privatisation process.

In the post-nationalisation period RJB also pursued an active policy of environmental awareness. In 1995 it stated:

> An important element in promoting the future of a competitive opencast mining industry is the implementation of management systems that maintain quality and improve environmental and safety performance.

The company's environmental policy statement claimed that that it was:

> committed to minimising the impact of the company's coal production and allied businesses both on the natural environment and on local communities.

It established a six-point programme which covered all aspects of opencast mining and development. To implement this policy

> a seven man environmental team has been established to ensure that all RJB sites—which number more than 200— operate to the highest environmental standards

In earlier periods of opencast expansion, opencast sites had a bad reputation. They were seen to be poor employers; some planning conditions were ignored leading to problems of noise and dust; some sites were not fenced; some were worked on a continuous basis, and some were not restored satisfactorily after coaling had finished. Another recurring problem related to coal transport from the sites and complaints became commonplace:

> outside contractors [were used] to transport the coal....Once a lorry axle broke in the middle of the road...lorries trailed mud right through to the other end of the village. The roads were torn apart by the traffic. It was a worry for those people going out for country walks...there was a real fear that someone was going to get killed.[1]

In the 1960s, as the coal industry contracted, opencast production was also cut back. However its reputation remained a vivid popular memory. This reputation proved a handicap as the industry was revived in the 1970s; a fact recognised in the repeated reference by the newly fashioned OE to the 'bad old days'.

In the late 1980s, British Coal Opencast produced a series of extremely attractive publicity brochures. They illustrated, through the use of diagrams of microscopes and photographs of computers, how opencast mining was a technically sophisticated activity. It also illustrated how the industry developed new sites in sympathy with the local countryside. In its account of the industry's activities BCO identified how:

> Opencast mining has a vital role to play in the low-cost recovery of shallow coal reserves that cannot be extracted by deep-mine methods. BCC aims to maintain opencast output at between 14–18 million tonnes per annum in the foreseeable future, subject to market requirement and the acceptability of individual projects as determined by the planning system.[2]

It went on to outline how opencasting was a very efficient method for extracting coal in shallow seams, thin seams, and seams that have been previously partially extracted by earlier mining, as well as reserves in areas of industrial dereliction, and those that would otherwise be sterilised by 'major road projects or the development of industrial or housing estates'.

These points were generally uncontentious and mirrored arguments in favour of opencast mining contained in the planning policy *Guidance* documents issued by the Department of the Environment. They were supported by photographs that showed how 'large areas of industrial dereliction have been cleared' and how abandoned coal mines in Derbyshire are 'now in full farming use'. The account, therefore, stressed the *restorative* features of opencast mining; contrasting it intriguingly (and provocatively) with a dereliction of a previous industrial age. But while the restorative role of opencast mining could be justified in relation to sites of industrial dereliction, it was hard to justify as a feature of all opencast activity. In an era when agricultural land was being increasingly 'set aside', many farmers had an economic interest in encouraging opencast mining. It became common, in some rural locations, to hear coal described as 'the most economic crop', a veritable black harvest.

Such over-enthusiastic defence of its activities by the coal industry has not helped its case. Its sympathetic biographer has argued that 'too rosy a view was sometimes published by those in the industry'. Ashworth drew particular attention to the fact that:

> The biggest sites such as Westfield in Fife and Maesgwyn Gap, near Hirwaun in Glamorgan, were repeatedly extended and so were occupied for decades rather than years. The improved techniques, bringing the ability to reach greater depths from the surface, caused a few sites to be reoccupied and excavated a second time. And the proximity of sites in the same district often meant that restoration of one little bit was counterbalanced by new workings nearby.[3]

Ashworth explicitly criticises an article in *Opencast News* which had written of the lower Aire valley: 'many of the sites have long since been restored and are now occupied by a sports stadium, a Leeds city car park, a golf course and other developments'. In his view:

> A region such as the lower Aire valley, between Leeds and Castleford, where opencasting went on continually, first on one site and then another, for forty years, could not hope to look like a shining example of the achievements of restoration.[4]

By 1986, the situation was moving towards a crisis. In its final report of its investigation into the coal industry, the Select Committee of Energy noted 'the apparent reluctance of some local authorities to co-operate with the Opencast Executive'.[5] Opencast sites were 'among the most ugly examples of the ravages of industrial exploitation', and the Select Committee commented on the presence in the coal districts of 'articulate local objections to the environmental and social costs of opencast mining operations'.

In the face of these objectives it became common for BCO to highlight plans to restore the land with the addition of a new amenity—'planning gain'. Golf courses were frequently used to support the industry's environmentally friendly image. But while the golf courses were valued by some, they were experienced by others as the loss of public access to land and countryside areas. A more overt example of the kind of thinking which emerged in the 1980s and 1990s is provided in a publication which gives advice to the potential opencast company:

> It is not usually advisable [at an early stage] to ask the local residents whether they think planning permission should be granted because this will only start the opposition bandwagon rolling. [However]…companies have experimented with near neighbours to the site offering incentives not to object to the scheme. This is a good ploy in isolated rural locations where the amenity of two or three families is amplified at public inquiry. It becomes hopeless when whole villages border the site. In this case a communal benefit can be offered (such as a cricket pavilion, village hall, etc.) but usually residents plump for total war.[6]

The decision by BCO (and later by other private operators) to sponsor selected conservation schemes represented a more sophisticated approach. In the 1980s and early 1990s it provided sponsorship and vehicles to various County Wildlife Trusts and, most dramatically, it supported the World Wildlife Fund (later renamed that Worldwide Fund for Nature). For several years BCO publications carried the WWF's panda logo. To its critics this provided further cause for cynicism, and a certain amount of distrust of the recipient trusts. People we talked with felt strongly that trusts like these should not have allowed themselves to be incorporated as tacit supporters of the opencast industry.

A QUESTION OF RESERVES AND ENVIRONMENT

This process of distrust, associated with inadequate or misleading data and information, was seen in relation to debates over the scale and nature of opencast coal reserves. The technological advances which had taken place in the opencast sector redefined the coal reserves which were mineable. By the 1990s opencast workings routinely extended to seams at depths in excess of 100 metres. At the Westfield site, in Scotland, for example, the workings descended to 215 metres. Opencast sites were mining coal that, until comparatively recently, would have been taken from deep mines. Indeed, many opencast sites were and are returning to old underground workings in which coal was left as old mines closed in the 1960s or earlier.

There is a large amount of coal available at such depths— but precisely how much remains uncertain.[7] In the 1980s BCC began to be criticised for its refusal to share its monopoly of information with others. As a consequence, one research report argued that 'information about coal reserves has only been released in a fragmentary way'.[8] In criticising the conclusions of this report, Mr Cotgrove of the OE argued that:

Its authors misunderstood the background data. Unlike its colleagues in deep mines the Opencast Executive has never sought to identify the total reserves which might be made available to it. Rather it has sought by its detailed drilling to provide enough information for its business uses....Our geological assessment of remaining total reserves available in England has doubled over the last ten years.[9]

The need for the industry by its nature to be involved in a process of establishing new sites raised questions about its development in the longer term. A report from consultants CICS distinguished between the elements that go to make up 'estimated' reserves.[10] Estimated reserves comprise those which had been 'proved' (measured by drilling), 'indicated' (limited amount of borehole information) and 'inferred' (little or no sampling). In 1982 the OE estimated its reserves at about 600mt, of which approximately half had been proved. Subtracting opencast output in the 1980s, and allowing for the additional new reserves, we are left with a likely total of below 500mt as a measure of opencast reserves in 1985. Again around half of this total will have been proved.

Assuming a national output of 15mt, reserves of 500mt imply a maximum life of 35 years; proven reserves of 300mt a more certain one of just over half of that. These are comparatively short time periods in the context of planning energy supply. Moreover, the picture is complicated by the uneven spatial distribution of reserves, both estimated and proved. Three districts in England and Wales (Castle Morpeth, Northumberland; Amber Valley, Derbyshire; and Cannock Chase, Staffordshire) contained approximately 26 per cent of the proven reserves of these two countries, whilst the leading 11 districts contained 56 per cent of the total. The importance of these reserves has increased with the dramatic sterilisation of reserves in the deep mines. In commenting on this, Mike Parker, former economics director of BCC noted that while

> reserves of oil and gas have increased broadly in line with output...assessed economic coal reserves have collapsed.[11]

THE ECONOMICS OF OPENCAST

Michael Spicer (Parliamentary Under-Secretary of State for Energy) in his preface to the BCO brochure gave a general statement, about the economics of opencasting which accurately described the reasoning used by BCC in its dealing with MPAs and the general public. As he put it:

Opencast coal is important to this country because it can be produced profitably and at low cost. In many coalfields it provides high quality coal that can be blended with lower quality deep-mined coal to produce a more attractive product. Opencast mining also provides special coals—anthracite and coking coal—which are in short supply and which we would otherwise have to import.[12]

These arguments had been developed in greater detail by BCC at numerous opencast inquiries during the 1980s. They came to form a complex and often impenetrable web of closely interwoven argument, constructed to serve as the industry's shield. In the hands of astute barristers they also provided the sword with which to deal with the complaints of local protesters and recalcitrant mineral planners. It is helpful to separate out the various components of these arguments and relate them to the practices of the industry.

The first, and most simple, relates to the question of production costs. Here too, however, there are complications. The principal argument used by BCO in favour of developing new opencast sites concerned the relative costs of opencast and deep-mined coal:

Production costs per tonne of opencast coal are significantly less than those of deep-mine coal. The profits earned from opencast coal production are substantial and are of great benefit to the industry and to the economy of the nation.[13]

The question of production costs of coal seems at first glance to be straight forward. For example, the 1990/91 *Annual Report and Accounts of BCC* showed that the average costs of deep-mine coal were £41.18/tonne while those for opencast coal were £31.79/tonne. This seems, in itself, to be a powerful argument for developing opencast coal reserves. However, in the 1980s, BCC was encouraging the expansion of one source of supply (opencast) while closing another in the deep mines at considerable public cost, struck some economic commentators as perverse. These criticisms became more pointed with the announcement of future deep-mine closures in the 1990s.

Researchers documented the economic costs involved in the closure of deep mines, through loss of revenue to the exchequer and the need for high redundancy payments to the workforce.[14] Others questioned the kinds of techniques developed by BCC to cost deep-mined output and the costs of closure.[15] Other economists questioned the reliance by BCC upon average costs. While average costs were helpful in offering a static comparison between the two sectors, it was argued that they may not be the best guide for planning future developments in the context of alternative sources of supply. In this view, the deep mines, operating as they did with much higher fixed costs and with a much longer life cycle than opencast sites, could *expand* production at the margin with little additional cost. Thus, when one opencast coal site ceases production it may be more sensible to compare the costs of opening a new opencast site (producing say 200,000 tonnes per annum) with the additional (or marginal) costs of obtaining that additional tonnage from existing deep mines. Viewed in this way it was arguable that there would be many occasions when the presence of excess capacity in the deep mines would make deep mine coal more attractive in terms of cost.[16] Support for this view came from Malcolm Edwards when we interviewed him in 1995. At that time Edwards was Chairman of Coal Investments plc and we pressed him on his plans with regards to opencast mining in England. In marked contrast to his expressed views when with BCC he said this:

> I don't believe we have to create an opencast coal subsidiary—there are rather a lot of people in the business at

the moment…and I have to say that in many cases the variable costs of producing extra coal at a deep mine are in fact lower than the total costs of an opencast site—by a considerable margin. And I don't want to be clobbered with substantial tonnages of £1/GJ coal from opencast sites.[17]

This approach is an interesting one, and one which was presented on several occasions at opencast public inquiries. However, BCC never responded seriously to it or published a model of coal output to show that this approach is flawed. It repeatedly referred to it, disparagingly and dismissively, as 'academic'. The flaw in the approach, and the reason behind BCC's reluctance to debate it seriously, lay in the financial and legal arrangements which dominated the industry. BCC did not 'own' the opencast sites in the same way as it owned the deep mines. It related to them very much in the way of a merchant capitalist; it provided the sites and occasionally provided loans for the equipment and other forms of financial assistance; the civil engineering contractors delivering the coal at an agreed price. In a period of ever tightening Treasury controls the OE represented a critical milch cow for the Corporation and this was its attraction. It was easy money.

The marginal cost argument did not, of course, apply to those firms operating exclusively in the opencast sector and, as we have seen, these were often the most aggressive in putting forward the claims of the industry. In the wake of privatisation, such firms dominated the coal industry in Scotland and Wales. In England, RJB Mining continued to operate an equivalent regime to BCC, but without the support of public funds. Hancock pointed out that:

Had RJB failed in all its privatisation bids it would have produced around 2.5 million tonnes a year…and would have been heavily dependent on replacing opencast sites to maintain this level of output. Now it can expect to produce around 30–35 million tonnes in 1995. In 2001 (even without new planning permissions) RJB could mine around 33 million tonnes….For RJB opencast should as a rule be the most straightforward part of its business…however certain opencast sites may cause the company headaches, especially where planning permission has been left in 'suspended animation'.[18]

In 1993/94 BCC reported that the cost per tonne at its remaining deep mines had fallen to £33.38 (£38.33 in financial year 1992/93). BCC's opencast output had a total cost of £29/per tonne in financial year 1993/94 (£32.12/per tonne in financial year 1992/93).[19] The levels of profitability for both BCC's deep mine and opencast output during this period were dramatically affected by falling coal production (due to the colliery closure programme) however. Nevertheless, in financial year 1992/93 deep-mined saleable output of 61.4mt produced an operating profit of £5.55/per tonne, while saleable opencast output of 15.0mt had an operating profit of £10.69/per tonne.

In the post-privatisation period the mining companies have been reluctant to publish detailed financial data concerning opencast and colliery production costs and profitability. Anecdotal information indicated that RJB Mining had continued to reduce the operating costs of its deep mines. Overall deep-mine costs were also reduced further by the closure of four high-cost/loss-making collieries in 1996, 1997 and 1999 (Point of Ayr, Bilsthorpe, Asfordby and Calverton). The 1996 *Annual Report and Accounts* from RJB Mining[20] had revealed that coal sales from its underground operations had generated a pre-tax profit of £169.382m (27.7mt output), while sales of coal from its opencast sites had a profit of £51.975m (7.2mt output). Using these crude figures RJB Mining's deep mines achieved a pre-tax profit of £6.11 per tonne, while its opencast sites had pre-tax profits of £7.22 per tonne. However, this level of profitability was linked to the high price paid for coal by the electricity generators—something RJB inherited from BCC. As this price declined, deep-mine profitability fell sharply. In spite of the mine closures, the gap between opencast and deep-mine profitability widened.

THE QUESTION OF QUALITY

If there was some substance in the opencast industry's arguments about costs, its claims about the superior quality of opencast coals were more open to challenge. Nevertheless these claims gained credibility through continual repetition. This is how the case for quality was presented in the 1980s:

> Coal produced by opencast mining methods is usually of better quality than the deep-mined product. Indeed, some deep-mined coal would not be saleable if its quality could not be improved by being blended with opencast coal.[21]

The opencast industry often turned to this argument to justify mining in areas where it would have a considerable environmental impact. In our researches we frequently heard this argument repeated by local planning officers, officials in the Department of Energy, DTI, DoE and in the House of Commons. We were assured that coals mined by this technique possessed certain inherent qualities which made them superior. The chemical and physical processes which had produced this happy outcome were less clearly specified. The further we investigated this issue the more did we realise that these claims were exaggerated and sometimes supported by questionable evidence.[22] Coal is a heterogeneous substance composed of a number of different chemicals with differing physical properties. It has been described as:

> a solid fuel formed from plant derived organic remains plus some non-organic minerals. The organic components of coal basically constitute its combustible parts.[23]

Coals are customarily classified in terms of their fixed carbon content, forming a natural progression from peat and lignite through to bituminous coals and finally anthracite. In this series the carbon content varies from under 29 per cent to over 95 per cent. Coals are given a rank or classification in terms of this increasing carbon content. Coals of certain ranks have historically gone to different markets. For example, coals with a high carbon content, especially anthracite, are prized for their high calorific values which provide a high quality domestic and industrial fuel. Lower rank coals, such as many of the coals in the Midlands and Yorkshire, are predominantly used for their steam-raising properties in the power station market.

Twenty years ago there were over 60 collieries operating in Britain which were capable of producing a range of coals, some for specialised markets. The collieries of West Durham produced prime quality coking coals (notably Rank 301b), as did others in parts of the Lancashire coalfield and the coal mines of Kent. In South Wales there were many anthracite mines and other collieries specialising in dry steam and other coking coals. However, with the exception of limited anthracite production in South Wales, all of these 'specialised' collieries have closed, not through exhaustion of reserves but as part of the general market crisis which affected the industry. That opencast sites emerged in the 1980s as the dominant source of supply for some specialised coals is a result of economic and not natural processes. Furthermore, the economic forces which led to the closure of the deep mines still press upon the markets for specialised coals and will be experienced as severely by the opencast mines as by the deep ones. The market space for producers of these specialised coals has been dramatically squeezed by imports over the past twenty years. So much so that the overwhelming bulk of UK coal production (from the deep mines *and* the opencast sites) goes to the electricity generators to be burnt in their boilers. It is here and not in the specialised markets that the claims of quality need be tested.

As we have noted, coal varies in its chemical and physical properties. One of these properties is referred to as its 'ash content', the non-combustible mineral matter which remains after the coal has been burnt. Power stations require coal in which the ash content is not high and optimum efficiencies (and lower operating costs) in most power stations are achieved using coals with an average ash content not greater than 15 per cent. The purchase price for coal is partially related to its ash content, with penalties (set out in the supply contract between the supplier and generator) imposed on coals with high ash levels. Most of the deep-mined coals in Britain usually fall below this critical level. However, there have been collieries which, due to geological problems, consistently produced coals with a very high ash content. Coals from these collieries needed to be blended with other coals to make them saleable. For example, the Whittle colliery in Northumberland consistently produced coals with an ash content of nearly 30 per cent. These were blended with coals from local opencast sites and other collieries before they were dispatched to either Blyth power station on the South East Northumberland coast, or to power stations on the Thames Estuary. However, Whittle was seen as an exceptional colliery, as were the others with very high ash levels. More significant perhaps, Whittle has been closed along with the others. None of the existing deep mines consistently produce coals with such ash levels. Almost all the deep-mine coal produced in the UK has an ash level which is consistent with the requirements of the power stations and to this extent the claims of BCC with regard to the needed quality of opencast coal can be seen as an exaggeration.

Coals, however, do possess other impurities. One of these is *chlorine*.[24] This element and the associated alkali metals have a deleterious effect on power station boilers. This was described in 1986 by Mr Clayton, Head of BCC Marketing operations in the following way:

> The significance of chlorine to the combustion of coal in the power station is that through complex chemical processes it causes corrosion of the boiler tubes which contain water and steam at both high temperature and pressure. As the tubes become progressively eroded there reaches a point where they have to be replaced at considerable cost in non-availability of the plant.

Mr Clayton also explained the possible dangers involved when:

> in the worst cases the tubes might actually fail under load

resulting in a serious disruption of power supply, again at considerable cost…chlorine has no advantages and hence the generating companies require the lowest possible chlorine level.

In the UK deep mines, coals have higher levels of chlorine than most opencast coals. The mechanisms that caused this to occur are not fully understood. However, it has been argued that the low chlorine levels in opencast coals are related to the shallowness of the coal seams. This was used as a powerful argument to justify opencast mining by BCC. The privatised industry has continued to stress the importance of low chlorine levels. This has tended to disregard the fact that most of the coals from British deep mines have chlorine levels within the acceptable limits.

In assessing this problem it is important to establish the view of the generating companies. Like the CEGB, National Power and PowerGen consistently argue that they require coal supplies with a chlorine content which does not exceed 0.35 per cent. However, chlorine content does not need to be consistently below 0.35 per cent as long as the total amount of chlorine passing through the boilers between planned shutdowns is kept to an average which is below the critical level. Therefore, a batch of coal with 0.6 per cent chlorine would be acceptable if it was followed by an equal batch of coal with a 0.1 per cent chlorine level. This arrangement clearly gives UK coal producers a much greater degree of flexibility of supply than would be possible if strict blending was required.

Once again it seems to us that the UK coal industry's arguments exaggerated the advantages of opencast coal. The chlorine problem remains specific to an increasingly small number of collieries. The repeated emphasis upon the technical merits of opencast coal served to shift attention away from their real source of attraction which lay in the realm of economics. It was also diversionary in another sense: it inhibited discussion of other technical solutions. For example, the installation of high performance co-extruded tubing could dramatically reduce the corrosion problems in power station boilers and allow the generators to burn a wider range of coals. Such tubing has a higher capital cost than existing tubes but has a much longer working life, so recouping any extra cost in reduced maintenance.[25] Gradually, over time, the opencast industry came to recognise the weakness of a case that rested on coal quality and blending. Since privatisation, the management of RJB Mining have acknowledged that most coals are no longer physically blended. At the Dawley II Opencast Coal Public Inquiry near Telford in 1998, the company's marketing manager conceded that:

> Blending is not a physical process, it represents the average chlorine content taken into the power station, not the actual taking of coal and mixing it together to get a homogeneous blend.

Rather it is:

> the provision of a portfolio of coals over a fixed period of time, normally a week, to meet an overall average chlorine value of balance.

One quality issue relates the high *sulphur* content of the coals in some opencast sites. Coals extracted in Scotland and South Wales (mostly from opencast sites) have mainly low sulphur contents (below 1 per cent), although there are some high sulphur coal seams. In England the picture is different. A substantial proportion of opencast coal has a sulphur content exceeding 2 per cent (and sometimes up to 3 per cent). Most English deep-mine coal has a sulphur content of below 2 per cent and usually 1.6 per cent or less. One comparison between the two sources of coal was made at the Berryhill Inquiry in Stoke-on-Trent in 1992. Coal in the Berryhill opencast site had an average sulphur content of 2.45 per cent, but half the coal had sulphur levels of 3.15 per cent.[26] Given concern over acid rain, high sulphur opencast coal is now marketed under statutory regulations. Coal-fired generating plants will increasingly require less and less coal with high levels of sulphur. Under the

Environmental Protection Act (following the ratification of the Second UN Sulphur Protocol in 1996) regulation of sulphur-dioxide emissions became more stringent. At the time, only 6GW of UK coal-fired generating capacity had flue gas desulphurisation (FGD) equipment retrofitted.

CHECKING 'HANDLEABILITY'

In discussing the marketing case for opencast mining, it is understandable that the role and requirements of the electricity supply industry take centre stage. Most of the UK's large coal-fired power stations were built in the 1960s and 1970s and designed to burn a wide range of lower-rank steam coals produced in deep mines. Due to the enormous coal requirements of the larger coal-fired stations, British Rail and the CEGB designed the merry-go-round (MGR) train system which enabled large volumes of coal to be delivered on a continuous basis from the deep mines. Without this transport system the larger coal-fired stations would not have been developed. This system emphasised the way in which the deep mines were seen to be the dominant supplier of coal to the power station market. However, as collieries were closed, those that remained were mechanised with coal cut by powerful face-cutting equipment. These cutting machines tended to produce coal of a smaller size (known as fines) and a larger proportion of coal containing rocks and clays. Interestingly, BCC began to argue in the 1980s that opencast coal was preferred to deep-mined coal by the generating companies. It was claimed that (unlike deep-mined coal) opencast coal was bulkier, had not needed washing and was less sticky and easier to handle. The notion of 'handleability' soon came to dominate debate.

Consider again the Berryhill Public Inquiry. In his evidence, Mr A. Clayton (Head of BCC Marketing Operations) defined 'handleability' as follows:

> Handleability refers to the ease with which coal can be discharged from trains and conveyed through bunkers and chutes. It is a function of the proportions of very fine coal

and free moisture in the product, high proportions tending to cause coal to adhere to conveyors and chutes.[27]

In this view the fine washed coals produced by modern deep-mine methods cause problems when they arrive at power stations. They stick when they are discharged from the coal wagons into chutes and bunkers.

This seemed to be a credible view. It was subsequently developed and refined by the opencast industry over a number of years. In our researches we contacted several companies involved in bulk handling. One engineer pointed out to us that each time coal is moved it undergoes degradation and attrition, which increases the fines content (reducing any handleability advantages). Such processes apply to all coal and will occur when coal is moved on an opencast site, transported to a disposal point or stocking yard and put into stock at the site of a final consumer prior to use. We interviewed Mr Braybrook, head of the British Rail (BR) coal freight section. BR, prior to the privatisation of the rail freight business, owned and operated a fleet of 10,500 MGR coal wagons—and its research department had been closely involved in their design. In its view BR has:

> always responded rapidly to the increased requirements of BCC and the CEGB/generators and this shows the great flexibility of the rail system to carry coal.

We asked Mr Braybrook how BR assessed the problems of coal handleability. In his view, many of the problems experienced in coal transportation related to opencast coal.

> Opencast can cause problems to BR. Its lower density means that there is less coal in the wagon. Opencast coal is lighter, drier and dustier. It sits higher in the wagon causing a higher crown. During long journeys the coal can cause a number of problems: there can be loss of cargo onto the track; this can cause a contamination of the ballast and also, of course, dust problems to communities surrounding the tracks.

So, opencast coals can occasionally have handleability problems, but of a different kind. When we asked Mr Braybrook directly about the kind of problems associated with deep-mined coals he was clear that: 'there have been far fewer problems from the denser, wetter deep-mine coals.'

In his view, such coal would have to be very sticky or extremely wet to cause handleability problems. He conceded that if wet coal had been standing in wagons for long periods it might cause problems but he felt that this was not a common occurrence. He expressed great confidence in the structure of BR's wagons and their ability to discharge materials effectively. In his view, the coal handleability problems were not serious enough to warrant BR investigating the use of different lining materials or different wagon designs.

This account led us to re-examine the evidence being developed by BCC and the opencast industry in relation to the physical characteristics of the coals produced by the different methods of mining. If deep-mine coal presents problems of handleability these, in the view of the transporter, are neither general nor very common. Equally, it needs to be recognised that the dry state of opencast coal can also present problems. Taken on balance, therefore, it seems unlikely that issues of handleability justify the general preference of opencast over deep-mine production.

Should the issue of deep-mine coal's handleability be seen as an important one to tackle it could be argued that this should be resolved by an engineering solution. For example, coal (like other dry bulk products) can stick to conveyor belts. Plant operators usually install belt scrapers or run the conveyors for a few minutes at the start of a shift to warm them up—so that most of the coal that has stuck to the belts falls off. In addition, a wide range of lining materials (including specialised plastics, stainless steel and glass tiles) have also been developed during the last 20 years which have greatly reduced the problems encountered in handling bulk materials such as coal. That BR did not consider it necessary to invest in such technical solutions, and was not pressed by BCC to do so, suggested to us that the issue of handleability was not of critical importance.

At the Rose Hill Opencast Public Inquiry in Co. Durham in 1986, BCC was concerned to establish that the steam raising coal in the site was an important part of the Corporation's contribution to the electricity generation market. To justify this at a time of concern over the futures of the deep mines operating on the Durham coast it argued, that when transported by sea to the Thames Estuary power stations, cargoes of deep-mine coal (with higher moisture contents) could become unstable, increasing the risk of ships capsizing. It justified this view by citing the example of the loss of a vessel off South Wales in 1975.[28] This new tack on the issue of handleability managed to raise eyebrows, even those of the seasoned mineral officers responsible for the appeal. Muffled giggles from the audience greeted the oral presentation of this argument by BCC's head of marketing in the North. As chance would have it, a retired sea captain who lived in the village happened to be present at the time and heard this account. He voiced his disbelief in the local pub and was pressed to give evidence. In a way which must have been nightmarish for the BCC team, he explained how, in his long experience of transporting coal by sea from the North East to London, no incident approaching the one described by BCC had occurred. He was, moreover, extremely sceptical that such an incident could ever occur.

A visit to the coal terminal at the Port of Tyne in 1989 (then operated by BCC) showed that the staff did take the issue of ship safety seriously. Sampling of coal being loaded into ships for export or for dispatch to the Thames power stations was regularly carried out by terminal staff. However, it soon became obvious that the vast majority of coal delivered to the terminal (by MGR train or lorry) could be loaded onto the ships without having to be blended to reduce moisture levels. Many of the sampling methods at the Port which we witnessed at that time were also rather crude—with detailed analysis of cargoes usually being undertaken at BCC's Laboratories in Yorkshire.

Following the closure of the last of BCC's Durham deep mines the issue of blending to improve handleability has virtually disappeared in the North East region. However, the companies that operate the few remaining mines and the opencast sites in the post-privatisation period continue to raise the topic—creating a mixture of entertainment and exasperation at public inquiries.

OPENCAST EMPLOYMENT

The final part of the economic case developed by BCC and followed by the opencast industry subsequently related to the way in which opencast coalmining generates employment. Looked at in an historical context, this argument might well seem implausible. One of the reasons why opencast mining was seen to be so profitable related to its lower levels of wage costs in comparison with the deep mines. Ashworth is quite explicit on this point:

> at the end of 1981–82 only 1,000 (mostly non-industrial staff) of the NCB's 282,000 employees were in the Opencast Executive, and the contractors' labour force in opencasting, though fluctuating a good deal, was usually under 10,000. The relatively small labour input was a major reason for the higher profits.[29]

With the enormous decline in deep-mining employment, it became more credible for BCC to argue that its operations created jobs in places that needed them. As with the other issues we have discussed, this was raised regularly when opencast sites were presented for approval by mineral planning authorities. As it put it in 1988:

> Opencast sites are worked by contractors operating on behalf of British Coal. They provide up to 7,000 jobs in civil engineering as well as additional indirect employment in the private sector.[30]

Ironically, this small group of workers which has often been seen as quite marginal to the coal industry had, by 1995, come to form a third of the total labour force. This was an argument which was put to us by Richard Budge:

When you consider direct employment, there must be nearly as many people working in opencast as there are in the deep mines. I can remember some of the objectors to opencast and consultants pointing to the higher ratio of jobs in deep mines (to opencast). That was only the case because the deep mines were grossly overmanned. I wrote a letter a few years ago pointing out that should manning levels be brought down to international levels we would employ more people in opencast than in the deep mines.[31]

It is a strong argument and one which local authorities have needed to take seriously. This is particularly so given that most opencast reserves are located in districts where the unemployment levels for men greatly exceed the national average.

However, the reality is again more complex than it might initially appear. To begin with, it has often been the case that the jobs 'promised' with opencast applications don't materialise. For example, at two major opencast sites in Northumberland (Stobswood and Plenmeller) BCC argued that a total of 620 jobs would be created. These promises were significant in the difficult balance of discussion which eventually led to both sites getting planning permission. However, on monitoring the employment levels it was found that once coaling had started 102 men were employed. Councillor Kevin Flaherty (then Chairman of Northumberland's Planning and Economic Development Committee) said:

Councillors have expressed extreme disappointment that jobs are being promised which are not realised. We are also very worried that government inspectors are mentioning employment creation in their reasons for approving sites where the actual jobs created bear no resemblance to those promised.[32]

In discussing these problems the OE's Northern Regional Director, John Stevenson conceded that he:

would be the first to accept that new technology and other factors have meant fewer jobs have been created on our larger sites than was at first envisaged.[33]

This problem of technological development was exacerbated by a change in employment practices on these sites. On larger sites like Stobswood, the contractors stopped employing specialist fitting and maintenance teams, preferring to sub-contract these activities, often to companies based outside the locality. As a result, local employment levels on opencast sites declined through the 1990s. This was often accompanied by local outbursts of anger over the failure of opencast sites to live up to the promises of local employment made at their commencement. Such was the case in the Swansea Valley in 1998. Workers at the Brynhennlys site became worried when nine local men were laid off. Many of them felt that they had been betrayed:

> It is a totally unacceptable situation. The miners from this area argued in favour of opencasting because [the coal owners] promised to employ people locally. Their attitude has been underhand—they make promises then, when the site is up and running, the local miners are turfed out

One of the local residents agreed:

> We have all been taken for mugs. [they] employ local men as and when they feel like it, and get rid of them when it suits them.[34]

The characteristics of the opencast labour force are such as to make events like these commonplace. Opencast sites are worked by specialist contractors which for the most part operate nationally. Their concern to maintain a regular workforce has led them to move their employees as sites close to new ones that open up. As such, a large proportion of the opencast workforce is not recruited locally, jobs 'created' as one site opens are obviously 'lost' as another one closes. Even here, however, it has been difficult to maintain 'permanent' jobs. In recognising this, Peter Cotgrove of BCO explained how:

> With the average life of an opencast site contract only four

and a half to five years, employment terms have to be somewhat different from those normal within British Coal. The
civil engineering industry, and indeed its labour force, are
well versed in the field of short-term employment contracts
which attract relatively high wages but smaller termination
benefits.[35]

It is this which has often led analyses of local labour markets
to compare 'opencast jobs' unfavourably with 'deep-mine
jobs'. This argument has been progressively weakened as the
deep mines closed. In Scotland, South Wales and the North
East and North West England, such a comparison is no longer
credible. In parts of Yorkshire and the Midlands however it still
carries some force.

The employment problems faced by the districts where
opencast mining predominates are often severe. In these areas
the various local authorities (together with other Government
agencies) are concerned to generate new jobs. As with questions
relating to the quality of the coal, the employment claims made
by the industry have tended to be over-generalised and exaggerated.

In the 1990s, several MPAs and local authorities began to
argue forcefully that at a time when regional development agencies were trying to attract inward investment, particularly from
large overseas corporations, opencast sites could have an
adverse economic impact on the locality. This was dramatically
demonstrated at the Hathery Lane Opencast Inquiry, in
Northumberland. As part of its investment strategy the South
Korean corporation, Lucky Goldstar, was considering a number of plant locations including Newport in South Wales and
the West Hartford Farm site north of Cramlington in
Northumberland. The company sent a lengthy questionnaire
to Blyth Valley Borough Council asking, amongst other things,
whether there were any sources of shock waves or dust pollution near to the site. The council was able to answer that there
were no quarries or opencast sites in the vicinity. At the
Hathery Lane Inquiry the borough used this as part of its case,
calling a consultant, David Napier, to give evidence. He argued

that, 'If the Hathery Lane site had been operational at that time then they would not have been able to give that answer.'

He also thought that when an investor actually visits an area the poor appearance of the local environment can be a significant deterrent to investment.

> It is very much a question of perception and it is clear that opencast mining has a very poor image in terms of its effect on the environment. It is difficult to find specific examples where sites have been blighted by opencast mines as mining has not in recent times been permitted in such close proximity to major inward investment sites. However, the response of inward investors is likely to be similar to that of Searle [pharmaceutical company] who objected strongly to proposals for opencast mining close to their site to the west of Morpeth. Had they been aware of the proposals, or even the prospect of opencast mining at the time of their initial site investigations then quite clearly they would not have located where they did.[36]

A further problem facing opencast mining relates to more indigenous economic activities being developed in the coal districts. One growth area of the UK economy in recent years has been tourism and leisure-related activities. During the 1990s many local authorities in the old coal districts have made serious efforts to encourage tourism. Anticipating this trend several coal companies began to argue that their working sites could be seen as potential tourist attractions. At inquiries we have attended, these claims have invariably produced laughter from the public. Indeed, many local authorities, tourist boards, owners of hotels and bed and breakfast facilities, and even publicans have come to view opencast sites as a deterrent to potential visitors. In the 1990s, it became common at opencast public inquiries for local businesses (including the licensees of public houses and hotel operators) to give evidence against the development of proposed sites.[37]

It seems likely that such opposition will continue to grow, and it relates to conflicting understandings of the use to which an area might be put. This is seen most starkly in the impact of opencast mining upon the property market. Many people who are thinking of buying homes in coalfield areas have asked us: 'Will there be an opencast site near my home?' fearing both the potential environmental impacts of the site (such as dust, noise, visual impact, and increased traffic volumes) and the effects on the value of the property. It has been made clear to us that to answer 'yes' will end any interest in the sale. Little systematic research has been carried out on the impact of opencast developments on property values and few local studies have been attempted. However, Trigg and Dubourg[38] carried out a short survey of the potential impact of an opencast site in North Staffordshire. The research project involved a survey of local estate agents with both experience of the housing market and of opencast mining in the area. They concluded that the adverse impact of the site on housing prices totalled several million pounds—equivalent to most of the profits from the sale of the opencast site's coal. A further research project carried out by staff at the University of Newcastle upon Tyne examined the potential benefits of developing the Dewley Hill opencast site (now called the Crescent Farm site). Using modelling techniques they concluded that the extraction of the coal in the site would incur large social costs.[39] These research findings confirmed the intuitive feelings of many people living around opencast sites. It is to a discussion of these that we now turn.

4
LIVING WITH OPENCAST

As opencast production expanded and became an important part of the British coal industry, so too did groups organise themselves in opposition. By this time, the coal districts had changed dramatically. As coal mines closed down, a pattern of living emerged that was separate from coal mining. Old coal mining villages died, or were transformed through owner occupation and the arrival of a new commuting way of life. Local authorities were involved in environmental projects which removed 'the scars of the past'. In this context people who, hitherto, had accepted dirt and dust as a part of a necessary economic activity and a 'way of life', began to take a different view of the environment and the context in which their children and grandchildren grew up. Repeatedly in council chambers, local meetings and public inquiries, a series of issues emerged with great regularity. These considered the economics of opencast expansion, but increasingly focused upon the social and environmental damage it caused. Throughout the exposed coalfield people drew upon similar experiences and gave voice to arguments which although locally differentiated had many common themes.

THE PERCEIVED THREAT

For people living on the exposed coalfields of Britain, the prospect of an opencast site opening near their homes began to be viewed as something little short of disastrous. When news of a new site is announced rumours spread and environmental activists talk with people about 'what it will be like'. These accounts all turn on the ways in which the new site will affect everyday life. People turn to friends and neighbours who have experienced opencast mining in the past. At protest meetings 'survivors' of previous opencast sites also recount in detail the disruptions caused by their development and working. The perceived threat to the local community is a powerful force, coordinating opposition. Extracts from one public inquiry into a proposed site, located close to the village of Sharlston, in Yorkshire illustrate these fears.[1] Michael Appleyard commented that:

> Deep mining did not, unlike opencasting, adversely affect the health of children or old people living in the area. Nor did it generate very much road traffic since all the coal traffic came in and out by rail. (Para.2)
>
> Some 90 per cent of the buildings in the village are down wind of the appeal site and would be affected by dust, noise, traffic and fumes from vehicles. The existing hedges would be little protection. The death rate in the village is about 2.5 times above the average. People with dust related diseases are understandably fearful of the proposal....Many buildings on Weeland Road have no gardens or any amenities of their own and people are quite frightened about the effect of heavy goods vehicles. The access rights on the appeal site would be permissive and would be no compensation for what people already have there. The Parish Council has promoted a number of projects in the village, including a smokeless zone, a traffic-calming scheme because of the accident rate, removal of spoil from the colliery, an annual clean-up campaign, the 'Sharlston in Bloom' competition for the best gardens, flower boxes maintained by local people and amenity use of the village green. The Parish Council has worked hard to involve local people and to develop these new initiatives. It is a travesty of justice that, less than six months after the deep mine closed because there was said to be no need for the coal, there could be an application for opencasting this site. Yet it would only produce during the working period the amount of coal which the colliery could have produced in 8–10 weeks. There would be no benefits

in the appeal site being worked whatsoever. (Para. 3)

The local MP, Bill O'Brien, stressed his support for the community and his opposition of the appeal. He noted that:

> This application was made very shortly after the closure of the colliery in Sharlston in July 1993 with the loss of more than 500 jobs directly and a similar number indirectly. Many opencasting sites would be needed to make good that loss. There is still an abundance of coal in the colliery site, but people were told that too much coal was being produced. The appeal proposal would not recover these jobs and would do nothing to regenerate the area. Indeed the reverse would apply. (Para. 7)

It is not common for church ministers or parish priests to give evidence at public inquiries. However, at the Weeland Road Inquiry the Right Reverend John Finney, Bishop of Pontefract, said that he was only too well aware of the effect of opencasting on local communities. He thought that people feel that they are being dictated to by outsiders and in particular those from London. The Bishop highlighted the effects of the recent colliery closure at Sharlston. He believed that Sharlston needed to turn its back on coal extraction and begin again—adding that:

> Communities have reacted in two ways to the closure of many pits in this area (West Yorkshire). Some have reacted with feelings of hopelessness and apathy with symptoms of vandalism, violence and truancy. Others are trying to pull themselves up by their own efforts by diversifying employment and trying to make a new life. Sharlston is one of the latter areas. The locality needs more employment, but the appeal proposal would deter people coming to set up new activities in Sharlston, which is already suffering from planning blight because of this opencast proposal...(Para. 13)
>
> This site is too close to the community particularly as the residents of Sharlston have been devastated in the recent past by the loss of the colliery. The impact of the proposed work-

ings would not only be visual and aural, but also would adversely affect the morale of the whole community. Extraction of opencast coal makes such a mess of the neighbouring countryside that people do not want to live nearby or to work there. The proximity of the site to Sharlston is bound to have a serious effect on the village and the accesses to it. A child attending the primary school next September would spend much of its time surrounded by opencast working and its effects. This proposal would be kicking local residents in the teeth again after the closure of the colliery. It is a question of justice. The proposal would not bring employment and very little of any positive worth. (Para. 14)

THE IMPACT ON THE COMMUNITY AND DAILY LIFE

Once permission has been given for coal extraction on a piece of land, it changes in nature. It is no longer a field or an area of woodland or even a derelict area: it is a major civil engineering site and a place of work. The purpose and use of the land changes with a suddenness that people often find deeply disturbing. Large ('monstrous') earth moving equipment is moved onto the site, and the existing trees, vegetation and top soil are stripped away. Within days the appearance of the landscape (peoples' 'views') is completely changed as the countryside is torn apart. The possibility of screening varies from site to site, depending on such factors as the lie of the land, the proximity of properties, roads and other rights of way, the depth of working (which controls the amount of rock overlying the coal that is available for creating baffle mounds) and the size and shape of the coal deposit. The screens of earth may themselves be highly intrusive as is the floodlighting at night. In the view of Andrew Purkis, former Director of the CPRE:

With an opencast pit every blade of grass is wiped off the face of the earth, sometime for at least as long as it takes a child to grow up, to be replaced by the desolation of a gigantic grey hole, spoil heaps, filth and noise.[2]

We have observed many people react with intense emotion at the thought of losing an established landscape. Familiarity with (and love of) a local environment may be as strong a human emotion as the relationship between two people. Often loss of part of a local landscape (trees, meadows, moorland, wildlife) can be as traumatic and intense an emotion as bereavement. These feelings are invariably underestimated by mining companies and developers, and were graphically described by the author Richard Girling:

> Landscapes are much like buildings. They can be large or small, humble or majestic, deliberate or accidental in their charm. Like buildings, they are human creations made from the materials that nature provides, and they deserve to be respected and cherished in exactly the same way. If an ordinary vernacular cottage, in an ordinary village in Middle England, deserves the protection of the law, then so too does the land on which it stands.[3]

The emotional impact of opencast site developments is usually compounded by a series of physical changes, of which dust and noise emissions are the most obvious. These are often examined in some detail in official reports.[4] What these often lack however is a detailed and personal commentary of the ways in which these environmental changes affected communities. And this is not because people do not have their own views, or that they are reluctant to express them. As the opencast industry has developed, local people have often commented in vivid ways on what it has meant to them. We have spent a lot of time listening to these views.

Dust is probably the complaint which is most often voiced by local people. The initial removal of soils on an opencast site needs to take place in dry weather, so as to preserve the structure of the soil for subsequent restoration. There is, therefore, an inevitable dust problem at this stage and at the conclusion of working. Major dust problems also occur when coal and substrata are dug up and moved about. Dust suppression measures (such as sprinklers and wheel washing) may help, but they cannot cope with strong winds and bad weather. As a result, people living close to opencast sites complain of being unable to sit pleasurably in their gardens, of clothes on washing lines being dirtied, of windows needing frequent cleaning and so on. For example on the Godkin site in Derbyshire one person commented on how:

> Dust is a major problem. Considering we live away from a main road and in a cul-de-sac—window sills, windows and net curtains are *black*. When it rains, the paintwork, front door, porch etc., have to be washed down to remove black silt.

Noise is a problem which is inevitably associated with opencast sites, due to the involvement of extremely heavy machinery, blasting and large coal wagons. Vehicles like draglines, dump trucks and motor scrapers can be particularly noisy. Lilly Ross lived in Burnhope Co. Durham near the former Chapman's Well site:

> They're only allowed to coal from 7 in the morning to 7 at night but the draglines are going 24 hours a day to remove the overburden. I can hear the bucket dropping on the dragline some nights, and the site's over half a mile away. There's lads living in Pavilion Terrace, which is only about 200 metres from the site boundary, work night shifts and so need to sleep during the day—but sometimes they can't because of the noise.

She remembers, with some humour, how:

> A few years ago British Coal fitted a new device to the draglines which goes 'beep, beep, beep' when they move in a certain way. When they first fitted it, I kept going down to my kitchen at night to check if my microwave was still on— eventually I realised it must be the draglines![5]

Some of the worst noise problems occur at the beginning of the site's working life as soil is stripped and placed into overburden mounds around the perimeter of the site. The nuisance is repeated as the site comes to the end of its working life and the mounds are removed. When the mounds are in place they serve to muffle the noise. However, on some sites (such as those in valleys) noise can sometimes carry for great distances. In addition, residents often complain of the 'off-site noise' associated with the transportation of the coal and the everyday to-ing and fro-ing which surrounds a productive opencast site. In this, the attempts by BCC and the other opencast companies to reassure people were often counter productive. In the case of the Plenmeller site, for example, local residents were particularly worried by the prospects of a rapid loading system which would transport the coal on British Rail tracks. They listened in disbelief to a statement which compared the noise levels involved here with the sound of 'cornflakes falling into a bowl'.

Whether noise is a nuisance or not will vary with personal circumstances. For example it will be influenced by work and leisure patterns, the proximity to the workings, and an individual's overall tolerance. One man in Durham explains how the quality of his life was adversely affected:

> I used to be able to go out and work in the allotment at the back peacefully, away from the noise of the traffic on the roads. All you could hear was the singing of birds in the trees. Since British Coal started working, we've lost that tranquillity.

Views such as this were frequently expressed at public inquiries and they persuaded one inspector to the view that:

> Although technical measures to ameliorate the effects of noise and blasting could be provided, they are subjective issues. I am satisfied that these, together with the general disturbance and nuisance arising from site-related activities, would lead to a serious diminution in the quality of life presently enjoyed by local residents.[6]

'Experts' are often dismissive about the comments made by local residents. Mr Charles, a witness for RJB Mining, commented that: '...People hear what they want to hear.'[7] The unstated implication is clear—local residents will tend to exaggerate the problem. Others mention the absence of complaint as evidence of compliance and satisfaction. However, a survey carried out by the Building Research Establishment highlighted the general reluctance of people to report noise disturbance.[8]

Blasting can be particularly troublesome, and involves more disturbance than the immediate noise it makes. Opencast mining usually requires the physical movement of large quantities of rock to gain access to the coal. The rock above the coal can most easily be loosened by the use of explosives. This causes ground vibration and surges in air pressure. Blasting is carefully regulated (via maximum charge sizes for example) and this is usually sufficient to prevent physical damage to buildings. However, due to the variability of geology, there can occasionally be excessively strong blasts which arouse extra worries and create uncertainty about future blasting levels. Nuisance from blasting can easily be the most offensive aspect of opencast coal mining, and even when operators satisfy the conditions laid down in their planning permissions there may still be cause for local concern. Despite continued assertions by the opencast industry that blasting is of an acceptable level, it remains a problem with regard to both damage to property and the fear of having the house and contents shaken several times a day.

Residents around the Godkin site in Derbyshire were asked if they had experienced any problems from blasting. All answered in the affirmative. These are some of their comments:

'The whole house shakes, pictures come off the wall.'
'Fright—I remember saying "what the hell was that" as the house shook. It threw me off the settee—terrified me and my dog, it knocked a clock off my wall and broke it. I live on my own, my husband is in hospital, and I am frightened to death...'[9]

People wrote of 'the whole house moving', of experiencing something 'like an earthquake as everything in the house shakes and rattles including people'. More worrying were the comments which mentioned blasting contributing to 'a general feeling of insecurity' and of how 'when there is a bad blast it affects you emotionally—it makes you feel like crying'. At a meeting organised by the Shilo North Action Group in 1989, Mr Stott, Regional Project Manager of the OE, attempted to dismiss such fears with the assurance that the vibrations were similar to the 'slamming of an internal door'.[10]

Opencast workings can also present a *general nuisance* to the areas in which they are located. Unlike a factory or an office block, they exist *outside* and are difficult to secure. Which gives rise to fears over the security of children. At the Godkin site in Nottinghamshire BCC insisted that all fences were two metres high with a basket wiretop, and were virtually impenetrable. Residents, however, were sceptical and testified that:

> We often see children and youths on motor bikes on the site which to me seems dangerous. I have seen children on the Godkin site close to steep drops collecting blackberries.

Opencast sites need to have deep lagoons around them to drain the water from the workings which are a constant worry for parents. This account from Co. Durham is not unusual:

> It was only last October some kids from Quaking Houses had a raft on one of the lagoons and a young lass fell in. She couldn't swim, and they had to throw her a lifebelt to keep her afloat while they dragged her out. That was with the barbed wire round the lagoon, and the kid was only about 4 or 5 years old. So now British Coal have put barbed wire coils inside as well.

These fears continued through the 1990s. In July 1997 RJB Mining warned about the dangers of children playing on its opencast sites, sending delegates to local schools and requesting its employees to take the message home. As the company's safety manager Paul Fairlamb put it: 'We want children to enjoy themselves, but not on our premises.'[11]

As a consequence of processes of economic change, peoples' homes had therefore been moved from an established local neighbourhood to one which approximates to a major industrial site. The openness of these sites means that unpleasant incidents are virtually unavoidable during their life. People complain of a loss of amenity, of losing a place to walk the dog, of rats infesting houses once old (underground) coal workings and drains are disturbed. From the standpoint of the operator these are all part of the painful facts of a life of doing business. To local residents they signal a marked and deleterious change in the quality of their daily lives. This is made clear in the following account:

> One of the main reasons we had for moving to Burnhope was the countryside at the back. The view was lovely when we first arrived—it was wetland, and there were three ponds with heron on, and other wading birds. Less than a year after we moved here, the Chapman's Well site started working. Only one of the ponds was saved, and we've never seen the heron since the opencast began.
>
> There were hedgerows too, and a variety of trees and hollybushes. We could go out on Autumn mornings and pick mushrooms, then come back and have them for breakfast. We'd see lots of other people mushrooming and blackberrying too. It was a place where we could meet people.
>
> That's one of the saddest aspects of opencasting. Here we are in the middle of the countryside, but there's very few places we can go which haven't been, or aren't being opencasted.

THE CUMULATIVE EFFECT OF OPENCAST WORKING

The 1988 edition of *MPG3* certainly made explicit the assumption that opencast coal mining involved 'a temporary use of land'.[12] In spite of this, many people on the exposed coalfields (and especially in South Wales and the North East of England) have experienced near-permanent opencast working as a succession of sites close down and open up. In these places, residents have experienced the *same* site being reopened and reopened as the improvement in equipment and changes in markets have made viable the extraction of coal from deeper seams. The area around Tow Law in the West of Durham has been sequentially mined by opencast sites for over thirty years. Maps indicating the extent and duration of this form of mining often bring gasps of astonishment and anger when displayed at public meetings. While Tow Law might be an extreme case, the cumulative impact of opencast workings upon local communities had, by the 1990s, become a significant issue in each of the major coalfields (see Figures 4, 5 and 6).

David Armstrong was brought up near Crook in Co. Durham, and moved to Butterknowle when he married. He is all too aware of the effects of cumulative opencast mining upon his local community:

> When I lived in Butterknowle I commuted to Ushaw Moor. During one period I passed 14 sites on the way to work, though it was only a twenty-mile journey. The hills still bear the signs of that opencasting. There are areas around Stanley Village used to be surrounded by beautiful countryside. Opencasting's taken most of that away. As a kid I used to walk the fields and wood where first the Nackshivan site worked, and now the Tanners Hall site is working. From Stanley Village the pit men would walk down a country lane to Wooley pit. From the gates you could walk all the way to Brancepeth or Oakenshaw through the woods. Now there's just barbed wire across, and a 'DANGER—KEEP OUT' sign. Everything else has been destroyed.[13]

George Bramfitt, Land Drainage Officer for Durham County Council since 1971, has lived in the Deerness Valley in Co. Durham for most of his life. Like Dave Armstrong, he has seen the countryside he grew up with gradually eroded by opencast mining:

A lot of the hedges and mature trees on the land are ripped out, but not replaced. Those that have been replanted aren't growing properly, so a lot of the wildlife habitat has been destroyed. Most sites look bare even twenty years after being restored. Some of them will never recover, such as the Hedleyhope site, because the restoration was so poor. Their ecology has been destroyed.

A few years ago I conducted a guided country walk, in conjunction with the County Council, along one of the restored railway lines. Along the way I spent most of the time describing what the landscape used to be like before it was opencasted. The people who came on the walk really enjoyed themselves, and I was asked if I'd like to do some more. I had to decline the offer, because I'd become so depressed by seeing exactly what opencast and deep-mining reclamation had done to the area.[14]

In areas like this one, objectors have argued that account should be taken of the cumulative impact of near-permanent opencast operations upon the quality of life in the area. Occasionally such objections are viewed sympathetically. The inspector at the Whiteside Farm Inquiry noted in his report that while small sites 'may appear to involve only marginal disturbance of communities or disruption of traffic or of the landscape, collectively their impact could be serious and largely unforeseeable'.[15]

THE EFFECT UPON HEALTH

In the 1980s there began to be some concern that active opencast sites adversely affected the health of people in surrounding communities. For some time there had been numerous anecdotal stories and concerns expressed about the impact of dust and noise upon health. This was often discussed with us in quite emotive terms, as people expressed sincere worries about the health of children and old people. However these concerns seemed to have little scientific foundation and the opencast industry was routinely dismissive of suggestions that its activities could endanger health.

However, in 1983 the West Glamorgan Health Authority noted that the Glynneath medical practice was prescribing drugs for asthma at a disturbingly high rate. As a result, the Glynneath practice started to audit its treatment of new asthma episodes:

> As a consequence of this audit the practice became concerned that local industry was aggravating its patients' asthma. These fears were voiced at a public inquiry into proposals to open an opencast site to the north of the town.[16]

Permission was granted to open the site and the practice extended its investigations (primarily carried out by Dr Mark Temple) into the number and frequency of asthma episodes amongst its patients. The investigation into these records seemed to indicate a correlation between the increased incidence of asthma and opencast coal mining activities. In their *British Medical Journal* article they concluded:

> Our findings are *prima facie* evidence to support the practice's concern about the risk to the general population from the opencast coal site. The results of this small study give cause for national concern in view of the current increasing trend towards opencast mining in Britain.

The article was extremely controversial. The findings, if sound, presented an enormous threat to the future development of the opencast sector. They also raised the question of legal responsibility and the prospect of financial compensation to asthma victims. At the time they also presented a significant threat to the privatisation of the industry. For these reasons, BCC took the evidence extremely seriously and commissioned research of its own in the hope that it would challenge the conclusions of the Glynneath doctors. Peter Weaver (then South Wales Regional Projects manager for the OE) in an article in *Mineral Planning* wrote:

> THE EXPERTS' VIEW. A number of epidemiologists have

examined the allegations, both as a result of submission of evidence to public inquiries and in response to the BMJ article. The overwhelming conclusion of these experts in the field is that, whilst not questioning the general practitioners' motives or bona fides, the methods employed and conclusions drawn are seriously flawed, and in any event not sustainable as a theory. In contrast, there are many well documented and well recognised factors which can exacerbate asthmatic conditions, and which could be expected to be present in Glynneath.[17]

The article made clear that BCC had commissioned 'independent consultants' from the Institute of Occupational Medicine (IOM) to investigate the health of workers on opencast sites as a way of checking the perceived link between opencast coal dust and asthma. 1249 employees involved in a variety of different jobs on a number of opencast sites were subjected to medical examination (including checks for lung diseases, lung functions and the incidence of asthma). The IOM report[18] concluded that there was no link between opencast working and asthma or chronic bronchitis. However of the 1249 workers, five were found to have established silicosis. As a result it was recommended that there should be widespread use of technology for control of dust emissions on opencast sites. They also saw the need for further research linked to the installation of dust monitors on site boundaries and in some adjacent communities.

This research was seized upon by the opencast industry and various government departments to neutralise the Glynneath findings. It was regularly cited at public inquiries throughout Britain. However the IOM study has been criticised as not being a comprehensive epidemiological study of the general population, being narrowly focused on the workforce of the sites. Findings from a sample drawn from a population of active men in good health should not be extended to a general population that included asthma sufferers, children, women, retired people and those with chronic illnesses. Far from alleviating public concern, the IOM report (and the controversy that sur-

FIGURE 4

**Opencast coal mining—Tow Law area,
Co. Durham 1953–86**

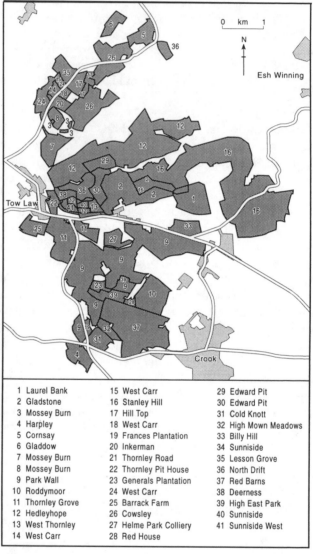

1 Laurel Bank	15 West Carr	29 Edward Pit
2 Gladstone	16 Stanley Hill	30 Edward Pit
3 Mossey Burn	17 Hill Top	31 Cold Knott
4 Harpley	18 West Carr	32 High Mown Meadows
5 Cornsay	19 Frances Plantation	33 Billy Hill
6 Gladdow	20 Inkerman	34 Sunniside
7 Mossey Burn	21 Thornley Road	35 Lesson Grove
8 Mossey Burn	22 Thornley Pit House	36 North Drift
9 Park Wall	23 Generals Plantation	37 Red Barns
10 Roddymoor	24 West Carr	38 Deerness
11 Thornley Grove	25 Barrack Farm	39 High East Park
12 Hedleyhope	26 Cowsley	40 Sunniside
13 West Thornley	27 Helme Park Colliery	41 Sunniside West
14 West Carr	28 Red House	

SOURCE: Co. Durham Planning Department

rounded it) tended to exacerbate the situation. In the conclusions of her report from the Weeland Road Public Inquiry[19] the inspector, Mrs Brushfield, noted that:

> It is not disputed that opencast sites produce dust, and that measures need to be taken to control it…the residents here are most concerned about dust blowing from the workings into the village and therefore the environment of the local people, including those already affected by respiratory diseases. (Para. 13.7.6)
>
> The health record of people in Sharlston is not good, the mortality rate being 251 per cent compared to the national average. This, together with the workload of the medical practitioners, confirms that local residents have a high incidence of lung disease and ill health, much of which may be linked to the employment of the majority of its male workforce in the colliery before it closed. Smoking in combination with these factors may exacerbate the problems. The increasing number of asthma cases in the area, particularly in children, corresponds to similar statistics seen nationally. (Para. 13.8.1)
>
> The unemployment rate in the village is high, at 27.8 per cent, and many people are therefore likely to be at home on the days when the workings on the site would be taking place. The effects of dust from opencast workings are disputed between the parties; the significance of the studies on dust is, and may remain, inconclusive. However, if dust does cause harm, then the health of people in this community is at particular risk, with a physical susceptibility well above the normal, and with most people living downwind of the site. Those affected by noise from the workings and site traffic would include the people suffering from industrial deafness who may be affected differently by noise events. (Para. 13.8.2)

Mrs Brushfield also added in her conclusions that the site could increase the *levels of stress* in the local community.

> Local people are worried about the accident potential of the traffic from the site, the health and safety risks for children, and personal distress from noise which might disturb the bereaved visiting the cemetery. With these factors, the recent

FIGURE 5
Opencast coalmining—Garswood, St Helens, 1995

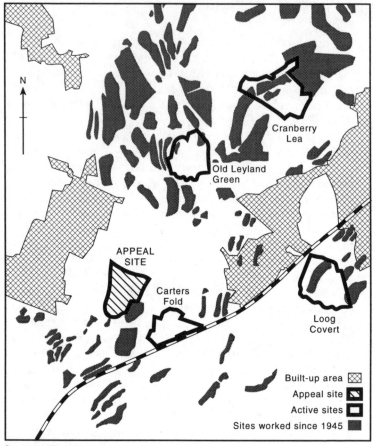

SOURCE: H. J. Banks & Co. Ltd

closure of the colliery, and local people's less than satisfactory experiences of opencasting in the locality in the past, the population in the Sharlston area is likely to be more stressed by the effects of the proposed workings than would otherwise be the case, with the potential for further ill health for that reason. Taken alone, these health considerations are not, in my view, sufficient to justify refusal of planning permission, but they do add to the need for the appellants to demonstrate that the development if permitted would be carried out with the interests of local people very much in mind. (Para. 13.8.3)

During the early 1990s a number of well organised action groups pressed for further epidemiological research to be undertaken. They carried these demands to British Coal, to Government Departments and to the EU. In 1994, partly in response to these demands, two locally based research projects started. One was a pilot study carried out by the Department of Epidemiology and Public Health at the University of Newcastle upon Tyne, the other a study by local councils and health authorities in West Glamorgan. Both studies were concerned to examine the impact of opencast mining upon children's health, and attempted to develop an approach which would allow them to disaggregate the variety of emissions which accompany opencast production.[20]

In a society where issues of risk and health have become increasingly salient it seems likely that opencast developments will be subjected to increasing scrutiny. As the economic advantages of the activity became less certain it is likely that these risks will acquire greater force in the decision-making process. This is especially the case where derelict sites and on land containing toxic wastes are involved.

RESTORATION OF SITES

Once the coal has been removed, operators are required to restore the site to its original or an improved condition. In 1985, Mr J.H. Atkinson, a former Land Commissioner for MAFF with responsibility for all opencast restorations in the North East of England spoke at a CPRE conference.[21] In this he argued that in describing the landscape which followed opencasting the word 'clinical' was the most appropriate. He continued:

This is best illustrated by a little exercise I did on a proposed site in Northumberland. With the help of a botanist from

FIGURE 6
Opencast coal mining Co. Durham 1943–96

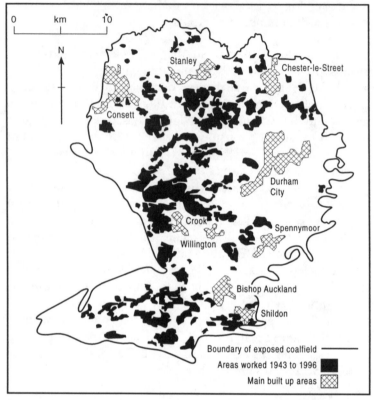

SOURCE: Co. Durham Minerals Local Plan (Deposit Version) 1997, p.43

Newcastle University, in the course of one-and-a-half hours we were able to identify 151 species of plants native to the British Isles. This was not an area particularly rich in plant life and the survey was not extensive as you will appreciate. By contrast, a restored site of some ten years could only support 30 species of plants including the grasses and clovers planted in the sward, the trees in the wooded areas, together with hedges and trees planted by MAFF. If you accepted the principle of the ecological chain you will appreciate what an environmental disaster this is.

When I was planting hedges, I had to keep them weed free. I used herbicides. When you consider this has been going on for forty years in a big way in certain parts of the UK it is small wonder that people are getting alarmed. Is it a living landscape or a dying landscape?

Mr Atkinson's comments were echoed by Mrs Rush, a local resident who opposed the Weeland Road site application at Sharlston. Mrs Rush thought that opencasting leaves behind a 'plastic model village look'.[22]

Critical comments on restoration schemes were also included by the inspector in his report following the inquiry into the Ellerbeck West site in Lancashire:

> There was some discussion at the inquiry as to the Corporation's capacity to restore the landscape of the area to some semblance of its present form and character. I recognise that the Corporation's Opencast Executive has won well-deserved praise for the sensitivity of many of its restoration schemes, that these have embraced more than the quality of the agricultural land in question, and that in the present case the Executive propose to extend the area of woodland within the site, plant other trees, re-establish hedgerows with a variety of species, provide new wetlands and return the contour of the land to approximately its present levels. However, common sense insists that the restored landscape would for many years appear 'man-made', more- or-less devoid of the countless natural features and eccentricities which are part and parcel of its present charm and result from the passage of time rather than man's artifice. None of the restored sites referred to at the inquiry or which I saw when I was in the locality lead me to conclude otherwise.[23]

These problems of restored land were highlighted in other ways. A study, funded by BCC, found that earthworm populations were reduced to 4–10 per cent of pre-opencasting levels during storage in topsoil mounds. When the soil was respread, intensive cultivation further devastated the remaining earthworm population. As a result, it could take up to twenty years for earthworm populations fully to recover from opencasting. Farmers have commented on the implication of these changes. Mr Forsyth rents land from BCC which was worked by the NCB in the 1970s as part of the Radcliffe site, on the coastal plain in Northumberland. The land was returned to him in 1983. He describes the effects of opencasting on the agricultural quality of the farm as follows:

> The productive capacities of the soil are reduced dramatically. The land is now very heavy clay-type soil. It is fibreless, structureless, and there are few worms to be seen. When preparing seed-beds it is very difficult to break down. It is not uncommon, when preparing for grass seeds, for the Ministry of Agriculture to go over the same ground twenty times or more with assorted implements to get the required tilth. The land does not stand the extremes of weather well, and gets very wet in winter. In the summer it dries out, shrinks, and huge cracks appear. Any crops that up until then had looked good, particularly wheat, will by midsummer struggle to find the moisture to swell in a dry season.
>
> Likewise with grassland....Fertiliser requirement is higher, which we assume is due to shallow rooting, a result of the compaction of the subsoil. The need to subsoil [subsoiling involves the use of a single vertical plough to produce drainage channels in the soil] therefore is paramount, but the cost is excessive. Whereas on virgin land any subsoil problem is about 12–16 inches, where continuous ploughing has over the years done the damage, here the compaction is down to drain depth, and nobody can afford to go down that far.[24]

Bob Pendlebury graphically described such problems on agricultural land in the West of Durham:

> When the land is put back the farmers need to apply a tremendous amount of fertiliser to put some productive capacity back into the soil.
>
> You can tell where a lot of opencast working has taken place by walking on the land. Its very hard. When you get a

dry spell, the grass goes yellow much sooner than land which
hasn't been opencasted.[25]

Another problem associated with reclamation relates to the
drainage of opencast sites. Speaking at a conference we organised on the topic in Durham in 1988 George Bramfitt, Land
Drainage Officer for Durham CC explained how:

> You can't properly start to drain a site for at least three to
> five years after the site's been worked, to give the land a
> chance to settle. During this period there's a lot of surface
> run off, which can lead to flooding. Slumping is fairly com-
> mon on restored land, and creates real problems where
> restored gradients are shallow.
>
> The opencasting of the hillsides feeding the streams in the
> West of Durham has induced a high flow, short duration
> flood situation with regular silt coloration problems. Most of
> the smaller rivers have reduced natural flows as natural
> ground water release has been affected.
>
> It costs £1,000 per acre to drain land properly, so there's
> a possibility that sites don't get drained properly because of
> the cost. Even when the drainage is done perfectly, you still
> get problems. Natural draining through man-made slopes
> takes years to mature.
>
> On a natural landscape the soil absorbs 90–99 per cent
> of rain-water. On an opencast site, particularly during the
> five- year period when it can't be under-drained, about 90
> per cent of the water runs off.
>
> Even when the sites are fully restored the land doesn't
> drain like it did before. On a site where there's a lot of mud-
> stone near the surface the soil becomes virtually
> impermeable, even when its been properly drained. The mud
> silts simply clog the drainage spaces in the ground.

He elaborated on the impacts on rivers and fish:

> There was a good trout pool next to the Rag Pathside site,
> but it became three feet deep in silt. This silt had run off from
> the opencast site, and it affected the fishing two miles down-
> stream, causing fish loss and migration…the proper recovery

time on the river life exceeded five years.

Before opencasting the flood water in the River Browney was greeny-grey in colour. Now when it floods, the river water is yellow with silt...

Everywhere you find opencast workings you always get these sandy/silty discharges. I've fished the River Browney for thirty-five years, and I've seen countless natural catchments that kept the river clean disappear. They've either been destroyed, or they're full of silt, even though these sites were worked more than ten years ago. Nobody knows what long-term effects this might have on fish life.

It was damaging criticisms like these which pushed the opencast industry into laying increasing stress upon its environmental policy. At times this stretched credibility to breaking point, as on the occasion when Peter Cotgrove of the Opencast Executive gave a lecture in Durham in 1989. Here he presented a carefully argued defence of the organisation's approach to opencast mining and the environment. He came equipped with slides for the overhead projector in which, somewhat to the embarrassment of the speaker himself, the diagrammatic representation of stock piles of coal were coloured green!

BREACHES OF PLANNING CONDITIONS

An often cited criticism of opencast mining relates to the ways in which the operation of the site fails to abide by the planning conditions which applied to its acceptance. A study by the County Planning Officers' Society, published in 1984, examined 30 sites involving twenty different opencast companies in six counties. It found 60 examples where conditions had been breached. In one county alone, serious breaches of planning conditions occurred on 6 out of 11 sites which had been granted planning permission since 1981. In our researches we interviewed several mineral planning officers who informed us that breaches of conditions had taken place on many sites in this same period. Even with the most severe breaches however,

MPAs have been reluctant to proceed with enforcement action. In cases where the site has been worked in the wrong direction, enforcement action is not a practical option. Given that any enforcement action takes place after the disturbance has been created, it can seem of doubtful relevance to hard pressed Local Authorities who are aware that the operator has the right of appeal and that this can be a long and expensive process.

However, the industry has been made aware of the criticisms and, in response, BCC set up a consultative system to relate to the local communities during the operation of a site. Each site was required to have a Site Liaison Committee which would listen to and act upon the complaints of local people. This system was an improvement but here too there was a suggestion that the Corporation was concerned with public relations rather than with the problems of residents. At the Billingside Public Inquiry, BCC told the inspector that its employment of a contractor to carry out work on the site would not make it difficult to monitor the site operations properly, since the setting up of a Liaison Committee 'would be helpful in solving any problems that might arise'.[26]

Following the Linton Lane inquiry in Northumberland in June 1988, the inspector reported BCC's views about Liaison Committees as follows:

> One of the matters raised in communities adjacent to opencast coal sites is that residents may not know whom to contact to discuss any aspect of the operations which appear to affect their interests. To overcome any such difficulty, British Coal would set up a Liaison Committee which would operate throughout the life of the sites. Aspects of the working of the site would be discussed at such committee meetings.
>
> ...free press access to Liaison Committees is inappropriate because people feel inhibited in fully expressing their views in the presence of the press.[27]

There was disagreement at the inquiry between Northumberland County Council and BCC as to whether the purpose of the Committee was to resolve complaints. The inspector concluded:

> ...In my view the resolution of complaints must remain in the hands of the operator or result, if appropriate, in the MPA taking enforcement action.[28]

Yet at the Marley Hill Inquiry in Co. Durham in November 1989, John Stevenson, the Area Director of the OE, stated in his proof of evidence that:

> British Coal would set up a Liaison Committee...to provide an opportunity for any queries to be brought forward and for information about future activities on the site to be given to those concerned.
>
> The Committee would meet on a regular basis to discuss any general or specific problems which might arise with a view to action being taken to enable them to be overcome.[29]

At the Public Exhibition relating to the Ryehill proposal near West Rainton, Co. Durham, one of the display boards stated:

> British Coal are [sic] willing to set up a Liaison Committee consisting of local residents and representatives of local authorities, the contractors working the site, and British Coal. This practice has been successful on other sites in highlighting particular areas of concern felt by the local community and in dealing with any problems which may arise.

There appear to be conflicting views as to the purpose of Liaison Committees. The view expressed by BCC at the Billingside and Linton Lane Inquiries was that the main purpose of establishing such Committees was to keep people informed of progress on the site as workings developed, and to ensure that local people knew to whom to complain. Its primary purpose was not to hear and resolve complaints. However at the Marley Hill Inquiry, the Ryehill exhibition, and in its publicity, BCC gave the impression that the Liaison Committee *was* to resolve both general and specific complaints. This confusion is symptomatic. The policy of consultation was developed in a rather *ad hoc* way, as a means of dealing with persistent criticisms rather than a wholehearted commitment to a new kind of relationship with local communities. In our researches across the coalfields we were regularly informed (as late as 1996) that many of the operators 'hold liaison committees in contempt'. Some of these Committees, notably in the Midlands and especially in Leicestershire, had been involved in effective local liaison. We were told by a councillor in Leicestershire that the effective Liaison Committees invariably linked to good site practices, but that operators usually behave well if their site operations are under 'the watchful gaze of the local residents'. But when highly intrusive site activities take place (especially blasting) there are nearly always some complaints to the Liaison Committee or to the MPA.

However, the most common approach by the operators seems still to be one which sees the Committees as a useful way of informing local communities of their future plans. This is better than nothing, but it failed to provide an institutional solution to the many problems experienced by local residents.

In its defence, BCC frequently stated that it received few complaints. As a result, inspectors often concluded that sites were normally being operated in a sensitive manner and that these operations did not cause unacceptable disturbances. Our researches have shown this not to be the case. The fact that many people do not complain often relates not to the level of the nuisance, but to the institutional processes that are in place. Sadly, for most people who live around sites, complaining is frequently viewed as being 'a complete waste of time'.

PLANNING GAIN

During the late 1980s, major opencast developments invariably involved the issue of 'planning gain'—the term used to refer to the financial payments or new community facilities provided by the opencast company as part of its planning proposal. Alternatively referred to as 'community benefit payments', these practices have been the source of conflicts in many mining districts. In 1997, RJB Mining's Hathery Lane opencast site application in Northumberland was accompanied by an offer of a £300,000 payment towards community facilities. This led to open conflict between individual County Councillors and between Northumberland County Council and Blyth Valley Borough Council. These rows were not prevented by the County Council's detailed guidelines and procedures covering the offer of community benefit payments. The issue was discussed at length during the public inquiry.[30]

A similar conflict had broken out in Leicester the previous year when Measham Parish Council dropped its objections to a planning application by RJB Mining. Chairman of the Local Action Group Mike Hodges argued that:

> with offers of...money it must be difficult to give weight to the parish council's objectivity on the issue. Moreover, it flies in the face of the overwhelming opposition expressed at the public meeting held at Measham village hall and attended by several hundred people.

For its part, the Parish Council contested the numbers of people who attended the meeting and insisted that it had never given full approval to the proposal. Parish Clerk, Susan Redman agreed that no firm plans existed, although:

> Budge has agreed to set up a community trust fund that I believe will benefit all the parishes that are affected. The trust fund will happen if permission is granted without going to public inquiry.[31]

The offer of financial payments from opencast companies has frequently led to angry outbursts, with public cries of 'bribery' from local residents. Such a charge was shouted at the Cutsyke Road Opencast Inquiry when a local councillor angrily told the inspector what he thought about the offer of a financial payment from the appellant, Miller Mining.[32]

In these ways people have become concerned about the offer of large sums of money to cash-starved local authorities. Throughout the coal districts we have heard serious allegations voiced on a regular basis. This issue assumed such prominance that it was considered by the Committee on Standards in Public Life (chaired by Lord Nolan). The Committee published its third report on 8 July 1997, covering the *Standards of Conduct in Local Government in England, Scotland and Wales*.[33] An important section of the report dealt with Planning Gain or Obligations and Agreements. These were considered to be 'the most intractable aspect of the planning system' with which the Committee had to deal. The Committee's report notes that: 'The potential problems have little to do with corruption, but have a tremendous impact on public confidence.'

Lord Nolan and his Committee took evidence from interested parties, indicating that there was a very sharp divide between the views of local authorities, developers, conservation and environmental groups. While the *DoE Circular 1/97* sets out 'clear and proper guidance' concerning planning gain, Nolan comments that:

It appears that pressures on the ground, particularly the restrictions on the capital expenditure of local authorities, are too strong to be overcome by guidance alone. After all, by using planning gain, many local communities have secured benefits and improvements which would otherwise have been impossible.

The report highlights the views of objectors to planning gain. They believe that inappropriate planning permissions were being given because of the infrastructural improvements offered by developers. In other words, planning permissions were being bought and sold. Conversely, developers felt that they were frequently being held to ransom by local authorities. They also felt that planning gain was being too loosely interpreted, so that in some cases the gain had little to do with the development. Nolan added that:

There have indeed been some celebrated occurrences of planning gain which seem to fit that description.

The Committee made several recommendations on this issue. It thought that the Department of the Environment (and the Scottish and Welsh Offices) should consider whether present legislation on planning obligations is sufficiently tightly worded to prevent planning permissions from being bought and sold. It was felt that local authorities should adopt rules on openness that allow planning agreements to be subject to discussion by members of the authority and the public. They should not restrict access to supporting documents except where justified by the requirements of commercial confidentiality, which should be interpreted narrowly. Clearly the adoption of tighter procedures covering planning gain would be one way to improve public confidence in local government and the planning system.

5
THE STATE, THE PUBLIC AND THE INQUIRY

In the 1970s, applications to mine opencast sites were normally given approval without too much discussion by MPAs. By the mid-late 1980s few applications passed easily. When an MPA refuses an opencast planning application, the developer has the right to appeal and appeals can be highly rancorous. For the coal company the site is an important source of potential revenue and a key part of its business strategy. But councillors, often under pressure from local communities and other pressure groups, have their own political agenda—which may be at complete variance with the views and aspirations of the company.

Commenting on this process from the standpoint of companies involved in opencast operations, Justin Hancock observed:

> opencast planning is...High Politics (as anyone who has observed the machinations of a typical council chamber knows well). There is little likelihood that someone who has recently left college with a good degree in Town and Country Planning could understand the logic in a random cross section of opencast planning decisions.[1]

In his view:

> The essence of local democracy is that the councillors can choose to ignore the advice of their professionals completely. Often they do so with little thought of justifying their refusal with adequate refusal reasons. The officers are then given the unenviable task of creating some believable refusal reasons and defending them at a public inquiry. They do

have the power to distance themselves from the decision, in which case the councillors themselves have to fight the appeal. This would make for a very interesting spectacle but very rarely happens.[2]

For many developers, the planning mechanisms and the appeal systems are not viewed as a legitimate part of the democratic process, but rather as a set of obstacles which have to be overcome. Given the implications of a 'good' or 'bad' decision on the company's finances, the planning system became the site of increasingly acrimonious debate during the 1980s.

The planning and appeals system can also be lucrative. Various planning consultancies and firms specialising in public relations have developed services to help companies obtain planning permissions for potentially difficult applications such as opencast coal sites. Many of them seem to specialise in undermining and limiting the effectiveness of local opposition. Ridgemount Public Relations coined the phrase '*Don't let the locals dig a hole for you.*' They stressed that employing communications consultants experienced in this field to work alongside the applicant's managers and other consultants should not be viewed as an additional expense but as an investment towards success. Others such as Harvey Wood, Director of the Clean River Trust, have employed a less competitive approach, insisting that the industry has nothing to hide or be ashamed of—it simply needs to adopt a less defensive attitude when opposed by the 'environmental lobby' and develop a clear message of its own.[3] Nevertheless, our discussions with anti-opencast action groups produced several accounts of 'dirty tricks', which included the case of a PR consultant, reputedly working covertly for a mining company, who tried to infiltrate one group, recommending tactics that would have significantly damaged its reputation.

What is clear is that the development of economic activities associated with opencast mining requires, as part of its operations, the construction of a set of arguments and a discourse which legitimises these activities. As we have seen, this discourse is increasingly subject to challenge within the planning process.

When serious objections are raised, and planning permission is refused, the different perceptions and aspirations of the companies, the planners and local people openly surface. This clash of interests is resolved by the state through a complex set of procedures, regulated by planning law and the Planning Inspectorate. It is this Inspectorate which has the responsibility for any public inquiries which may result from intense disagreement between the applicant and the local planning authority.

THE INSPECTOR AND THE INSPECTORATE

The Planning Inspectorate is one of over 100 Executive Agencies established since 1988 under the Conservative Government's 'Next Steps' initiative with the aim of bringing greater efficiency and accountability to those parts of Government with executive functions.[4] These reforms involved a fundamental change in the structure of Government, and led to nearly one-half of all civil servants being employed in Agencies by the end of financial year 1995/96. The Inspectorate has been a joint Agency of the Department of the Environment and the Welsh Office since 1992. These two Government Departments are also the principal source of funding for the Agency—with other work (housing, highways, etc) being charged to the relevant Departments.

The Planning Inspectorate's aims and objectives were formally agreed in the context of the preparation for Agency. The agreed function is that:

> The Planning Inspectorate serves the Secretaries of State for the Environment and Wales on appeals and other casework under planning, housing, environment, highways and allied legislation.

Its objectives are:

- to provide as efficient, expeditious and economic a service as is compatible with the maintenance of quality and high professional standards;

- to maintain the integrity of each inspector as an independent tribunal, not subject to any improper influence;

- to provide clear and readily available information and guidance for all who come into contact with the Inspectorate;

- to achieve all financial and performance targets that are set for the Inspectorate; and

- to maintain an efficient, properly trained and well motivated workforce.

The Planning Inspectorate has also outlined a 'vision' of its role:

> For the Inspectorate to be the prime source of impartial expertise for resolving disputes about the use of land, natural resources and the environment.[5]

This notion of 'impartiality' is central to the Inspectorate's view of itself and critical to its success as a legitimator of the planning process. In the run-up to Agency status, however, it became clear that other criteria were also considered, by others, to be of importance. For example, the Minister for the Environment, Michael Howard, indicated that he expected:

> ...the Agency to be ever more efficient. And I do expect— as does the public you serve—the Agency to give better service in terms of cutting out the unfortunate delays which now dog the system. These benefits will surely come from better organisation, more responsibility and greater freedom for your management to manage.[6]

The workload of the Inspectorate increased in the 1990s. It was particularly high from 1994 onwards when the unusually large number of local plan inquiries took place which needed to receive priority. Local plans (and their policies) evolve in a series of stages: the consultation draft, followed by a deposit version.

After a period of consultation, a public inquiry is held to hear any objections and amendments to the plan. These can be submitted by any body, company or member of the public (inside or outside the authority's boundaries). The inquiry inspector's report is subsequently published. The report may recommend modifications before the Plan is finally adopted by the MPA.[7] In 1994 the Government made it clear that these appeals received priority in order to achieve a full plan coverage as quickly as possible. So other work was delayed. Such was the case in Durham.

Durham County Council published the consultation draft of its *Minerals Local Plan* in September 1995. The Council hoped to identify opencast coal sites which would form part of an agreed programme, and asked all opencast operators in the county to identify potential sites for which they might planning permission. The operators identified 43 sites, but the publication of the list, and maps showing their locations, caused widespread anger and public opposition. Approximately 3,800 comments were submitted to the Council concerning opencast mining. The Council's Environment Committee was told that the main issues raised were the impact on local communities from noise, dust, traffic and visual intrusion; impact on the landscape and wildlife; cumulative impact; the effects on health; and the impact on the County's economy.[8] As a result, there was an increase in the number of local plan inquiries from 73 in 1983/84 to nearly 100 in 1995/96. More importantly, the average inquiry duration increased from 40 weeks to an estimated 50 weeks over this three year period.

In an effort to anticipate these developments, new rules were established in 1992 aimed at simplifying and rationalising procedures. Under its new Agency Status, the Inspectorate embarked upon an appraisal of its own performance and W. S. Atkins was commissioned to produce a 'Customer Survey'. This revealed considerable 'customer dissatisfaction' with the system: too intimidating and too repetitious. These points were picked up immediately by the then Secretary of State for the Environment, John Gummer, and eventually incorporated into a Departmental Circular.

'Customers' also complained about delays. But as a consequence of the ongoing squeeze on public finances in the 1990s, there was a halt in the recruitment of new Inspectors. This exacerbated a situation in which the time between an applicant appealing against refusal of planning permission and the subsequent public inquiry could be one year or more. However, in the Inspectorate's 1995/96 *Annual Report and Accounts* it was reported that a new intake of inspectors had been appointed to help reduce these delays. It also included the results of another 'customer survey' which revealed high levels of satisfaction among local authorities, the general public, and the planning professions. This was written with some relief and in a way which was indicative of the beleaguered state of the Agency in the 1990s.

A sense of the ways in which these changes have affected the job of an inspector can be gleaned from a recruitment leaflet distributed in 1995. At this time, potential applicants were informed that:

> You will need to be sufficiently robust, both physically and mentally, to undertake long, arduous and controversial inquiries, and make detailed site inspections.

The leaflet also stated that inspectors:

> need maturity, a good presence, sound judgement and the ability to think clearly and to draft clear, concise reports and decision letters.

There are potentially at least 183 different categories of work on which Planning Inspectors (Reporters in Scotland) can be deployed. However, the bulk of their case-load relates to general planning appeals, enforcement appeals, development plan inquiries and highway inquiries.[9] As a consequence, the Inspectorate was concerned to recruit people aged between 35 and 55, with an active background in one of several relevant professions. Exceptionally, applicants were considered without a professional qualification if they had had experience of special value to the Inspectorate.[10] Short-listed candidates were required to undertake a series of exercises, tests and interviews at the Civil Service Selection Board. These last one full day and part of the following morning. The exercises include small group discussions in which general topics and those relating to planning and housing are considered and followed by written tests which include the drafting of reports. The Board selects a final short-list for interview. Successful candidates are then investigated by the Commissioners to ensure that they are trustworthy and qualified for the appointment. If satisfied, the Commissioners issue a certificate of qualification.

In many respects the position of the inspectors in the Agency carries on established 'civil service traditions'. Following the training period new Inspectors will usually start with simple work (such as written appeals), before moving on to more complex appeals. The work of each inspector is graded and assessed depending on the quality of the work handled and the quality of the output. If an inspector is considered suitable (s)he is given higher grade or more specialised work. However, the pressures of Agency status have produced some important changes. Most significant of these has been the appointment of 'non-salaried inspectors' engaged on short-term contracts or as consultants on a fee-paid basis. These are seen to provide a 'flexible resource' which has been used mainly for written representation casework. In the view of the inspectorate the availability of this flexible workforce has enabled it to cope with a rapidly varying load of appeal cases at the same time as meeting increasing demands for experienced inspectors for the local plan inquiries and the new environmental work.[11] This flexibility can also be found on complex appeals where the inspector can be assisted during the inquiry by 'assistant inspectors' or 'specialist assessors'. In September 1996 the Planning Inspectorate advertising the posts of three Planning Assistants to help and assist inspectors in very long inquiries, including those dealing with local plans.

FORMS OF APPEAL

Following the reviews of the Inspectorate, the Department of the Environment issued *Circular 15/96* on 20 September 1996. This Circular—*Planning Appeal Procedures*—governs all aspects of the appeal process in England and Wales. If an application for a site's development is rejected by the MPA, an appeal must be submitted within six months of the date of the MPA's decision notice.[12] It should contain an explanation of why the appellant disagrees with each of the MPA's reasons for not granting planning permission.

Appeals can take three basic forms: an appeal based on written representations; a hearing; or a public inquiry. While most appeals concerning opencast coal applications are dealt with at a public inquiry, there is a growing trend for appeals concerning smaller site applications to be dealt with either by written representations or at a hearing. Appeals by *written representations* are by far the most common procedure involving 80 per cent of all appeals. Generally they offer the quickest, simplest and cheapest way of deciding appeals (the procedures are described in detail in Annex 1 of *Circular 15/96*).[13] A timetable is set out in the regulations for the notification of the appeal to the various parties, plus the starting date. Third parties can submit representations about the appeal within 28 days, and are allowed access to the relevant documents submitted by the principal parties. The process also involves a site visit by the inspector. On these visits the inspector can either be accompanied by representatives from the appellant, the planning authority and other parties, or they can (in some circumstances) be unaccompanied.

A *hearing* is considered to be a suitable method for considering an appeal when the development is small-scale; where there is little or no third party interest; where complex legal, technical or policy issues are unlikely to arise; and where there is no likelihood that formal cross-examination is required to test the opposing cases. Hearings were introduced in 1982 and have grown in number each year. By 1995, 12 per cent of all planning appeals were considered at hearings. The procedure is intended to save the parties time and money and to allow the inspector to lead a round-table discussion about the main issues. The aim is to give everybody, including interested third parties, a fair hearing and to provide the inspector with all the information necessary for a decision—but in a more relaxed and less formal atmosphere than at a local inquiry.[14]

It is for the Secretary of State (through the Planning Inspectorate) to decide whether a hearing is a suitable means for considering an appeal. This decision will be reached after consultations with the MPA and the appellant. Once a decision has been made the regulations state that it is the aim to hold the hearing within 12 weeks. Normally a hearing will be informal in character, with the inspector and the various parties sitting around a table. *Circular 15/96* suggests that a small committee room is usually satisfactory for a hearing—that 'the more formal atmosphere of a council chamber should be avoided.' The proceedings will commence by resolving any residual doubts about the application, then the inspector will outline what (s)he considers to be the main issues, and indicate those matters for which further explanation or clarification is required. However, the parties present can still refer to other aspects of the planning application and appeal which they consider to be relevant.

Appellants usually present their case at a hearing through an agent or advisor—but such representation is not essential. *Circular 15/96* notes that legal representation should not normally be necessary (though experience has shown that some appellants do employ solicitors at hearings). In addition, the parties involved in the hearing are expected to have circulated and exchanged written material well in advance so that this need not to be read out at the hearing. In order to prevent delays and lengthening the proceedings, the parties are also requested to avoid introducing new material and documentation at the hearing. The appellants will be allowed to make any final comments before the discussion is closed. Unlike a public inquiry, the hearing system allows the inspector the option of adjourning the proceedings to the site, allowing it to be concluded there. The inspector will only do this when (s)he is satisfied that the discussion can proceed satisfactorily, that all the participants can attend, and that no-one involved would be at a disadvantage. Normally a formal site visit would be held on a separate day.

In contrast with these two procedures, the public inquiry (which covered 8 per cent of all appeals in 1995) is much more formal and legalistic. These are quite dramatic events which can last for weeks and are therefore both time consuming and strenuous. A public inquiry can take one of two forms. In the first category (usually involving smaller opencast sites) the inspector hears the evidence from the various parties and reaches a decision himself at the end of the Inquiry, which appears at the end of his report. An example of this type would be the appeal by Ward Bros Mining Ltd., concerning its proposed site at Arch Lane, Garswood, St. Helens MBC in June 1995. In this case, the inspector, Keith Durrant, refused the appeal, having found 'harm to matters of acknowledged importance'.

The second category of public inquiry is the 'call-in' by the Secretary of State. The circumstances for this type of appeal in England and Wales are defined in the Town and Country Planning Act (1990). Such a 'call-in' takes place where appeals are controversial in nature; involve complex issues; involve large-scale development; or involve another government department and government policy considerations.[15] Here the inspector hears the evidence and produces a report and recommendation on the outcome of the appeal. This is then submitted to the Secretary of State who makes a final decision, which normally confirms the inspector's recommendation.

In 1995 the Secretary of State for the Environment, John Gummer, called-in the appeal by H.J. Banks & Co. concerning refusal of planning permission by the City of Wakefield MDC for the Weeland Road opencast site application at Sharlston. The Secretary of State's letter (28 March 1995) noted that the reason for his decision to determine the appeal himself was because 'the appeal relates to proposals giving rise to significant public controversy.' The department had been inundated with letters of objection from local residents and the issues surrounding the Weeland Road appeal had been raised in the House of Commons by local MPs.

Occasionally, after consideration of the evidence, the Secretary of State disagrees with the recommendations of the inspector. In these cases, the inspector's view is overturned. One such case occurred in 1997 and concerned the inquiry relating to the appeal by Coal Contractors over the former New Stubbin Colliery opencast site in Rotherham, South Yorkshire.

THE PUBLIC INQUIRY

A public inquiry is an highly orchestrated event which works to an established set of rules set out in documents produced by the Lord Chancellor's office.[16] In many ways it resembles a court of law, with the inspector serving as judge, in others it is like a board of examiners, with the inspector acting as the external independent overseer of internal wars and disagreements. In both respects the inspector represents an authority which is national rather than local. However, the dynamics of administrative justice are such that the discussions and disagreements are all aired in the local place, usually in venues close to the site of the proposed development, and this adds a unique element to the inquiry process.

Depending on the scale of local participation, inquiries can be held in diverse settings, including sports, leisure and community centres, church halls, public houses and hotels, working mens' clubs, local government offices and civic centres.[17] As part of our research we have sat and admired the civic grandeur of Bolton Town Hall, reflected on the Methodist tradition in South Wales and seen a variety of working men's clubs in the North East of England. In each and all of these occasions we have been struck by local particularities and the ways in which these insert themselves into the fabric of the inquiry.[18]

The venue can greatly affect the conditions experienced during an inquiry. In winter a venue with inadequate heating can be a serious problem; others can also be uncomfortable or noisy. The Plenmeller Opencast Inquiry (held in Haltwhistle, Northumberland, 1986) had to be interrupted due to the noise

3. A typical cast of characters portrayed by Bob Peck a member of the Shilo North Action Group

being generated by a children's playgroup on the next floor in the building. Occasionally the venue can become a part of the Inquiry. At the Barcus Close Opencast Inquiry (Stanley, Co. Durham, 1984) a witness for the appellants (Ward Bros Plant Hire Ltd) was being cross-examined on the risk of flooding from the potential site. It was argued that thunder storms and heavy rain showers were regular features of the area. At that moment heavy rain and hailstones pounded the roof of the building so loudly that it was difficult to continue the cross-examination.

Many of the administrative and procedural matters of a large public inquiry can be dealt with at a *Pre-Inquiry Meeting* (PIM) which is usually held a few weeks before the main event.[19] As in the case of the main inquiry, the date and venue of the PIM. has to be formally advertised in a newspaper circulating in the locality. In addition, it is usual practice for the relevant MPA(s) (under instructions from the Planning Inspectorate) to write to other parties taking part in the appeal with the PIM details. The MPA and appellants will have already identified the key issues that they would raise at the inquiry. It is common for inspectors to press both to arrange meetings before the commencement of the inquiry to consider whether statements of agreed facts can be compiled and whether some draft site working conditions can also be agreed.[20] In such complex and lengthy inquiries, the inspector will often ask the planning authority to appoint one of its staff to act as the inquiry's programme officer to deal with practical issues. Evidence from all the main parties is exchanged four weeks prior to the start, to allow the inspector, lawyers and other participants a chance to prepare cross-examination questions and any necessary rebuttal evidence. In the 1990s, participants were requested to minimise the number as well as length of supplementary/ rebuttal proofs, and submit them to the inspector and other parties in ample time to allow for reading and preparation prior to possible cross-examination.[21]

The inspector officially opens the inquiry at 10.00am on the first day (frequently at an earlier time on subsequent days). The various parties (starting with the appellant and the MPA, and ending with members of the public) are requested to list their witnesses. The inquiry proper begins when the appellant's barrister or solicitor presents a concise *opening statement* in which the main elements of the appeal are described. This is followed by the presentation of evidence through the calling of witnesses. Under the 1992 Inquiry Rules witnesses are no longer allowed to read laboriously through their 'evidence in chief' (their proofs of evidence and appendices). They are asked instead to produce summaries of 1,500 words which at worst can be presented in no more than one hour. However, subsequent cross-examination on the information in the full proofs of evidence of a witness can take several hours or sometimes, even days.

All inquiries have a standard physical layout. The inspector, resembling a judge, sits in a central and often elevated position at the front of the inquiry room with the appellant usually sitting on his right side and MPA to his left. At venues such as clubs and church halls, the inspector may have the table and chair on a stage which provides a commanding position. Third parties, such as District Councils and amenity groups, comple the circle of main participants. The general public congregate at the back of the room. Ashforth has described such inquiries as 'theatres of power'. Yet in the way the inquiries bring such groups together, emphasising openness and freedom of speech, they appear to elevate the state above the ordinary wranglings of daily life. In Ashforth's view these are key institutions which *legitimate* modern states.[22]

Around the sides of the room there are usually maps, wallcharts and photographs. During quiet periods of recess, people wander around the exhibits, pointing out features to their friends and companions; sometimes arguing. The tables behind which the inspector, barristers and witnesses sit are usually piled high with boxes of evidence. This veritable baffle bank of paperwork can include proofs of evidence, maps, voluminous details of the appeal site's proposed development, previous appeal decisions, local planning documents, and other material. Inquiry staff spend many hours referring to these documents during the presentation of evidence, later during cross-examination.

At the start of the inquiry, the representatives of the local and regional newspapers, local television crews and radio reporters usually gather to interview the main participants. On the opening day local action groups opposing the opencast site's development frequently organise small demonstrations, often with banners; sometimes they chant slogans. Demonstrations may also involve children from local schools, and occasionally workers employed from the opencast companies and their contractors organise counter-demonstrations. It can become quite lively.

Usually the inquiry is concluded with a formal site visit by the inspector, accompanied by representatives of the other main parties. These visits may simply be a brief tour of the appeal site but they can include a lengthy tour of several other sites (possibly to highlight comparable restoration strategies carried out by the appellant or other companies).

The inquiry ends with the closing submissions by the MPA and the appellant. In the 1990s these speeches tended to be long-winded and rather tedious. As a consequence, the inspectorate asked for copies of closing speeches to be made available, in at least note form and preferably drafted.

At this point in the inquiry the appellant (and sometimes the MPA) can make an application for costs. Any application for costs has to be made and time may be allowed for a response to any claim.

Circular 15/96 notes that:

> parties should bear in mind the guidance in DoE *Circular 8/93* regarding the risk of an award of costs against a party who fails to comply with the Inquiries Procedure Rules so as to cause other parties to incur extra expense as a result of 'unreasonable' behaviour.[23]

Such 'unreasonable' behaviour might include the failure by one party to submit its written statement within the timescale prescribed in the Inquiry Procedure Rules. Sometimes these delays have been viewed as amounting to unfair gamesmanship or deliberate tactical delays. With this in mind *Circular 15/96* adds that:

> If an inquiry is prolonged as a result of a party's failure to submit proofs of evidence at the prescribed time, or failure to provide a required summary, so that the whole proof has to be read at the inquiry, an award of costs may be made against that party.[24]

While the DETR has made clear that the award of costs (and its threat) is disciplinary and not punitive, many MPAs clearly feel that they have been unfairly treated by the existing costs regime. In their view many awards have gone well beyond mere disciplinary action. In our experience of opencast public inquiries in the 1990s, applications for costs by appellants occurred at almost every appeal. Sometimes it seemed that the lawyers for appellants sought to intimidate the local MPAs. A significant award of costs (several tens of thousands of pounds) made against an authority is a daunting prospect, and we heard of several cases when planning permission for opencast sites has been granted, in circumstances in which it would normally have been refused, as a result of these worries over costs.

Following the conclusion of a public inquiry, the inspector will prepare his report, and recommendations.[25] The appeal decision must be notified in writing to all parties entitled to appear at the inquiry. Other parties who were given leave to appeal at the inquiry (such as local protest groups) will receive a copy if they have requested it. The decision must be justified with reasons which are full, clear and precise so that the appellant and other parties can understand the logic underpinning the outcome. Where the Secretary of State disagrees with the inspector's recommendation, he must explain in full why he has rejected it. In all these cases there is opportunity to challenge the decision on a point of law in the High Court.[26]

PUBLIC INQUIRIES IN ACTION

In his advice to *appellants* Justin Hancock indicates that:

> Lodging an appeal is a straight-forward process involving a succinct form to be filled in and a map to be attached. The only 'creative' input to the appeal form is the composition of the appellants 'grounds for appeal'. These must reflect the MPAs reasons for refusal or raise issues unfairly ignored by the MPA. The refusal reasons do not limit the areas of debate at public inquiry in quite the same way as the MPA.... Nevertheless it is good practice to write grounds for appeal which are comprehensive and will drive the inquiry in the direction the appellant wants.[27]

Hancock's comments are probably indicative of a general approach by mining companies to public inquiries. They frequently believe strongly that their application has been unfairly treated, the victim of political manoeuvring and the emotional and irrational objections by local residents.

At the inquiry the company, like the MPA, will have a room in which to conduct its operations. This often has the feel of wartime command and control centre—with facsimile machines, mobile telephones, computers and printers marshalled to counter the opposition with rebuttal evidence and penetrating cross-examination. Junior solicitors or clerks are often to be seen taking notes alongside witnesses waiting to give evidence or (later in the Inquiry) assisting with cross-examination. These people frequently rush back and forth from the 'war room' to the inquiry itself. Frequently another 'war room' can be located at the hotel where the appellant's barrister or solicitor is staying. Meetings to discuss evidence, cross-examination tactics and strategy often go on long into the night. Officers of the MPA and managers of the coal company often have to fit the inquiry into their other duties. By the end of a long inquiry the exhaustion and tensions on both teams is clearly visible.

This was the arena of conflict into which many MPAs stepped during the 1980s and early 1990s. It is fair to say that they went through a steep learning curve. Thrown in at the deep end, often against a determined appellant and an experienced barrister, the MPA staff adopted many of the tactics and strategies of the opencast mining companies themselves. They too recruited expert witnesses and barristers to lead their case; they had their own 'war rooms' and late night discussions. However, the MPAs worked within much tighter financial constraints than the appellants. In the 1980s it became clear that a series of major opencast appeals could put considerable financial pressure on an MPA. Senior barristers or QCs do not come cheaply and legal costs often reached £40,000. Additionally, these appeals were serviced through the overtime worked by the MPA's planning and legal staff. These administrative and financial strains began to tell with repeated threats of damaging costs being brought against them. Many MPAs began to feel that any solution would be preferable to 'another bloody inquiry'.

The MPAs evidence primarily revolves around the reasons for refusal of the planning application. It covers the key planning issues—including the increasingly important Development Plan and Local Minerals Plan policies. A large volume of evidence (including correspondence) can appear during the examination and cross-examination of the MPA's planning officer—sometimes going back to the pre-application discussions between the MPA and the applicant. The appellant's lawyers at an inquiry have been known to try to show (or imply) that the process was politically motivated. So the mineral planning officer and his colleagues can sometimes be drawn into acrimonious cross-examination concerning the MPA's policies and decision-making processes.

In order to produce authoritative proofs that can withstand detailed scrutiny and cross-examination MPAs have frequently employed *expert witnesses*.[28] Lawyers, expert witnesses and environmental activists appear at many inquiries, giving the appearance of a 'travelling roadshow', moving from appeal to appeal throughout the country. These witnesses, once recruited, are organised and coordinated by the legal teams.

Sometimes MPAs can use expert witnesses for strategic rather than technical reasons. There have been occasions when mineral planning officers have recommended the approval of opencast sites only to have councillors reject them. Facing an appeal, such planning officers are in an extremely difficult position, occasionally refusing to give evidence. Wakefield MBC refused permission for Miller Mining's Cutsyke Road site in 1993 under just these circumstances. Sensibly, they hired an outside planning consultant (the Manchester-based Robert Turney Associates) to present the Council's case at the inquiry in January 1994. This approach proved successful. Wakefield MDC has subsequently employed specialist witnesses at several of its opencast appeals.

There are a variety of views on the role of the expert witness in public inquiries. G.E. Warren (Chairman of Chapman Warren) sees them assisting an inquiry through their fairness, openness and impartiality.[29] But this Olympian view often conflicts with the client's objectives—a favourable decision. In fact, the role of the expert witness is far more complex. An alternative view has been presented of the 'hired gun' whose expertise is used to sift the evidence to create the interpretation most advantageous to the party paying the fee. As in all things, science involves a degree of partisanship. It is not an area of life in which values play no part. Furthermore, the adversarial approach adopted at public inquiries acts against the presentation of 'impartial evidence' for scrutiny by 'impartial observers'.[30] The fascination of the inquiry process (as dramatology) lies in the ways in which the different sides construct their arguments and conduct themselves. This is most poignantly illustrated in the behaviour and manner of the expert witness and the way s(he) is managed by the client and the legal staff. They will have been given a thorough briefing on what they can write in their evidence and what they can and cannot say when cross-examined. Not infrequently this process of negotiated reality leads to upset, as the cautious concern of the client comes up against the ego of the expert. At one inquiry in the 1980s we talked with a senior planning officer at a moment when he felt especially beleaguered. He was stuck, he said 'with a QC who appears to know nothing and an expert witness who thinks he knows everything'.[31]

Not all barristers are pleasant to know or to work with, however. So, in 1996, the Department of the Environment produced a guide to *Good Practice at Planning Inquiries*[32]—which dealt specifically with the issue of cross-examination. The *Circular* emphasises that all parties involved in an Inquiry should be aiming to assist the inspector, rather than seeking confrontation with each other. It adds that:

> Inspectors will intervene in inquiry proceedings wherever they consider cross-examination or witnesses' responses to be unduly lengthy or unhelpful or in order to protect witnesses from excessive or over-aggressive questioning. This is particularly important in the case of unrepresented or inexperienced witnesses. They will also be expected to make full use of their powers to refuse to permit the giving or production of any evidence, cross-examination of witnesses or the presentation of any other matter they consider to be irrelevant or repetitious.

This was picked up by the report on the appeal by H.J. Banks & Co. concerning refusal of planning permission for the Weeland Road opencast site. The Inspector, Mrs Brushfield, commented on the manner of cross examination adopted by the appellant's barrister in this way:

On those occasions at planning inquiries when appellants choose to question local people, they have a significant opportunity to emphasise their positive approach to the local community and to reinforce their credentials in that respect. This is not what occurred here. The manner in which many members of the public were questioned by the appellants, particularly in the second week of the inquiry, varied between the aggressive and the offensive. This was quite unnecessary, since the interested persons were perfectly willing to assist the inquiry.

In the face of what was described in closing by the appellants as 'cross-examination' of these interested persons, their oral responses brought to life (much more vividly than the written statements presented) the history of personal disruption and discomfort which opencast mining has brought to this locality over a long period of time. It is for the appellants to decide how they should proceed at the inquiry. However, it is reasonable to expect some consistency between their case and the way they present it.

If the information network between communities in Yorkshire opposing opencasting were to be as effective as the appellants have sought to suggest, knowledge of the appellants' treatment of local people at this inquiry will not be confined to the area a short distance to the east of Wakefield. The way in which local residents were questioned was, in my experience, unique; they should not let it deter them from appearing at other planning inquiries.[33]

These comments by Mrs Brushfield (a senior inspector with considerable experience of opencast inquiries) were significant ones and serve to highlight the changing attitude of the Inspectorate towards the conduct of inquiries and the treatment of witnesses.

PUBLIC PARTICIPATION IN OPENCAST INQUIRIES

The rules developed for planning appeals marginalise residents and local groups—putting them into the 'third parties' category. The appellant, the MPA and other parties (such as affected landowners, government departments, executive agencies and other bodies) have pride of place. It is they who have the first opportunity to present evidence and examine witnesses.

Members of the public most often feel alienated by the structure and proceedings of public inquiries. They arrive at an inquiry having little or no knowledge of procedures and the 'rules of engagement'. Many people soon drift away when they realise that their submissions won't be heard until the final days of an inquiry (which could be one or two weeks later). As a result, only a few activists and stalwarts are left to ask questions and maintain a presence while the professional witnesses for the appellant and the officers from the MPA present their evidence.

Some inspectors work at developing a genuine rapport with members of the public. Often this takes on a rather 'folksy' air. At Coalburn Farm Public Inquiry in Gateshead in 1992, for example, the inspector went out of his way to say how much he had enjoyed the refreshments that had been provided by the members of the local Women's Institute (telling one resident that his mother was also a WI member). Other inspectors take a different stance, seemingly viewing the public as little more than a nuisance.

The use of shorter summaries by witnesses has helped make the evidence at opencast inquiries more accessible, but technical evidence on issues such as noise, visual intrusion and planning policy is often presented in ways which are generally incomprehensible. When local people present their own evidence, they are frequently intimidated by the adversarial nature of the system they encounter. We have observed barristers acting for appellants taking a highly aggressive stance highlighting that local residents lack qualifications and technical knowledge. Their qualifications as a 'lifelong resident of a community' and having an 'intimate knowledge of the area' is openly belittled. Outsiders attending opencast inquiries are frequently struck by the tremendous patience and self-control which the members of the public exercise on these occasions. Local people are sometimes enraged by the views expressed by the lawyers acting for the mining companies, or by their witnesses, but it is extremely rare for their anger to develop beyond occasional bouts of shouting and swearing. While inspectors have the power to require any person(s) acting in a disruptive manner to leave the inquiry, we have never encountered a situation where this has been necessary. Inspectors tend to ignore the shouts or ask people to keep quiet and let the witnesses complete their evidence. Concerns by local residents for the effects of mining on their property, the local environment and their health are frequently denigrated as selfish and self seeking. The fact that these charges are made by barristers on exorbitantly high fees, living miles away from any opencast site is deeply ironic but rarely a matter of comment.

The nature of these criticisms frequently rest upon the idea of NIMBYism (not in my back yard), and in part it derives from the particular status afforded local people in these inquiries. They are placed last in line and their contribution and status derive from their local knowledge and interests. It is easy for this to be counterposed to more global and universal principles, as one form of knowledge is privileged over another. Thankfully, experience shows that local people can have an important role to play at appeals in opposing opencast applications. In their detailed study of such hearings in Canada, Mary Richardson and her colleagues have indicated ways in which the knowledge of the expert witness contrasts with the every-day understandings and commoners' case knowledge of the local people. In their view proceedings are normally constructed in ways which favour the expert, although on occasions this 'local knowledge' can break through, to positive effect.[34] This has also been the case in the UK.

Kate Burningham and Martin O'Brien have conducted research into local planning inquiries relating to motorway construction. In this they have observed that:

> objectors' knowledge about the locality and their every-day lives constitutes a sphere of expertise distinct from that available to the experts whose assessments they dispute. Although objectors are often unable effectively to challenge the experts they are pitted against, equally their authority as 'ordinary people' to speak of their concerns for the community and

locality cannot be easily undermined.[35]

This was also our experience of opencast inquiries. When a large proportion of the local community near the proposed opencast site turns out to object forcefully to an appeal and give its support to the MPA, it can be decisive.[36] One such case was the Marley Hill Public Inquiry involving the Gateshead and Co. Durham authorities in 1989–90. This inquiry dealt with an application from British Coal Opencast for a 2.8mt site which was scheduled to have a working phase of 8.5 years followed by a further 5 years restoration period. The local action group opposing the site (CAMHO) made the decision (like many other such groups) that evidence should be presented by people acting as representatives of the community and not as individuals. They in many ways acted like a local trade union branch. They emphasised the need for discipline and the advantages to be gained from a considered submission being made on a set of agreed topics. They were concerned to avoid repetition of the same arguments and of their view being dismissed as a cacophony of people 'speaking their minds'. The contributions to the general evidence were obtained by talking to villagers and other local residents and writing down their views in a way which was felt would express their feelings as well as their opinions.

When reflecting on this experience Eric Lee (then Honorary Secretary of CAMHO) addressed a conference organised by the North East Opencast Action Group in 1992. In his presentation he revealed that when the views of the Marley Hill residents they interviewed were collected together a common theme emerged. It was 'worry'. He commented:

> People 'worried' about what would happen if they had to move away to a new job and could not sell their houses. They 'worried' about those already afflicted with chest troubles and who might have the condition aggravated by the dust. They 'worried' about the extra housework to deal with the dust. But the worst 'worry' of all was about the safety and health of their children attending the local schools.[37]

Mr Lee added that CAMHO subsequently decided to empha-sise 'worry', the common aspect of most of the local concerns, in the Action Group's evidence.

CAMHO noted that the Inspector at the Marley Hill Inquiry would have taken countless pages of notes by the time its evi-dence was presented. The group therefore concluded that he would appreciate a copy of its evidence which ensured that he had clear and precise knowledge of its views. It concluded that Action Groups and local residents need to submit well-drafted and 'professionally-produced' proofs of evidence and other sup-porting documents in order to demonstrate that they understand and are capable of behaving according to the rules. In contrast many local residents who appear at inquiries (par-ticularly during evening sessions arranged to hear their views) do not submit a written summary or letters outlining their views. These verbal comments are often quite dramatic and evocative. But it is doubtful whether they are as effective as those supported by a written submission. This, of course, is a further indication of the inequalities of power involved in these proceedings. It reflects what Bourdieu refers to as 'cultural cap-ital'.[38] It is extended when we realise that, unlike the lawyers appearing for the mining company and MPAs, the majority of local residents are unused to speaking in public.

Photographic evidence can also assist the case of local resi-dents at a public inquiry. This was particularly true at Marley Hill. At the time of the initial application by BCC, CAMHO wrote to the CPRE assuring it of strong local support should it decide to oppose the application. The CPRE subsequently announced its intention to fight the application—as a test of the current mineral planning guidance (the initial version of *MPG3*). As part of its evidence it commissioned a leading pho-tographer to visit the site—producing a set of stunning photographs during the summer of 1989 prior to the inquiry (which commenced during late 1989, reconvening during February 1990). The photographs were also very effectively dis-played in the church hall in which the inquiry was held and were later reproduced in CPRE's magazine (*Countryside Campaigner*) and other campaign literature.

The Marley Hill planning appeal by the OE was rejected by the Secretary of State for the Environment (based on the report from the inquiry inspector). Following the result Eric Lee reported on the conclusions that could be drawn from the Inquiry and the inspector's report that could (then) be of value to other Action Groups. He noted that:

> The impact which opencast will have on the lives of the local population carries more weight than the devastating effect it will have upon the beauty of the countryside.

He thought at that time that some inspectors seemed to have a touching faith in the ability of BCC (and other mining companies) to restore sites in a way that improves upon nature and in a way that is a substantial improvement upon their best efforts in the past.

However, there appears to have been a significant change since the publication of the *Interim Planning Guidance* in 1993, shown in the decisions announced since the introduction of the *Revised MPG3* in July 1994. Less weight is now given to the 'creative' restoration abilities of site operators as opposed to the retention of existing mature landscapes.

But Mr Lee also added:

> …As far as practicable objectors should constantly urge the inspector to put himself in the position of a local person and to view the application from that standpoint. For example— 'How would you feel if it were your grandchild that faced the prospect of spending 10 years or more in a noisy, dusty environment created by the opencast site.' Or the inspector could be asked—'What would be your concern if you lived in a house adjacent to the site and were forced to obtain employment away from the area but could not sell your house, would YOU worry.'

Mr Lee stressed that Action Groups should avoid adding every possible objection to their evidence—so called 'make-weight' evidence. This can be easily exploited by lawyers from the appellants. He also concluded that Action Groups should:

> Seek a theme such as 'worry' to link up various aspects of
> your evidence in order to create greater impact. Take great
> care on the health issue—do not make direct assertions link-
> ing particular aspects of ill-health to opencast; these could
> be challenged to your disadvantage. Instead, use words such
> as 'concern', 'worry' and 'stress' which are more in the con-
> text of 'opinions' than 'facts' and can therefore be used to
> counterbalance the 'opinions' of the expert witnesses.
>
> Do not be afraid to use words, where appropriate, in an
> impressionistic way to reinforce a particular point. For exam-
> ple at Marley Hill, British Coal suggested that a view of the
> opencast site might be a tourist attraction in its own right.
> We responded by saying YES!, any obscene or macabre spec-
> tacle will attract some visitors whether it be badger baiting
> or opencast mining. Seek every way in which to show that
> the true reality of opencast is one from which every right-
> thinking person recoils in horror.
>
> The public inquiry system is a public performance in
> exactly the same way as a play. Those giving evidence are in
> exactly the same position as actors—so write and learn to
> play your parts convincingly and hope that the sole 'Critic',
> the inspector, gives you a good write-up.

We have used this theatrical analogy repeatedly throughout this
chapter.[39] It has, however, clear limits. Its explanatory force is
weakened when we realise that while playing their parts these
'actors' are involved in struggles which have real material consequences. A too heavy focus on the discursive dimension of the
exchange risks losing sight of the fact that profound asymme-
tries of power and resources characterise these relationships.
That when the curtain falls, some return to London, others to
a life in the shadow of a drag line.

6
DEMOCRACY! WHAT DEMOCRACY?

Not all opencast applications go to public inquiry. In fact most do not. They are presented to the MPA and after a sometimes extended period of negotiation and discussion planning permission is granted. During the 1980s and 1990s this sometimes led to resentment, bitterness and recrimination. Such was the case with British Coal's application to opencast the site of the former Tinsley Park steelworks located in the Lower Don Valley on the eastern edge of the city of Sheffield (see Figure 7).

REGIONAL REGENERATION

The closure of this steel works in 1986 exacerbated the many problems which Sheffield City had faced in relation to the rundown of the coal and steel industries in the Lower Don Valley. This decline let to a collapse in employment between 1975 and 1988 from 40,000 to 13,000 jobs.[1] The area, which extends from just north east of the city centre to the border with Rotherham, was also left with a poor image, rundown physical appearance, severe dereliction and deteriorating infrastructure.

The problems of the Lower Don Valley were part of a general problem faced by the Sheffield City Council. During the first two Thatcher governments, the Labour-controlled Council had been mainly concerned with a policy of defending jobs and giving support to established local industries. Within the area represented by the Yorkshire and Humberside Development Agency, Sheffield and the South Yorkshire area generally was

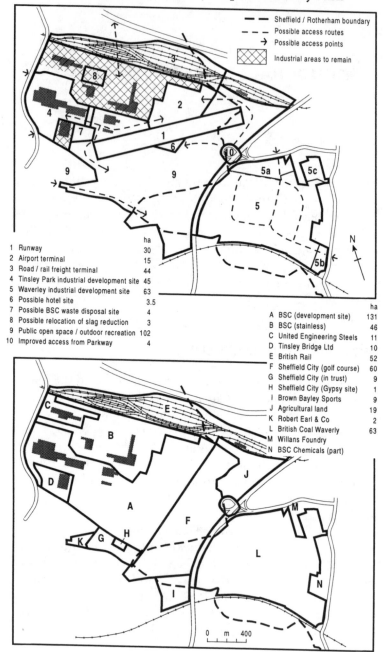

FIGURE 7

Opencast mining and City Airport—Tinsley Park

Legend:
- Sheffield / Rotherham boundary
- Possible access routes
- Possible access points
- Industrial areas to remain

		ha
1	Runway	30
2	Airport terminal	15
3	Road / rail freight terminal	44
4	Tinsley Park industrial development site	45
5	Waverley industrial development site	63
6	Possible hotel site	3.5
7	Possible BSC waste disposal site	4
8	Possible relocation of slag reduction	3
9	Public open space / outdoor recreation	102
10	Improved access from Parkway	4

		ha
A	BSC (development site)	131
B	BSC (stainless)	46
C	United Engineering Steels	11
D	Tinsley Bridge Ltd	10
E	British Rail	52
F	Sheffield City (golf course)	60
G	Sheffield City (in trust)	9
H	Sheffield City (Gypsy site)	1
I	Brown Bayley Sports	9
J	Agricultural land	19
K	Robert Earl & Co	2
L	British Coal Waverly	63
M	Willans Foundry	
N	BSC Chemicals (part)	

0   m   400

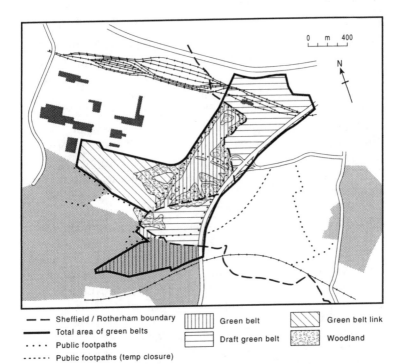

N

- – – Sheffield / Rotherham boundary
- —— Total area of green belts
- · · · · Public footpaths
- - - - - Public footpaths (temp closure)

Green belt

Draft green belt

Green belt link

Woodland

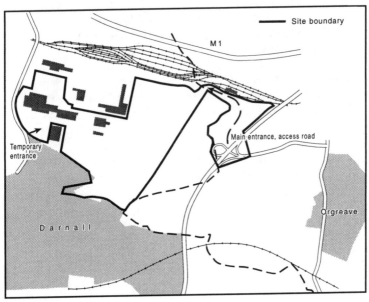

—— Site boundary

M 1

Main entrance, access road

Temporary
entrance

Orgreave

D a r n a l l

strongly linked with the coal and steel industries and the traditional Labour politics associated with them. After the defeat of the coal miners in 1985, there were calls for a new approach, emphasising the need to create new economic initiatives in the 1990s. As part of this, the council began to think in terms of establishing 'cultural industries' within the city and embarked on an ambitious plan to attract the World Student Games. In 1988 Sheffield was chosen as a site for one of the Conservative Government's new Urban Development Corporations. Clive Betts was leader of the Labour group at the time and he remembers:

> The Government's view, however, was that the regeneration of derelict areas, and in particular of an area of Sheffield which had lost 40,000 jobs following the collapse of the steel and engineering industries, was a matter for development corporations. David Trippier, the minister at the time, came to see me when I was leader of the council and asked what our response would be to a Sheffield development corporation with £50 million to spend. I said that I thought that the city council, in conjunction with Government and private industry, working on a tripartite basis, would spend the money better and with more democratic accountability. I added that if the Government were making it a take-it-or-leave-it offer, we would not wish away a development corporation with £50 million, which could benefit local people. Certainly, we opposed it in principle, but once it was established we would sit down and work with it and try to make it as big a success as possible.[2]

The question of Sheffield's links with Europe was also raised, and with it the idea that the city suffered from the absence of an international airport. This concern led to the plan for an airport (similar to the one in the London Docklands) within the city.

THE OFFER

British Coal had long established operations in South Yorkshire, and it prided itself on its local contacts and knowledge. In 1988, managers were well aware of the aspirations of the city council, and saw in them avenues through which they could advance their own interests. Large sites for opencast development were especially at a premium. But BCC had become attuned to the nature and scale of the opposition to this activity. The Tinsley site offered the prospect of mining 1.5 million tonnes of coal. Its location had also enabled BCC to present its case as part of a modernising project for the city. The planning application emphasised the urban dereliction of the Lower Don Valley, and the need to redevelop the site without sterilising the coal. BCC's plan stressed how the coal extraction would be phased in a way which allowed it to assist the renewal of the area.

> In addition to the recovery of valuable coal reserves, the working of the site would assist the redevelopment of a substantial part of the site as a Short Take Off and Landing Airport (STOLPORT) with an associated access road direct to the Sheffield Parkway...BCC can assist such a development by the provision of the proposed new access to reach the Sheffield Parkway which as well as being utilised for coal traffic from the site could be retained for the airport development.[3]

So, there would be real planning gain. In addition (though this wasn't included in the initial planning application), BCC would make a significant financial contribution to the costs of the airport itself. In short it made the city an offer it could not refuse.

We discussed the issues raised by the Tinsley application with two of the city council planners involved. It was the first opencast application with which either had dealt with. This was generally the case in the Sheffield Planning Department, and during the course of determining the application they had come to rely on advice from their counterparts in Rotherham MBC. Their general view was that BCC had behaved very well and had given their department all the information it had requested. They also felt that it would have been difficult to oppose BCC's application:

> With the background of *MPG3* it would have been very difficult to win an appeal, mainly because a large area of the site was derelict. One part of the site had been opencasted in the past and this had become partially wooded. However …most of the land was derelict or very degraded.

Nevertheless, they were very clear that without the linked attraction of the airport the application would have had a rougher passage through the city's Planning Committee:

> Without the airport there would have been a split between the various factions on the council—those who supported the NUM against those who saw the redevelopment of the site as an important part in the redevelopment of the area and the local economy. The airport proposal had attracted support from a wide range of groups and from local MPs. Without the runway it would have been a lot more difficult. The location of the site in a heavily built-up area, so close to the centre of Sheffield, made BCC think that sweeteners were necessary to avoid going to appeal.

A careful piece of economic and political planning, then, and one that was supported by both the Sheffield Development Corporation and A. F. Budge Mining Ltd, the chosen contractor for the Tinsley site. In the words of Hugh Sykes, Chairman of the SDC:

> This is what the region's business community has been waiting for; an ultra-modern airport on its doorstep, linking with the continent and providing fast transport to other UK cities. It will catapult Sheffield into the 21st century at a time when first-class communications are vital for business success. And it will be a bridgehead into Europe, handling business traffic between Sheffield and the continent as the city rises to the challenge of the new decade.[4]

Richard Budge, then managing director of A. F. Budge Mining Ltd, is reported to have been:

> delighted to be undertaking this vitally important development and acting as a catalyst in the regeneration of Sheffield.[5]

In this way the 'old economy' of coal became wedded to urban renewal.[6] The irony here was not lost upon many of the people in the communities surrounding the site. It was played upon regularly by local people who were also sceptical about both the efficacy of the plans and the need for such 'prestige projects' in Sheffield. One of the residents put his reservations to us in this way:

> I think Sheffield suffers from an inferiority complex and the council feels that the city must have a range of prestigious schemes and events to help bring the city to national prominence.

Another resident said this to us:

> How many new jobs will it create? We thought that the site was going to be developed as an industrial site—to bring in the so-called entrepreneurs and captains of industry who will create new employment. But what we have got is an airport and an opencast site. How many jobs will they bring? I've heard that less than 200 permanent new jobs have been created by the Docklands Corporation in London and that their STOLPORT is running at less that 25 per cent capacity.

Views like these contributed to the development of the Tinsley Park Action Group, which was set up to oppose both the opencast site and the proposed airport development.

THE OPPOSITION

Several communities surrounded the Tinsley Park site—the

closest being Tinsley to the north, Brinsworth to the north east, Darnell to the south, and Greenland and Carbrook to the west. Residents in each of these villages opposed the development, and were supported by Kevin Barron, one of the local MPs. In addition to their criticisms of the economic logic of the development plan, they were concerned about the loss of amenities and the noise and the dust associated with the opencast site. They were also worried about the noise associated with the airport and, following the M1 air crash at Kegworth, were fearful of having a runway so close to residential areas. As part of their campaign, members of the Action Group travelled throughout the UK visiting other communities affected by opencast sites and those living near to the London City Airport.

The key activists remember that the Action Group sprang out of local reactions to a series of consultation meetings organised by Sheffield and Rotherham Councils, and from the feeling that these meetings simply involved these councils in 'going through the motions'. The decisions, in their view, had already been taken. The accounts of the consultation process are interestingly different in tone. In the views of the local planners:

> The purpose of the meetings was to inform people about what was going on and then for them to ask questions. Minutes were taken at the meetings. The Planning Department, however, wanted views on paper and comment sheets were distributed at the meetings. Following the meetings a large number of letters—two large files full— were received, most of which were opposed to the applications. These responses were evaluated for the report to the Planning Committee. One of the major objections to the opencast application had been about the removal of the ancient woodland at the golf course. Following subsequent representations by the Planning Department, BCC took the golf course and most of the woodland out of the site application.

We asked about the airport, and in the planners' views:

> A wider survey was carried out…and people were generally in favour of the airport close to the industrial heartland as they thought it might provide economic spin-offs….However, the Council had been accused of selling the opencast planning permission to BCC because the council wanted the airport development, and many of the letters from the public did contain objections to both applications. However, the Planning Department had to separate the two applications … The Committee report on the opencast application makes few references to the airport.

In contrast, the members of the Action Group remember the process as being much less reasoned and even-handed. In the view of Geoff Deeley:

> There were three public meetings in September and October 1988; one organised by Rotherham MBC, the other two organised by Sheffield City Council. All the meetings were stormy and heated and the arguments expressed by the audience were violent and repetitive. 1,100 attended the meetings and everyone who spoke was against the developments. At one meeting the chairman was so concerned by the hostility that he called the police. By the time of the third meeting the representatives of the Opencast Executive would not go to the front because their arguments were being thrown back in their faces. At each meeting I moved resolutions against the airport and opencast proposals and they were carried virtually unanimously. However, we made the mistake of believing that the strong feelings expressed at the meetings would force the planners, planning chairmen and local authorities to rethink their policy on the whole idea.

The activists attended meetings of the Planning Committee and the City Council. They felt that the Planning Committee in Sheffield was 'little more than a farce'. While they put their views 'no one was listening'. Their feelings were reinforced by a letter written on 17 October 1988 by Clive Betts, Leader of the Labour Group, that had been leaked to them. In this letter, Betts stated that the city was definitely going to get the airport and the council was going to support the planning application for the opencast site. As such, they felt that at the meeting of the full council 'there was very little debate and the views of the local residents and our petitions were dismissed out of hand'.

As a derelict area, on the verge of redevelopment, Tinsley Park fell within the criteria identified by *MPG3* as environmentally sound. So, why was there such local opposition? To begin with there was some scepticism about the economic rationale of the plans for the Tinsley Park site. In addition, many people dreaded the prospect of several years of opencast working. They became aware of the potential problems associated with noise and dust from the opencast site and an increase in traffic, especially lorries carrying coal from the site. The news from South Wales that opencast sites could be associated with increases in respiratory illnesses became a major cause for concern, especially among mothers of young children and among older people.

There was also the concern about the local golf course: the site wasn't simply an industrial wasteland, nor was it isolated from the surrounding residential areas. For many people, the local woodland and the golf course represented a valued amenity—somewhere to walk their dogs; somewhere green to look over and reflect. While the amended plans protected most of the golf course, parts of it and the adjacent woodland, would be lost. It was this which persuaded Cyrus Heppenstall, a local churchman, to join the campaign:

> I am not a political animal and I have never been involved in politics. But I really felt that something had to be done to stop these plans going ahead. The council didn't seem to understand that on the Greenland side of the proposed site there are a large number of council houses and old people's bungalows. The impact of their proposals on these people, and all of the 60–70,000 people who live in the area would be unpleasant. This local community has been clobbered enough in past years from pollution and

other environmental problems. It's time we had some peace. The proposed opencast site and the airport was the straw that broke the camel's back. Apart from anything else, to have aircraft taking off over schools, old people's homes and the Parkway could be a recipe for a potential disaster.

We repeatedly found industrial communities angered by the return of coal mining after the promise of peace. 'We have suffered enough.'; 'Why is it always us?'; 'It's someone else's turn now.'; 'They wouldn't put it in one of those posh Tory areas.'— these are recurrent phrases which reflect a commonly held sense of grievance. Linked with this is a sense, strongly held within a settled community, of a stable landscape, and concerns about its proposed transformation. 'Brutal' is another word regularly used in conversations that we have had about the visual impact of changes brought about by opencast coal mining. In 1989 Cyrus Heppenstall insisted that we should appreciate what local people stood to lose if the development went ahead. In his view, we could only do this by walking around the area— words alone couldn't convey his concern, or the dimensions of what he stood to lose. The landscape was changing too fast, he said. For all of his adult life he had been able to see a local church spire above the horizon at a particular point on a pathway; it had regulated his evening walk. It is now obscured by opencast workings.

An important part of his world was being altered by external forces over which he had no control. This became 'the final straw' that brought community action in Sheffield and Rotherham. The leader of this group was Geoff Deeley.

Geoff Deeley had formerly been a local trade-union representative with the Iron and Steel Trades' Confederation. He had lived in Brinsworth for thirty years and had been made redundant during the steel industry closures of the 1980s. He emerged as the clear leader of the action committee:

I was the only member with any trade-union background and experience in public speaking. The only reason I became chairman of the action group was because I proposed the original motions at the three public meetings held in Sheffield and Rotherham.

Cyrus Heppenstall was also involved, and he remembers how:

The action group was formed after the third public meeting. At the end of the meeting it was agreed that a further meeting of all those individuals interested in opposing the site would be held in Brinsworth. A committee was formed which represented all the seven communities who were affected. A further three public meetings were organised by the new committee to help maintain public interest. The committee originally had thirty-six members though this shrank during the following months. Further weekly meetings of the action group were held which had good attendances. We had no trouble in finding individuals to help with the secretarial work and the campaigning.

Another active member of the committee was Stuart Butler, a former steel-worker who had been made redundant and taken a job with Rotherham Educational Department. Brought up in a mining family, he was concerned about the affect of open-cast mining on employment in the local deep mines. In his view:

Opencast sites may be in direct competition with deep mines, and any expansion could endanger the future of the deep mines. I was amazed when I discovered that councillors from deep-mining communities actually voted in favour of opencast proposals. I don't think that those councillors were really thinking of their communities.

In his view, people in the local communities were not fully aware of what was happening and ignorant of the implications of many council decisions on their lives. 'The information wasn't getting back to the villages'. He saw this to be the main role of the Action Group, as he felt that if people had a greater knowledge of what was happening, they would be in a better position to decide whether certain developments should or should not take place. Generally he felt that councillors in the area were insufficiently accountable. In his view, the public should be in a position to keep pressure on their representatives and question them about their actions. Stuart Butler had been particularly disturbed by his experience of the consultation meetings:

> The public had not been heard. They had complained and protested, but whatever they had done it hadn't seemed to matter. They had been excluded from the planning process.

These feelings were reinforced during the period when the Action Group organised its campaign.

Geoff Deeley remembers that they were referred to as 'pinkos and communists', as 'the paramilitary', and in the view of the Sheffield Development Corporation, a 'major force' and 'a stumbling block to progress, preventing continuity of progress as they didn't have the intelligence to realise that the development proposals were for the greater good of the area.'

In Sheffield, criticism of local political leaders wasn't particularly welcomed; nor was reference to the environment when jobs and development seemed to be at stake. Councillor Smith, the Deputy Chairman of Rotherham Planning Committee argued with the Action Group, saying: 'what are you worried about the green belt for? We've got 70 per cent green belt in this area around the boundaries...we've got too much green belt, let's have some for development.'

At Tinsley they felt that the media had been reasonably fair. Members of the Action Group had been asked to take part in several radio programmes and felt their comments hadn't been used out of context. They had a similar experience with the local newspapers. When the Tinsley site was 'news', the Action Group was newsworthy. Once the decision was made media interest faded; so did the interest of people in the local communities. It is this transient nature of protest and of news which typifies much of the responses to opencast mining and other environmental issues and was something the Action Group committee experienced as a source of frustration. Cyrus Heppenstall commented:

> We have done a lot to raise the issues in the area and to keep people informed. But I think that over 60 per cent of the people here have little or no idea of what could occur. There is still considerable apathy and ignorance in the community and this will get worse once the publicity about the opencast site disappears.

Partly as an attempt to maintain the momentum of the campaign, Geoff Deeley stood as an independent for Rotherham MBC in the local elections of May 1990. Although he was defeated, he easily polled the highest number of votes recorded in living memory for a non-Labour Party candidate in the ward.

THE PLAN IN OPERATION

Once the opposition had been dealt with, the plan for the development of the site got underway. One local newspaper described the situation in this way:

> Coal opencasting is expected to start at Tinsley Park in July [1989]. It means that if all goes well, work on a £11 million city airport for the site should start in the summer of 1991. The Sheffield Development Corporation, Sheffield and Rotherham Councils and British Coal are working together to see that the mining and airport are both completed for Christmas 1992.[7]

In its own announcement of the scheme Sheffield Development Corporation wrote of how in July 1989:

> planning permission has been granted by the City Council with extraction expected to start in September of this year continuing until February 1993. The opening date for the airport is June 1993.

Its tone was up-beat yet reassuring:

> the agreement together with the planning permission, will safeguard a number of interests, ensuring that noise, dust and traffic are minimised; that land is made available for Tinsley golf course to remain in operation, and that appropriate road access is provided to the opencast site...in total nearly £3 million will be spent on the golf course, landscaping works, environmental programme and access roads.[8]

Both the Development Corporation and the City Council commented on the importance of the airport. In the view of the Development Corporation:

> The creation of an airport for the city at the end of the opencast programme will be of great benefit to the city's regeneration. Top quality communications are essential for business development. Sheffield has suffered in the past from lack of access to a local airport and that obstacle to progress will now be removed.

Mike Buckley, Chair of the City Council's Planning and Transportation Committee commented that the development of the airport:

> marks the culmination of a major effort over the past few years by the City and Rotherham Councils, the local business community and, more recently the Development Corporation, who will now see the project through to fruition.

This concluding comment reflected the fact that future arrangements for the planning and development of the Lower Don Valley rested with the new groups and not with the Sheffield and Rotherham councils.

The other new party to the deal was the contractor chosen by British Coal to mine the site—A. F. Budge Mining Ltd. By May 1990, this company, along with the Development Corporation had extended the vision.

A *Financial Times* article made clear how an '£11 million airport' had been transformed:

> A £100 million airport and business park to be built in Sheffield by Budge Mining, part of the A. F. Budge Construction Group, a private company based in Retford, Nottinghamshire. Budge Mining plans to open the airport...in the summer of 1993. It will be built on a former industrial site and provide 3,500 jobs.

It went on to point out that:

> the development will be funded privately. Much of the capital is being provided by income from an opencast coal mine on the site which will be exploited until 1992 when construction work on the development will start.

Hugh Sykes, of Sheffield Development Corporation added to the hype:

> Until we launched this initiative, Sheffield was the largest city in Europe without its own airport. Now it will be able to assume its rightful place as a centre of manufacturing and commerce excellence.[9]

For his part Richard Budge, as managing director of A.F. Budge Mining Ltd, made clear that:

> We are bringing all our experience of major construction projects to bear on the airport scheme and we are confident of its success.[10]

In a communiqué which made little reference to Budge's ongoing involvement in the opencast mine, the Development Corporation noted on 18 May 1990, however, that:

> The Sheffield Development Corporation and Budge Mining signed the agreement for the airport's development and operation today. The airport will straddle a former industrial site

in Sheffield's Lower Don Valley where British Coal are currently carrying out opencast mining, and will have a 1200 metre runway....Under the agreement Budge mining...will carry out the development of the site, including the provision of accommodation for customs and immigration services. Budge will also be responsible for the earthworks on the adjacent Tinsley golf course...a new spine road... and...extensive landscaping.

It added:

Budge Mining are already contracted for British Coal at Tinsley, making them well placed to put in a successful bid for their project, building on the success achieved in their current £60 million opencast contract.[11]

There was no reference to the money for the airport or of 'planning gain'. Instead the talk was of team-work:

making the airport a reality has been a team effort. It is the culmination of work by many parties: the Sheffield and Rotherham Councils who gave initial planning permission; British Coal, British Steel and ourselves. It forms part of an integrated strategy to improve the infrastructure of the Lower Don Valley and makes the area increasingly attractive to inward investors, as well as providing much-needed facilities for local companies.[12]

However, in the life of the project disagreements emerged within the team in ways which made the local councils feel severely marginalised and which confirmed many of the worst suspicions of the local protest groups. Once the site at Tinsley was opened up and coal mining was underway, the situation changed. To begin with the tonnage agreement was altered. In its initial application BCC had requested planning permission for the removal of 1.5 million tonnes of coal. This was refused and agreement reached on the extraction of 800,000 tonnes, planned to link in with preparation for the construction of the airport. However, as Bryn Morris, corporate affairs director of

BCC explained:

> In May 1990, Sheffield Development Corporation entered into an agreement with A. F. Budge Mining Ltd for the construction and operation of the airport and the development of adjacent land.
>
> Subsequently, on 12 March 1991 the opencast contract between British Coal and A. F. Budge Mining Ltd was altered, with the tonnage to be extracted from the site increased. This was a consequence of the agreement between A. F. Budge Mining Ltd and the SDC with regard to the airport construction, which extended the time available for the operation of the opencast site.[13]

The new agreement lifted the tonnage limit to 1.1 million tonnes, which was later expanded to 1.5 million tonnes. This new pattern of extraction altered the planned working of the site. This alteration was exacerbated by the changes that took place in the Budge company in 1992. In the reconstruction which created RJB Mining, Richard Budge retained the contract for mining Tinsley Park. However, the responsibility for the airport remained with the A. F. Budge Group which in turn established the Sheffield Airport Company as its subsidiary. In this way a project which (in the minds of the local authority) inextricably linked opencast mining with planning gain through an airport became disrupted. This change did not require the prior approval of the Department of the Environment. Nor was the local authority involved as the Development Corporation had taken over planning responsibilities. In the words of Richard Page, then Under-Secretary of State for Industry and Energy:

> the variation in the Tinsley Park airport contract, releasing A. F. Budge Mining Ltd was agreed by the Sheffield Development Corporation....[14]

In his parliamentary adjournment debate in 1995, Clive Betts raised many of the issues and problems which have bedevilled opencast mining operations across the country. He asked 'who the opencast contract was with—British Coal or R.J. Budge Mining?' and went on:

> What were the main financial provisions of the contract?... Had there been any significant changes in the terms of the original contract?...Had there been any changes to the parties to the contract or any of the sureties for the performance of the contract?...Had the contract been satisfactorily performed, operationally and financially? When would it be completed? In what state would the site be left on completion of the contract?[15]

And with regard to the airport:

> What were the main financial provisions of the contract? Had there been any significant changes to the terms of the original contract? Why was the contract transferred to Sheffield Airports Ltd. Why was the contract not left with RJB Mining, perhaps retaining the A. F. Budge Ltd guarantee?[16]

These questions were all the more poignant given the events of 1993 and subsequent years. At the end of 1992, receivers were called into A. F. Budge Ltd. A spokesperson for Coopers and Lybrand confirmed that the company had significant debts of many millions of pounds. He added:

> The situation is very fluid. We have only just been appointed and this is a multifaceted group with interests ranging from equine to military to road construction and of course Sheffield Airport.[17]

At that time, the *Yorkshire Post* reminded its readers that:

> The airport is a major plank in Sheffield Development Corporation's regeneration plan for the Lower Don Valley and was seen as a key to economic prosperity, linking the city with Europe. The SDC signed a deal with A.F. Budge

Mining three years ago to opencast the airport site at Tinsley, using the £60 million profits to pay for the airport which was expected to create up to 3,500 jobs and carry up to 300,000 passengers a year.[18]

The Chairman of the Development Corporation Hugh Sykes commented:

> progression beyond this point will depend upon a number of factors but we will do everything in our power to maintain the momentum of development on this site and we remain committed to an airport for Sheffield and Rotherham.[19]

However, with the collapse of A. F. Budge Ltd, the future looked far from rosy. In this context the SDC began to look for alternative sources of funding and alternative companies to take over the construction of the airport site. Richard Budge was very active in these negotiations. As Clive Betts recalls:

> In January 1993 there was a bid for the open partnership fund, for a Sheffield aerocentre project. That bid came from a company headed by Mr Richard Budge, whose proposals required £2 million of government funds and another £1 million from Sheffield development corporation—as well as international development association grants of more than £2 million, which have subsequently been agreed.[20]

When this fell through, yet another company emerged to involve itself in the venture. The new company was called Glenlivet. Based in Chesterfield, it was run by Mike Shields, who had also been involved in the earlier aerocentre project. With Sheffield Development Corporation directly involved, the company outlined its moves toward the completion of the airport. When these were discussed in 1995, however, the project seemed to be less ambitious. As the *Yorkshire Post* recorded

> Developers are finalising technical details of a £6 million project on a site at Tinsley which will include a business park

creating 1,000 jobs.[21]

Mike Shields expressed cautious optimism:

> There are a lot of technical issues that need to be solved. We need to convince the funders that the project is viable and we are not saying that it is going to happen next week but we are on the first rung of the ladder.[22]

By that time the credibility of the scheme amongst local people had declined further. Several people we talked with expected it to collapse. In Geoff Deeley's view the viability was declining with each passing year. The reduced scale of the project and the problems posed by lack of funds, had meant that many of the environmentally supportive aspects of the original scheme (such as sound-proofing two nearby schools and the limitation of operating hours) were dropped.

In early 1997 the airport was ready. In the view of the *Financial Times* correspondent, 'the airport will be a specialised one, limited to short take-off and landing (STOL) aircraft... Sheffield will be chasing short-haul, time-conscious business travellers.[22] A view supported by Joanne Rawsley, the Director of Administration at the airport:

> This will not be a bucket-and-spade operation for flights to Majorca. It is going to be a business airport at the high quality end of the market, geared to European business travel.[23]

The first of the business park's customers was the South Yorkshire Police which established a twenty-four-hour depot for operational patrol cars and police helicopters. In February 1998, Air UK opened a service for between twenty and fifty people between Sheffield and Amsterdam three days a week. However, demand was not buoyant. Reports of plans to convert the old military airfield at Finningley south-east of Doncaster into a commercially viable regional airport and the expansion of other regional airports seemed to put the long-term future of the STOLPORT in doubt. In March a school teacher took a class of junior school children to the airport as part of a local project. All that was on view was a police helicopter. Incidents like these convinced many of the local people we talked to that the airport was a white elephant. Although other services have been added since (these include tourist charter flights to Europe) in 1999 it seemed that the STOLPORT had yet to live up to the expectations that it would play a dynamic role in the region's economy.

7
CHANGING PATTERNS OF PROTEST

Opencast coal mining, together with other economic activities associated with nuclear power plants, new motorways, waste incineration and the like can cause widespread disquiet and concern amongst local people. This concern is most frequently reflected in opposition to planning applications. Many view the prospect of opencast mining as equivalent to the Four Horsemen of the Apocalypse riding through their communities: such a view was expressed by the Ashfield Against Opencast Group in Nottinghamshire in 1995. As part of its successful campaign against the application by Coal Contractors Ltd. to mine an opencast site at Skegby Junction this group produced a depiction of the opencaster as a marauding Viking. In its view:

> we shall be paying the Danegeld again! Naturally they will not go away but will return to Nottinghamshire for more and more and more.

The public response to opencast development has changed considerably over the past thirty years: there is resistance where there was once general acquiescence. This change has been obviously influenced by the changed position of the coal industry. As the deep mines have closed people have begun to question the very idea of the need for more coal mining.

UNDER THE HEGEMONY OF COAL

In examining this changing pattern it is possible to distinguish a number of clearly distinct periods. The first extended from the Second World War to the early 1970s. In this period there was a clear understanding of the national importance of coal, of the dominant role of the coal industry in the coal districts and the dominance of the NCB over coalfield society. This hegemony was expressed through the close working relationship between the NCB and the local authorities, and through the variety of ways in which 'the Board' involved itself in the social life of the coalfields. Many of the new industrial relations managers were ex-NUM officials who worked easily with local councillors (many of whom were miners) and local union officials. It was a hegemony which emphasised the uniqueness of coal mining culture through which it obtained a powerful and unstated ascendancy.[1] Often described as corporatist, patterns of protest and dissent were ordered though the trade unions. There was a variety of understood checks and balances within this system, which minimised the occurrence of unregulated conflict.

In these areas the state, through its ownership of the nationalised industries was by far the largest employer, and exerted a dominance which was only surpassed in the Eastern European bloc. In such state-controlled regions, social and economic relationships were highly regulated through the day-to-day operation of the planning system in which the interest of coal was paramount. Local authorities who attempted to build an industrial policy which might develop alternative sources of employment found themselves frustrated by the reluctance of the NCB to release necessary information. The economic planning of the coalfield districts in this period reflected their subservience to the NCB, as was revealed in countless decisions and documents. It is illustrated in the text accompanying the draft town map for Houghton-le-Spring in Co. Durham in March 1950.

It has frequently been said that the main weakness of an area such as (Houghton-le-Spring) lies in the almost complete dependence upon one industry—coal mining. However the National Coal Board has made it clear that as far as can be foreseen, the employment level in coal mining in the area should not fall much below its present level. In some senses, therefore this high degree of reliance upon coal mining does not present a real problem.

As a result, and in view of:

the importance of the coal mining industry to the nation as a whole it might be considered dangerous to propose any major diversification as this would almost certainly mean the attraction away from the mines of the young recruits so vitally necessary to the industry.[2]

Within such a system, the opencast sector was entirely subordinated to the larger number of deep mines. Opencast mines were located on the outcrop rim (the exposed coalfield areas) and frequently produced coal alongside the deep mines that had existed in these localities for generations. They were an integrated part of local industrial economies based on coal and the political hegemony of the NCB. As part of this logic, opencast production was reined in as the deep mines were closed in the late 1950s and 1960s. In this period there was very little opposition to the development of opencast mining, or to the overarching legitimacy of the NCB. Rather than see opencast sites as part of an environment that needed protection, they were understood, by the people of the coal districts, as one part of the normal activity of coal production.

DISSENT

In the early years of the 1970s this perception began to change. The miners' strikes of 1972 and 1974 are commonly identified as a critical turning point for the coal industry. These strikes came at the end of a period of dramatic decline, when over half of the deep mines in the country were closed down:[3] But after the sudden increase in oil prices in 1973, the coal workers realised that they were suddenly in a more powerful position. The success of the strikes changed the miners' union. After 1974, it was recognised once again as a force to be recognised in the country. Its members were better paid and they celebrated a more militant tradition of trade unionism. It was this, and the threat of more mine closures (on a par with those of the 1960s) which heralded the election of Arthur Scargill to the union's presidency.

These changes in the mine labour force were well understood by the NCB[4] and it developed its industrial relations policies accordingly. But the management was far less attuned to the changes that had taken place *beyond* the coal mines; across the towns and villages that made up the old coalfields. As a result of deep-mine closures, many of these districts had lost all of their deep mines. Across the coalfields generally, the NCB had lost its position of dominance. In the 1960s regional policies had encouraged new forms of employment in these districts. They were transformed from mining districts to centres of light manufacturing, rural residential areas or even commuter belts. Many of these areas introduced landscaping policies to deal with old waste heaps. The winding gear, which had come to symbolise the mine, was removed. In a way (and in spite of the fact that a minority of their residents were coal miners, commuting to the deep mines) many of these places had ceased to be a part of the coalfields. Yet it was to these areas that the NCB turned in 1974, in order to make good its commitment to increase opencast production to 15 million tons per annum under the *Plan for Coal*.

Looking back to this period it can be judged that the NCB barely appreciated the significance of the social changes that had taken place in these districts following its decision to close many collieries in the 1960s. Its intention was to expand opencast production through a mixture of large opencast sites and a number of small licensed operations. In line with its previous practices it established a production plan which received the general approval of local authorities and the NUM. Local 'quotas' were agreed as part of a national plan to achieve the targeted increase of opencast production. The degree of formality associated with these discussions varied throughout the coalfields. In some, like Co. Durham, the quotas were formally established within an agreed programme of site development. These plans met with increasingly organised local resistance. This emerged from outside the network of institutions that made up the corporatist society of the old coalfields.

Local planning officers had come to accept the standpoint of the NCB as orthodoxy, while the NCB had come to dominate debate through its virtual monopoly of information on reserves and markets.[5] Resistance and protest emphasised elements that were outside the Board's remit.

It focused on the environmental destruction and nuisance associated with opencast mining. Individuals objected to the loss of hedges and took legal action against the NCB, citing ancient statutes in defence. In the west of Durham, a number of individuals met together to express concern over the potential impact of opencast mining operations upon the Derwent valley. This valley had been at the centre of the coal and steel industry in West Durham, once dominated by the Consett Iron Company. In the 1960s all the coal mines in the valley closed leaving behind millions of tonnes of high-grade coking coal. With the mines closed, the valley gradually emerged as a site of enormous natural beauty. It was this that people felt was under threat in 1971 when the NCB announced its intention to open a large opencast site at Lofthouse along the southern scarp of the valley. The Derwent Valley Protection Society was formed which aimed to:

> protect the amenity of the valley' from its sources from the point where it enters the Tyne; to promote the protection and positive management of the countryside; to assist, advise and consult with the local authorities to that end.

The Society saw opencast mining as the main threat to the amenity of the valley, and this became the focus of its interest and of its relationship with the local authorities. Such was its success that it came to play an active role in fourteen major opencast planning decisions in the county in the 1970s and 1980s until the death of its founder Desmond Napier in 1988.

George 'Pitch' Wilson was the first person to join together

NO OPENCAST

DAY OF ACTION

5am (morning)
FRIDAY 31st OCTOBER

Meet: Ward Green Community Centre
Genn Lane
WORSBOROUGH
BARNSLEY,
SOUTH YORKSHIRE

The Community Centre will be open from 10pm Thursday
30th October for gathering/sleeping.
Bring food and warm clothing. See map on other side.

FOR TRANSPORT FROM LONDON & THE SOUTH
AND INFORMATION: PHONE 0171 603 1831

THE LAND IS OURS TO ENJOY
- NOT DESTROY

with Desmond Napier. At that time 'Pitch' was a boiler test engineer at Blyth Power Station and a Labour Party councillor on Gateshead District Council. He remembers:

> Our main argument at Lofthouse, our first public inquiry, was concerned with the protection of the beautiful countryside and the preservation of the rich woodland and denes, inter-dispersed with pastures. During the inquiry an NCB survey map came into my hands which showed the vast potential for opencast mining in the Derwent valley and it became evident that the Lofthouse site was not to be an isolated application but was the thin edge of the wedge. At the time, the Coal Board dismissed this notion and managed to persuade the County Council to withdraw its objection. In return, the NCB promised not to return for another site in the valley; they also reduced the size of the site by half, thus saving some of the woodland. Unfortunately, this map was to prove correct as regards the potential for opencasting in the valley. Despite promises made at Lofthouse no less than six applications were made in the following sixteen years.

The Lofthouse Inquiry ended with a recommendation from the inspector that the site be allowed to proceed. This decision was overturned by the Secretary of State, Peter Walker. The society regarded this as 'a victory for a small group of ordinary people with no experience of fighting such a campaign'. The experience of this inquiry proved to be decisive to the development of the society as a committed protest group. It learned three main lessons, which were to remain with the group through the next two decades. It also convinced them of the rightness of their cause. This was the first and most important lesson. It underpinned the second, which was that the NCB could not be trusted. When we met members of the society in the 1980s we were regaled with stories which in their view illustrated the perfidious nature of the NCB. It was their view that the board's arguments went unchallenged because the local authorities had no expertise on issues that related to the industry. This was the third lesson. At Lofthouse, the evidence from the coal industry emphasised the value of the coal that lay in the site, and its importance to the local coke works at Derwenthaugh. In Pitch's memory: 'we were told that they were on the edge of an abyss with only two days supply left. They referred to the 1967 Fuel Policy White Paper which showed a steeply rising demand curve'. This argument presented the needs of the economy and local employment in opposition to environmental considerations. The society was clear that in the long run it needed to equip itself to deal with these wider issues.

> It was decided that the need for the coal ought to be looked into; the underlying philosophy being that if we could successfully challenge and destroy the case, the environmental issues could be resolved. Thus, future applications were challenged using technical and energy arguments.

An example of what the society was up against was made clear at a meeting of the Durham County Council Planning Committee on 5 November 1975, which considered an application for another site in the Derwent Valley. The minutes of the meeting note that:

> In considering this matter we have had special regard to the following:
>
> ■ the worsening employment situation in the County as a whole and in the Derwentside District in particular;
> ■ the renewed threat of the loss of jobs at Consett Steel Works;
> ■ the Secretary of State's recent decision to grant permission to the Coal Board to undertake opencast operations at Michesons Gill, despite objections by the local authorities.
>
> Having regard for these factors we believe that in this instance the economic argument for the development outweighs the environmental arguments against the development and we have decided to withdraw the County Council's objection provided proper safeguards could be agreed with the NCB. Agreement has been reached with the NCB and the objection has been withdrawn.

At the same meeting the committee underlined its overall support for opencast mining and its commitment to the agreed plan for opencast production:

> we have decided to continue the County Council's policy of seeking to assist the National Coal Board to produce 900,000 tons of coal a year by opencast methods, providing this can be done without an unduly adverse impact on the county and its residents and that the production of private operators is included in the total.

By this time, however, opposition had become much tougher. The Society had affiliated to the CPRE, Desmond Napier lobbied local councillors and planning officers, expertise and advice was gleaned from all quarters. Napier and Wilson studied the NCB's evidence at Lofthouse and checked it out. They contacted the coke works and reinterpreted the Board's statistics; they examined the 1967 Fuel White Paper and the path of coal demand. They became clued up. They photocopied materials and pestered the local planning office in Consett. Desmond Napier was the driving force in this. At the time of the Medomsley application, he had gone a long way to convincing the local authority of the need to oppose and to develop more sophisticated arguments. He remembered how in the weekend prior to the inquiry he had commandeered the planning office and spent the entire two days working on the Society's proof of evidence. By 1978, the District Council had become openly critical of both the NCB and the County Planning Committee. This came to the fore when , in 1978, the NCB asked the County Council to consider its proposals for the mining of 68 potential opencast sites. The minutes of the meeting of 28 April 1978 note that:

> in making their comments on sites, the Derwentside District Council has asked that the County Council should question the National Coal Board's production target of 900,000 tons in view of the current level of demand for coal, the stock piles at colliery yards and redundancies in deep-coal mines.

They have requested more information and discussion with the County Council before any production target is agreed and before further discussions with the National Coal Board.

An Australian who had been a pilot in the Second World War, Desmond Napier and his wife Sonia migrated to Britain and established a business latterly involved in supplying specialist lining materials to large companies. By 1970, this was quite successful and he and Sonia lived in a large detached house in Rowlands Gill in the middle of the Derwent Valley. He was a member of the Conservative Party and happily contrasted his politics with those of George Wilson. But as he would point out regularly at public inquiries, he did not believe in the unbridled pursuit of profit; nor did he believe in monopoly power. He hated corruption, in business or in public life. He believed in everybody getting a fair share, and he believed in preserving the countryside. He devoted an enormous amount of time to the society and when we met him first in 1982, its activities and the campaign against opencast mining had become as important to him as his business.

The Derwent Valley Protection Society was therefore one of the first examples of organised resistance to the development of opencast mining. It was the first group to question, in a quite fundamental way, the hegemony of the NCB. In developing this resistance, it followed the progress of all new opencast site applications in the district, regularly pressuring and lobbying local councillors and planning authorities. Such was the dominance of the NCB and its control over information on the coal industry that the group soon realised that effective resistance needed to be conducted on a broader front. It joined forces with other individuals and groups across the North East of England. This network of supporters also included local politicians and university researchers. It developed sources of information and began to co-ordinate effective political lobbying. The group realised however that in order seriously to challenge the expansion of opencast mining, the rules and regulations which governed it would need to be changed. Rather than simply oppose each new site, it developed a sophisticated criticism of the way in which the coal industry operated. This was achieved through the formation of the Opencast Mining Intelligence Group (OMIG) and involvement in the CPRE. It was OMIG that first examined the issues of the marginal cost of deep-mined and opencast coals and subsequently presented it at public inquiries. An indication of the influence of OMIG can be gained from an exchange that took place during one of the sessions of oral evidence to the Select Committee on Energy in 1986. Peter Rost MP asked George Henderson of the TGWU whether he felt that campaigns against opencast mining had an impact in the coalfields. In reply Henderson (seemingly unaware that a number of the members of the group were sat immediately behind him) focused on OMIG, saying that he had received a communication from them in 1981 and that he believed that they were 'associated with a number of other groups'.[6]

Via involvement in OMIG, and in other ways, Desmond Napier and the Derwent group came to play a pivotal role within a growing network of individuals troubled by the effects of continued opencast production. In 1985, for example, when a planning application for opencast mining in the Forest of Dean was under consideration, Desmond received a phone call asking for help and advice. This was not unusual. Napier's influence was, however, felt most powerfully in the CPRE. As a result of his near-continuous pressure, the national organisation began to see opencast mining as a serious threat to the countryside and gave the issue a heightened national profile. The CPRE gave important evidence to the Flowers' Commission and continued to present the case for the tightening of opencast planning regulations.

Further national support was obtained from the NUM. Under the arrangements of the *Plan For Coal*, the NUM had given strong support to the expansion of opencast production, seeming to accept the arguments relating to an energy gap and the need for 'sweeteners' in the blend for many power stations. However as deep mines began to be threatened once again, the NUM's support weakened. In areas like Durham and South Wales, local union officials joined with communities and environmental campaigners in voicing opposition to new sites. In 1983, the NUM proposed a motion, seconded by Gloucester West Constituency Labour Party, which was severely critical of opencast mining and its role within a putative national energy policy. It referred to the:

> unnecessary exploitation of the environment caused by opencast coal mining and the fact that whilst deep-mined coal output has been reduced and stockpiled, the level of opencast operations has continued unabated at a level bearing no relation to need.

The involvement of Gloucester related to the development of opencast mining in the Forest of Dean and the worry that the alienated coal there 'cannot be used in future to obtain creeping denationalisation of the coal industry'. It prefigured the emergence of dissent on a national scale in the changed context of large-scale colliery closures and the privatisation of the coal industry.

ORGANISED OPPOSITION AND CONFLICT

In his own reflections on changes in the pattern of acceptance of opencast mining, George Hardy, when senior Planning Officer at Durham, noted:

> Since 1976 when the present County Council was established, I have been actively engaged in implementing its policies on opencasting , and I have seen the topic take a progressively higher profile. This is some indication of the environmental impact which people perceive opencasting to have, of the changing economic base of the County and the environmental expectations of its residents. The comparative indifference with which opencasting was viewed by the general public in 1974 had, by 1984 been superseded by an intense environmental awareness, and individual proposals were progressively brought under much closer scrutiny than they had previously been. In the process, I do not think that anyone will dispute that several old myths had been undermined.[7]

The 'changing economic base' refers to the large reduction in the number of collieries operating throughout the British coalfield, and the related reduction in the levels of mining employment. In all but a few districts in the UK, coal miners had disappeared as a significant occupational grouping. The rundown of deep mining was accompanied by a further programme of opencast mining, with an increasing number of private operators becoming involved. The changes served to strengthen the alliance between mineworkers and the local environmental protesters. Many local and regional groups sprang up at this time and opposition to opencast proposals became widespread. Opposition became common in all of the major coal fields and the character of the local groups varied with the socio-economic mix of the communities affected. In Scotland and Wales, the historical presence of large, continuous opencast sites combined with separate planning arrangements under the Scottish and Welsh Offices had seen a stronger consensus develop over the presence of the industry in those regions. This too began to break with the arrival of more extensive mining and the emergence of action groups around the planned sites.

In the mid-1980s, this pattern of difference often reflected the varied ways in which the various mining regions had experienced the year-long miners' strike. In many of the English coalfields the coal crisis had drawn the miners and the NUM into a radical reassessment of the dangers which the opencast sector posed to deep-mine jobs. During the strike the opencast sites had continued to work and this had produced flash points of conflict in Durham, Yorkshire and Lancashire. In Co. Durham effective picketing of an H.J. Banks & Co. site at Tow Law had resulted in an injunction being taken out against the union, whose officials were required to appear in the High Court in London. This seriously aggravated the views of the moderate leadership of the union; views which increasingly focused on the morality of the profit motive.

Matters were aggravated further by the fact that during the strike many miners viewed the extent of opencast mining for the first time. Comments on the extent of the opencast sites and the effects on the landscape ('It's like the moon out there…') were common place.[8]

The Miners' Support Groups, which had played a key role in the Durham communities during the strike, became closely involved with the action groups opposed to the extension of BCC's opencast mining in the county. In 1985 the Corporation had decided to press ahead with five large opencast site applications. The County Council had requested a moratorium on new sites and in its annoyance with BCC rejected all five applications, polarising the issue of opencast mining in the county. These sites (at Daisy Hill, Rose Hill, Hill Top Brasselton, West Carr and Billingside) were spread across the whole of the exposed coalfield and the public inquiries associated with them served to spread protest over a wider area. The Inquiry into the Billingside site was held in July 1986 and evidence from local people was organised by the Durham Area Miners' Support Group. It stated that:

> Durham Area Miners' Support Group is a federal organisation of the Miners' Support Groups in Durham County. The main objective of the Area Support Group is to co-ordinate the work of the different groups within the Durham Area. Like the separate groups it was formed during the miners dispute of 1984–85.
>
> Soon after the dispute ended, one Durham miner summed up the feeling of the mining communities as follows: 'The pits are all we have; that's why we went on strike for a year. They're still all we have and we've still got to fight for them.
>
> Many of the Support Groups meet to do precisely that. Indeed that is the first reason we are represented at this Inquiry. It is our firm belief that opencast coal mining (OCCM) is a major threat to deep-mined coal mining on a nation-wide basis. As such OCCM will inevitably lead to the further socio-economic decline of mining communities.
>
> The second reason we are here is because, in our experience, OCCM drastically reduces the quality of life of communities nearby.[9]

This evidence was presented by a disparate group and brought together sophisticated analyses of coal production and markets with direct experience of residents, supported by photographs and dramatic references to the changed pattern of daily life. It was something of a cultural shift from the normal pattern followed by inquiries in the county and represented the broadening and deepening of opposition referred to by Hardy. Dave Ayre, a resident of Crook and secretary of the Trades Council for the Wear Valley, recounted the experience of his area in the wake of the closures of the deep-coal mines.

Overall the sense of identity within the local villages together with the social fabric of the communities have been destroyed. The decline of the coal mining industry went hand in hand with the rise of opencast coal mining. Map 2 shows the scale of opencast mining around Tow Law….We have had to suffer excessive noise and dust, vibrations from blasting, heavy traffic past our houses and bright light shining though our bedrooms from the flood lamps. Through opencasting much of the natural environment of the area has been destroyed. A variety of wild life such as foxes, geese, ducks, rabbits and badgers, wild flowers, trees and shrubs have been driven out of the area or destroyed. As if this wasn't enough, one child was drowned in one of the lagoons at the Red Barns site when it was first opencasted fifteen years ago.

The supposed employment benefits to the area have proven to be spurious. In Billy Row, Sunnyside and Stanley Hill, no more than five people work on opencast sites. As in other places, most of the people who have started employment on opencast sites are from outside the area.[10]

This new form of protest group differed considerably in composition and perspective from the environmentally based opposition of the 1970s. Nevertheless there were moments when these different social groups came together. In 1986 Desmond Napier gave a presentation to a weekend school of miners in Durham. In his account of the struggles with the opencast industry he won the general admiration of the members of the audience who reflected that he had been the most radical speaker to whom they had listened. One lodge secretary commented that 'at least we have listened to one person who has beaten British Coal.'

In the aftermath of the strike, the large scale colliery closures and the direct protest of local people saw a build up of pressure within the NUM for a much more determined policy of outright opposition to opencast expansion. Union officials such as Billy Etherington had already begun to present evidence at public inquiries and the Research Department of the union had produced a substantial report entitled: *Opencast Coal: The Threat to the NUM.*[11] In so doing they enlarged the nature of the anti-opencast coal coalition and also added a new dimension to the kinds of evidence and expertise that was brought to the attention of the Inspectorate. This process was assisted by the formation of an opencast committee at the NUM's national headquarters in Sheffield. This committee was made up of union officials and sympathetic experts from the universities. The committee organised several meetings, assisted in the production of a series of position papers and liased closely with the newly established Coalfield Communities Campaign and with Labour Party MPs.

While Durham had been at the centre of both opencast mining *and* opencast protest in the 1970s, by the mid-1980s both activities had become widespread throughout the British coalfields. An indication of this can be found in the pages of *Hansard*. For example on 20 January 1986 Lawrence Cunliffe, an ex-mining engineer and MP for Leigh, in an adjournment debate strongly criticised the spread of opencast mining and asked the government to note that:

> Thousands of ordinary householders are suffering because of this great intrusion into their lives which is causing, in their opinion and that of my colleagues, wholesale havoc and devastation.[12]

He quoted an example from the Lomax site application in his own constituency.

In the following May, as part of an orchestrated national

campaign, members of parliament from England (Birmingham), Scotland (Strang) and Wales (Clwyd) asked for:

> a list by site and county of all opencast coal mining applications received since 1 January 1984, stating in each case, whether authorisation has been granted, refused or is still pending; and…for each approved, refused or as yet unauthorised case, the tonnage per year to be mined and the time period requested or authorised.

NEW PATTERNS OF PROTEST

The defeat of the Labour Party in the 1987 General Election and the subsequent publication of *MPG3* in 1988 led to a new national surge in opencast site applications—particularly smaller licensed sites. In the run-up to *MPG3*, the opencast industry increased its public pressure for more sites, arguing that its efforts were being thwarted, in illegitimate ways, by the operation of the planning system. Ray Proctor, managing director of the OE, orchestrated these complaints when he argued that:

> Under the new planning system we are not getting sufficient new sites even to maintain current output. In 1987–88 local authorities approved just 20 per cent of what we asked for. Of the sites that went to public inquiries we gained only one-third of the tonnage applied for. On this basis, far from expanding the opencast sector, we are facing substantial decline.

He had developed this argument by reference to jobs and employment:

> Thousand jobs in the civil engineering sector are at risk and, with less profit, there is less money available to support the deep mines. And the coal gap will not be filled by coal mines in this country.[13]

Statements such as these incensed many local planners who felt that BCC was playing fast and loose with the statistics and was undermining their attempt to run a rational planning system. Early in 1987 at a large conference on the coal industry at the University of Nottingham, one respected planner, Richard Tamplin, likened BCC to the Medieval Catholic Church. So uncontestable did it regard its view of the world 'that anyone who disagrees is branded a heretic'. In discussing this matter further we interviewed George Hardy who, through the County Planning Officers' Society, had been involved in the annual publication of opencast mining statistics. The first publication had covered the year 1983–84, and it was conceived as a device for providing accurate data which could rationally guide the planning debate. However this aim was not achieved without a struggle. As George explained:

> What British Coal have always done at the end of every year was to have a concerted campaign in the press about how they are being starved of planning consents. For example, here's a press cutting from 10 May 1988. At that time we were preparing the figures for 1987–88. 'British Coal Bosses Warn of Disaster' is the headline.
>
> 'The industry is heading for disaster in the light of the current poor success rate in planning applications.' They mention the possible affect of the current downturn on jobs, etc.
>
> The actual figures for 1987–88 show that the output for opencast coal was 12 per cent higher than the year and 7 per cent higher than the previous year. Nineteen square miles of land were dealt with, either approved or refused, of which 8 square miles were approved. Fourteen million tonnes of opencast coal were approved, and the amount of opencast reserves available at the year end with planning permission (and this is the important figure) were 74 million tonnes. That was only three million tonnes lower than the previous year, which in its turn had been the highest ever, as far as we are aware.

The bad feeling generated by these disputes united the planners and fuelled their determination to get *MPG3* amended. It also brought them into a sympathetic relationship with the environmental lobby at a time when there was a dramatic increase in protest in the exposed coal field areas.

Once again, the form of protest changed. Local under-standings became expressed less through party politics and more through questions of the environment. 'Communities' came to be understood as part of the sustainable environment and local life and custom expressed by way of references to landscape and permanent features of the fixed environment. Opencasting joined other forms of 'destructive development' as a focus for a more generalised protest against environmental damage. In part this was a response to the changes accompanying the *New Strategy for Coal*. In the pursuit of 'cheap coal', BCC had embarked upon a national programme of extraction, involving areas which had previously been undisturbed. The march toward privatisation confirmed in people's minds that issues of profit and money were dominating all else. In such a context evocations of the 'common good' and 'national need' began to have a hollow ring. In response some people raised general questions of environmental damage; others looked after their own interests. In odd ways, people emerged as new protesters.

Such was the case in the Erewash Valley—which straddles the border between Nottinghamshire and Derbyshire. The first application in the area was for the Smotherly site. The second site, known as Shilo North (containing 1.7m tons of coal and located near Eastwood), was strongly resisted, opposed by Nottinghamshire County Council and several local amenity and community groups. The public inquiry for the site was held in 1989. BCC appeared confident (perhaps overly confident) of victory over the unprofessional and inexperienced local people and the County Council. However, the Shilo North Action Group (SNAG) had spent many months in careful preparation for the Inquiry—preparing a raft of detailed critiques of the planning application and highlighting the potential impact of the proposed site on the local environment. During interviews with the members of the Action Group it became obvious that they had no respect for or fear of BCC. They worked closely with the County Council's planning and legal team—subjecting BCC's witnesses to detailed cross examination and occasional ridicule.

SNAG had mobilised a wide coalition of other groups to oppose the application—even local Conservative MPs, including Jim Lester, gave their support. Every opportunity for coverage in the local media was seized upon and the group's banners were regularly brought out. After the eight week inquiry came to an end SNAG's members felt that they had to continue a high profile campaign until the result of the appeal was announced. Follow-up activities included continuous press releases and media interviews, while a delegation from the Action Group visited the Department of the Environment and met with the Planning Minister and officials to press their case.

The result of the Shilo North Public Inquiry was announced during May 1990. The Secretary of State for the Environment upheld the recommendation of the inspector—that BCC's appeal be dismissed. In his report, the inspector, Mr Donnison, concluded that the environmental destruction involved in the site's development far outweighed the benefits of extracting the coal. He noted that although BCC had presented a plan to restore the valley:

> ...It would be 13 to 14 years before the basic structure of the landscape could be restored and perhaps 50 years before mature vegetation growth could be expected. The loss of this locally scarce, multi-use mature landscape in the greenbelt would be serious.[14]

The OE's Regional Director, Tony Palmer, commented after the appeal was dismissed that:

> The Shilo North Action Group put on a very professional campaign and they have won on this occasion....The coal hasn't gone away because of the decision. It is low cost and very attractive and a £60m national asset. We will reapply to work Shilo.[15]

Norman Lewis of the Nottinghamshire Wildlife Trust, who had given evidence regarded, this as 'a political move and is not good news.' However, in his view:

People are getting the message and have got their act together. The message to British Coal is still 'the valley is not for digging'.

Speaking for SNAG, Bob Peck said:

We hope our victory gives the people around other threatened areas the heart to join together and let the voice of the people be heard. It is very sad that the people of this area have to live under a threat from British Coal who can't admit defeat. We are certainly not going away and if they want to come back we will be ready for them.[16]

In commenting on BCC's intention to reapply David Lane of Cossall Robinettes Action Group (CRAG) wrote:

I have always believed that we in Britain live in a fair, democratic society but the attitude of Mr Palmer goes some way towards dispelling this belief. It is clear proof…that he doesn't care about the views of people, local councils or indeed central government. All I can say to Mr Palmer and his henchmen is that his contemptuous attitude towards people's opinions in general and society as a whole only strengthens our resolve and, I am sure, that of other action groups to continue to represent the voice of the majority.[17]

The activities of SNAG had served as a catalyst in the area, especially down the road in the communities threatened by BCC's proposed Robinettes site (located near Cossall). There, the local parish councillors were criticised for failing to notify local residents about a meeting they had had with BCC to discuss the proposed site. Mr Maurice Cresswell told a local parish meeting that individual communities were simply 'bleating in the wind' when they negotiated alone with BCC and its well-funded professional team. At that meeting in 1989 Mr Cresswell said that 'the (Parish) Council's docile attitude would be interpreted as lightweight opposition and only encourage British Coal to proceed more positively and at a faster pace.' He argued that without sustained opposition the little island of

Cossall 'will be marooned in a waste land in 10 to 20 years.'[18] As a consequence of this meeting the Council endorsed a five-point *Resident's Charter* aimed at defeating opencasting in Cossall and in the country. The main points of this charter instructed the Council to:

- Recognise its residents as being totally opposed to open-cast.
- Liaise with, and join surrounding action groups.
- Lobby MPs for a change in the law leading to a total ban on opencasting.
- Appoint a press secretary to liaise with the media.
- Recognise that opposition to opencasting is its funda-mental priority.

Local pressure groups like these gradually became linked together in informal national networks which exchanged infor-mation and advice in increasingly sophisticated ways. Following the Shilo North Public Inquiry a special meeting was held near Eastwood to bring together the various action groups and amenity organisations in the area. It proved to be highly suc-cessful and a new umbrella group emerged—known as People Against Opencast. The new group decided to bring the issue of opencast mining to the attention of MPs of all parties. To this end it was subsequently agreed to organise a mass lobby of Parliament during 1990 and continue to pressure the Government for changes in opencast planning policy.

The lobby of Parliament took place on 13 June and involved people from all the coalfield areas of Great Britain; mostly they were directly involved in protesting against a particular open-cast site application. Although it had received the support of the CPRE, it was organised entirely by People Against Opencast. In a way which became common throughout the 1980s, these people had little previous experience of public protest or political activism: for all of them this was their first Parliamentary lobby. They learned as they went along, receiv-ing a helping hand from some time served politicians. A 'photo-opportunity' was arranged at the Jubilee Gardens alongside the old County Hall, where Dennis Skinner and a number of other MPs talked with the crowd and mingled amongst the variety of environmental banners (see p.198). The Jubilee Room had been booked at the Houses of Commons by Jim Lester. Mark Fisher, the MP for Stoke on Trent was one of the speakers who addressed a meeting during which it became clear that while these people were relatively new to political protest, they knew a great deal about opencast mining and the planning process. During the meeting many of them left for brief discussions with their own MPs, pressing the case against opencast mining. The lobby was by far the biggest meeting of anti-opencast campaigners that had taken place in the UK. The organisers were both surprised and pleased by the level of support and interest provoked by their demonstration. It was one of the important forces which influenced the Labour Party and radicalised its view of opencast.

Once the Party had published *Opencast Mining—too high a price?* local councillors and prospective MPs adopted a largely belligerent tone in discussing opencast mining. The *Nottingham Evening Post* led with a headline 'We would ban opencast mines'[19] and quoted Paddy Tipping, Labour's prospective parliamentary candidate for Sherwood, as saying:

> Opencast mining has blighted many parts of Notts. Labour's policy statement will give added protection to the countryside and the people who live in it.

In spite, or perhaps because, of this success, the life of People Against Opencast was a short one.

Without financial support, such national umbrella organisations, aimed at co-ordinating local protest, have always been difficult to sustain. In contrast, regional groupings have proven to be more durable. In the North East , for example, several of the local action groups had met to co-ordinate travel arrangements for the lobby and their media coverage. At a subsequent meeting they decided to join forces and form the North East Opencast Action Group (NEOAG). This group built upon the experience of strategic lobbying in the area and aimed to 'reduce opencast coal and associated mineral production to a level which does not adversely affect either peoples' quality of life or the quality of the local environment.' It produced a regular newsletter and held quarterly meetings and occasional seminars on opencast-related issues. Similar groups were formed across the Midlands (Midlands Against Opencast) and Yorkshire (Yorkshire Opencast Objectors). In Wales and Scotland groups were also formed (Scottish Opencast Action Group, and Wales Against Opencast) in a way which made up a patchwork of regionally organised activity. This phenomenon of emerging local action groups and changing patterns of networks became a central feature of the protest movements in the 1990s. In this period national conferences and the lobbying of government and parliament became regular events. Patterns of intense national activity (in response to a particular issue or event) were followed by months of relative quiescence as activity focused on particular local issues or died away.

The defeat of the Labour Party in the General Election of 1992 and Heseltine's subsequent announcement of large scale colliery closures can be seen as decisive moments in the pattern of coalfield protest in this decade. One of the features of the protests against opencast mining was the fluidity of its organisation and the heterogeneity of its social base. Something of this diversity and heterogeneity had been seen in the social support the miners evoked in 1985.[20] It was also clear in the massive demonstration that took place in torrential rain in October 1992. Protesting against the closure of the deep mines, people also talked about the immorality of politics and the importance of employment linked to sustainable community life. The contingent from Cheltenham and Gloucester included Lord Neidpath, heir to the Earl of Wemyss whose estate in Scotland had been involved in a contentious dispute with BCC over opencasting. In 1995 he wrote:

> I seem to remember it was shortly after the Black Wednesday devaluation. The government had behaved outrageously at the time by pretending that nothing had happened. They were in general bad odour and they decided to shut down

half the pits in the most brutal way. Everyone was outraged. It seemed appropriate to demonstrate to show contempt for that decision. I used to be a Tory voter, but not any more.[21]

The subsequent failure of this protest was marked by the closure of almost all of the deep mines outside of North Yorkshire and the Midlands. It totally marginalised an already weakened NUM, which was forced to close its national office in Sheffield and make most of its staff redundant. In regions like South Wales, Scotland, Durham and Lancashire where once the NUM had had powerful regional bases, the organisation's membership bled away. In these areas, the occupation *coal miner* had changed dramatically. Where once it was dominated by men who worked in the deep mines, by the mid 1990s they had been replaced by surface miners in the opencast sites. This altered local politics in important ways. To begin with, these miners (with the support and encouragement of their employers) began to demonstrate in defence of their jobs and in support of the continuous development of opencast mining. Their trade union, the Transport and General Workers Union (TGWU), had been at odds with the environmental protesters for over a decade. Furthermore, and in spite of a *rapprochment* with the NUM in South Wales in the 1980s, it had not been able to develop a common cause with the unions representing the deep miners. The marginalisation of the NUM, however, created the space for a more aggressive approach by these organised workers in defense of *their* jobs. In Durham, the Sunshine Miners Action Committee (SMAC) organised marches and activities in defense of opencast mining. In Derbyshire Bring Opencast Back (BOB) appeared.

As a consequence, in many districts, local protest groups began to feel that they could no longer rely upon the support of an organised trade union. Increasingly, they looked to organisations like the CCC and the CPRE for information and for the development of a national strategy in relation to opencast mining. Both of these organisations had a strong background in local economic and environmental planning, and this alliance was strongly in evidence in the co-ordinated response during the consultation period for the revised *MPG3* in 1993–4. Successful as this had been, however, it hadn't squared the circle of maintaining sustainable communities in the context of the market. It didn't prevent opencast sites being opened when and where people didn't want them. It didn't halt the growing cynicism in the coal districts.

Occasionally growing cynicism was reflected in a dark humour. In Nottingham the newsletter *Around Robbinettes* offered advice to people facing a future of opencast mining at a 450 acre site near Cossall. It offered a translation service of the official documents they would read. We have represented this in Figure 8. In justifying their publication, Reg Connor, the spokesperson of the Robinettes Action Group made clear that:

> These are the sort of words you can pluck out of the material they used at the exhibition about what they proposed to do. Having looked at the lively words they used and compared them with what we have seen on other sites, they don't gell.

BCC declined to comment in detail, but was clearly upset by the tone of the publication.

> We are not going to be drawn into a comedy slanging match. We have many examples of restoration activity and operate stringent guidelines in stringent planning conditions.

By this time however nothing was going to be good enough to appease a growing angry resistance.

The opencast companies continued to apply for sites in places where people objected strongly and some of these obtained approval. One such place was Garforth near Leeds where H.J. Banks & Co. started mining coal in 1995 (See Figure 8). The village was described as 'Siege Town' in the *Yorkshire Evening Post*.[22] The article compared the opencast contractors to 'an army encircling a medieval city'. In spite of the efforts of the company to reduce the intrusiveness of the site, the noise and dust levels became the source of major irritation. This was exacerbated by the feelings of injustice expressed by Garforth residents. They had campaigned in a sustained way to prevent the site from receiving planning permission. But without success:

> Garforth Against the Opencast—GATOC—had mounted a vociferous and well-organised campaign to keep the contractors out. The group has, without doubt, the support of the vast majority of residents, evidenced by the turnout at a local rally and march in defence of the town and its surrounding countryside.
>
> The Government's decision to override the wishes of the community, its elected councillors and Leeds City Council met first with incredulity, then anger and now a continued bitterness. Added to that is the knowledge that more and more potential opencast sites are being identified around the town by Banks and other contractors.
>
> Against that background H.J. Banks and other developers have little hope of appeasement, whatever they did. Garforth Labour Councillor Shirley Haines chairs Garforth Against the Opencast. 'They are not wanted' she says. 'They are gouging up the countryside.... We will resist them in every way possible.'[23]

These sentiments and experiences were common ones. Across the coalfield districts at this time, the mood was of cynicism and despair. People began to see the need for more direct forms of action.

DIRECT ACTION

Something happened to political life in Britain in the 1990s that had not been predicted. After more than a decade of Thatcherism it had been assumed by many that there had been a triumph of individualism, and a general acceptance of the market as the rational and just basis of social action. Inequalities increased but no one seemed to care. Environmental protests were often interpreted in this light: NIMBYism (not in my back yard) was seen to reflect the dominant interests of a vocal middle class who wanted whatever it

TABLE 4

A protester's guide to opencast speak[24]

Short-term working	Six to sixty years
Initial void	A big hole
Final void	A bigger hole
Operating in harmony with our neighbours	Dirty, noisy and difficult to evict
We instruct the contractor on how we want the area worked	He does his own thing
Woodland feature	One each – acorn, conker and hazelnut encircled by a post and rail fence
Enhanced woodland feature	Plus a concrete badger set
Wetlands	Any 'restored' opencast site after it has rained
Greening over	Sow with grass seed

was to be dumped or dug elsewhere. But things were clearly more complex that this. The Community Charge (Poll Tax) produced a genuine sense of outrage even amongst many who benefited from it. The public protest brought about a change in the Government's policy and effectively finished off Mrs Thatcher.

By 1995, the *Observer* newspaper was announcing that 'The middle class goes militant' and reflecting upon the opposition that had built up to the export of veal calves to France. Its reporter had visited Brightlingsea and had watched the police forcing lorries packed with sheep and calves through lines of placard-wielding women, children and pensioners and reflected that:

> animal rights, the Government's attempts at Twyford Down to drive its roads programme through the shire counties, the Criminal Justice Act's perceived restrictions on ramblers, even the attempt to stop broadcasting Radio 4 on long wave, have brought a new kind of demonstrator to the streets. The middle class is tending to militancy.[25]

Two years later *The Economist* reporting protests over the Newbury bypass quoted Rob, a local resident who had joined in the protest:

> I think you'll see the direct-action movement beginning to diversify more and more. Fairmile is the university of direct action: we are teaching our methods to people from all over the world.[26]

Five times as many people were members of green groups as were members of the Labour Party. In public opinion polls between 80 and 90 per cent of people routinely answered that environmental issues were of importance to them. As Geoffrey Lean pointed out:

> MORI measuring what people actually do rather, than just what they say, describes over a third of Britons as 'environmental activists'[27]

In the coalfields popular protest began to take on more and more direct forms. Protesters were supported by a number of highly charged statements by Frank Dobson, the Labour Party's shadow minister responsible for environmental issues, which severely criticised the industry:

> Opencast undermines people's quiet enjoyment. We are contemplating getting people jailed for being unneighbourly. But when it comes to opencasting it's a mega-lout 'it's the

Genghis Khan for bad neighborliness.' It should only be permitted where there is a direct benefit to the local community
and to the environment. Otherwise we think there should be
NO opencasting.[28]

In the same speech he developed his populist hyperbole even
further:

> We have now got cowboys wall to wall. We'll get pressure for
> them for more opencasting and a more cowboy attitude.
> Opencasting needs to be cut back. Coalfield communities
> have been thrown on the scrap heap by this government
> which is refusing to start talking to protect the environment.
> My party's policy would be to give this issue a high priority.

The privatisation of the industry had a decisive effect on attitudes. While the nationalised industries were not universally
admired, they could at least call upon a level of tolerance from
amongst their publics. When the Water Boards had asked for
voluntary rationing of water during periods of drought, there
was compliance. Not so with the privatised utilities, and their
'fat cats'. Water consumption actually increased in the hot summer of 1996 in several areas, in spite of publicised pleas for
frugality. Similar processes were at work on the coalfields.

At this point, in the mid-1990s, a split began to emerge in
the opposition to opencast mining. The dominant position of
persistent lobbying and contesting of site applications and
plans continued. Organisations like the CPRE continued to
play an important supporting and coordinating role. This form
of opposition had become highly professionalised and quite
successful. Such successes were clear in the responses made to
the publication of new draft local mineral plans across the
country in 1995. One such plan, in Co. Durham, aimed at fore-
stalling expensive public inquiries by establishing a set of
agreed sites for opencast mining across the west of the county.
This produced concerted opposition.

The first meeting of the new CPRE Derwentside Group was
held in Lanchester on 16 February 1996. It was dominated by

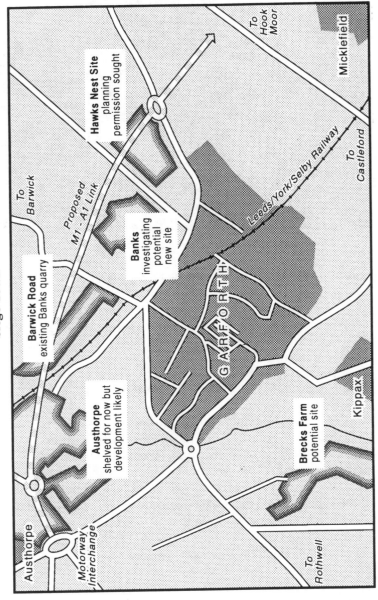

FIGURE 8
'Siege Town'

5. Demonstrators at the Houses of Parliament, June 1990

the issue of the local plan. Branch Chairman Neil Piper told
the meeting:

> We have consistently fought against opencasting. We believe
> much of the finest landscape in the county has been saved
> by our contribution to the debate. Some of the sites on the
> new list are on people's doorsteps and there is always that
> threat hanging over them. It is a great worry.

Opposition was organised and coordinated through letter writing and local Labour Party branches. Such was the public
opposition during the consultation stage that all hope of drawing up an agreed programme of future opencast sites in the
County was formally abandoned during July 1996. Councillor
John Alderson told the media that issuing a list of potential sites
had been a disaster because it had raised unnecessary fears.
The Council decided to change tack and adopt a criteria-based
approach. Councillor Alderson added:

> When it comes back to this Committee, members will find
> the criteria will be very much tighter than anything we've had

in the past, so much so, that there are doubts in some minds about whether it will be approved by the Secretary of State.[29]

The new criteria-based policy was included in the Minerals Local Plan Deposit Draft, published in March 1997. As well as several general policies covering all mineral developments there was a specific policy (M6) relating to opencast coal mining. It noted that within the exposed coalfield area of the County, proposals for the opencast mining of coal will only be approved where:

■ A significant part of the site is land which can be demonstrated to the satisfaction of the MPA to be derelict or contaminated and in need of treatment and the proposal provides for its comprehensive reclamation; or
■ Significant resources of coal would be sterilised by another development which is permitted and where extraction would enable the preparation of the site, provided the development would not be significantly delayed or impeded by the opencast working and restoration; and
■ They are acceptable in terms of other relevant policies of the Plan.

When the Deposit Draft was published it generated considerable comment in the local media. There was speculation that tighter planning controls would lead to the disappearance of opencast mining in Co. Durham. The mining companies attacked the proposals strongly and claimed they would be effectively prevented from developing new sites in most of the County's exposed coalfield area. The Sunshine Miners' Action Committee (SMAC) also protested. Copying the chants of deep miners a decade earlier—'Coal not Dole'—two hundred opencast miners marched through the streets of Durham City. Richard Bland of Tow Law worked at the RJB Mining site at Prior's Close:

Durham is more or less adamant it doesn't want any more opencasting. It is about time we took some action, make a bit of noise and approach the council with our views.[30]

Jackie Hindmarsh (secretary of SMAC) was firm in her view:

> We have ample evidence to prove that there is a bias against coal when it comes to planning approvals and that has to stop. The industry has been quiet for too long and we have got to stand up and fight. We want a fair deal for coal and for every application to be considered on its merits.

She wanted to know:

> from Durham County Council why they are trying to throw more than 500 men and women out of work and deprive their families of a livelihood.[31]

This change in rhetorical tone reflected the fact that, with the ending of the deep mines, the employment argument rested squarely with the opencast industry. Its opponents, as a result, began to give increasing stress to environmental concerns. In Durham, they won the argument. It was clear, in conservationist areas of the county, that any amendment to the Plan by the new Labour administration would be seen as a retreat from its policies whilst in opposition. It would also play into the hands of a new and more militant style of opposition to opencast mining which emphasized direct action.

The sources of direct action as a tactic on the coalfields are numerous. It grew out of frustration and annoyance with the perceived failure of the planning system to take account of local people's views. It gained impetus as many of the remaining deep mines closed. Opencast mining was increasingly seen as an illegitimate economic activity which had taken away other deep-mined jobs. It borrowed from a tradition of sit-ins and sit-downs used by women on Greenham Common and by the 'eco-warriors' in their anti-road campaigns. Activists like 'Swampy', 'Muppet Dave' and 'Animal' gave prominence to views that things were going wrong, and that individuals' had a responsibility to do something about it.

New protest groups were formed across the coalfields. One such was No Opencast.

The No Opencast group operated in England and brought together an interesting collection of groups and individuals. It was supported by the NUM as well as by Earth First! and Friends of the Earth. In Yorkshire, a number of the miners' support groups, which had emerged during the miners' strike of 1984–85, gave active support and the organisation attracted a number of unemployed trade unionists and local community campaigners. Its programme was one of complete opposition to opencast mining. It aimed to publicise this through its own policy programme and through a series of daring adventures and direct intervention into the workings of opencast sites.

In 1995, the group dug up the grounds around Michael Hestletine's house:

> By lamplight and headtorch, 50 people from mining communities, ex-miners, trades council members and environmental activists were digging for coal with pick-axe and spade. They were already a foot deep in places.

The group had applied for planning permission to mine the site and this was their 'preliminary site visit'. In the view of Steve Parry:

> One man wakes up to one of the finest views in Britain yet whole communities are on the dole. All over Britain land as beautiful as this is being destroyed.[32]

The group repeated this action in 1997: this time focusing on the home of Richard Budge, the owner of RJB Mining. *The Times* reported that:

> Mrs Scargill, 52, was amongst five demonstrators arrested at 5am at Wiseton, Nottinghamshire, for alleged breach of the peace. She then returned to the scene, about half a mile from Mr Budge's property, where she was again taken into custody. After being released for a second time, again without charge, she said: 'I was there as a member of the

No Opencast campaign group, not as Arthur Scargill's wife, and I was there to protest against Budge's policies'. He doesn't know what it's like to wake up in the morning and look out upon an opencast site'.[33]

This policy of 'demonstration' by transferring experience from one place to the other had great visual effect. It encouraged others to think imaginatively about new ways of organising and communicating. In Derbyshire, campaigners against a proposed opencast site dumped a large pile of coal at Chatsworth House, the home of the landowner, the Duke of Devonshire. Hugh Ellis of the campaign group remarked 'let's see how the Duke likes having a coal tip on his doorstep'. Ellis rejected the idea that an opencast site would bring needed employment to the area. Rather:

> We feel that Chatsworth are selling us out. The duke is immensely rich and he makes a lot of money from Chatsworth House. But this site is high quality countryside which people can enjoy for no money. Why change it into yet another industrial site?

His fellow campaigner Ann Syrett had talked with the duke. 'He told us that we were very selfish and we should be happy for jobs to be created in the area. I don't think he's been very well advised'.[34]

In South Wales opencast mining had been carried out alongside deep mining for decades. During the crisis years of the 1980s a rapprochement had been established between the trade unions which represented both sets of workers. A 'gentleman's agreement' existed which tolerated the continuance of opencast mining, emphasizing its effectiveness in relation to derelict sites. But in 1993, the last of the deep mines closed down. Tower eventually survived in a new form, but this did not affect the general sense of an ending. However opencast mining continued as the main activity of Celtic Energy. The company developed plans for a major increase in both the scale and extent of its mining operations, concentrating upon the anthracite belt in the West.

John Vidal explained the situation graphically:

> There are more than thirty sites known to be of immediate interest to the privatised opencast companies in the whole crescent-shaped anthracite belt. Another 40 have been mentioned. If they are all developed—as the valley communities believe is inevitable because no application to mine has been turned down in more than 45 years—together they would make Europe's largest opencast site, in effect a 40 mile scar from Hirwaun in the east to Kidwelly in the west.[35]

In this new context, the opposition escalated. West Glamorgan County Council granted Celtic Energy permission to mine the Selar site near Cwmgwrach, an unspoiled location in the Neath Valley which included a designated Site of Special Scientific Interest (SSSI). With a projected acreage the size of 800 football pitches, the Cwmgwrach development was planned to work coal to a depth of 180 metres. In order to obtain planning consent the company agreed to move the SSSI further down the valley. It also concluded a 'planning gain' agreement which involved Celtic Energy ploughing back £1 million into the three villages nearest to the site. Margaret Minhinnick of Wales Against Opencast was outraged:

> The valleys have been opencast-mined before but this time it's different. The destruction will be worse, the scale is now immense. The communities built on coal are no longer behind the work or trust the companies who talk of 'voids' not mines, and 'overburden mounds' not tips.

And she adds: 'For whose benefit? Whose economy is it?'[36] These questions drew in the involvement of the radical environmental organisation, Earth First! Local meetings were organised, and the plight of the people in the Welsh valleys compared with that of indigenous peoples the world over struggling for *their* land. A group of Earth First! activists moved to the site, camping in tree houses. A spokesperson complained about the way the site was being despoiled:

> They did it by slicing up 8ft by 4ft lumps of SSSI, plonking them on the back of a truck and driving them down the road...It will take centuries to replace the hundreds of mature oaks because of a scheme which will only last a few years.[37]

John Vidal talked with some of the villagers about the involvement of these 'outsiders'. One said:

> I felt it was all over until these people arrived. We were fighting as locals. I feel a hell of a lot better now. They've inspired us to stand up.

Another commented on how:

> They entertain the children, they are very interesting people. It's a marvelous inspiration for the village. Now they understand what opencast is.

In this changed context, opposition became more generalised. Several County Councils began to turn down applications for opencast sites and residents living near working sites complained more vociferously. The Brynhenllys site near Ammanford was one example. Local activists complained about the reduction in their standard of life and of the impact upon the value of their houses. They protested to the valuation officer who, it seems, agreed with them. Hywel Gwyn Evans was at the center of the local campaign:

> Brynhenllys has generated more complaints than all the other opencast sites in South Wales put together. Following our success with the valuation officer, who reduced most of Ystradowen properties by two tax bands, we intend to sue Celtic Energy for the money we have lost on our homes.

His fellow campaigner in the nearby Lash valley intended to follow this example and insisted that: 'our campaign won't be over until the last element of blight has been lifted'.[38] In this they sympathised with the activities of groups like Earth First! In March 1997 the South Wales group's newsletter reported that:

the opencast mine at Brynhennllys was successfully closed
down for the day as workers were caught completely
unawares and every working machine was occupied....
Workers were mainly quiet, apart from the odd one or two
that were itching to use physical force to eject people from
the machines. Indeed anyone with a camera was particularly
in danger with one guy away from the safety of the main
group being attacked and having his camera smashed to
pieces. Anyone who had been on the previous occupation of
this site though, considered this to be nothing in comparison to the violence against protesters then. Apparently the
workers are now under orders to stay calm and not to use
violence. It is a shame that they did not follow these instructions....Altogether there were six arrests for alleged criminal
damage. Many outlandish stories had appeared in the local
press....One of those lies was that the whole action was being
put together by people outside Wales. This was simply not
true as local people, both Earth Firsters and others being centrally involved in the planning.[39]

Friends of the Earth was also active and building upon its
involvement with the No Opencast group. In 1997 it
announced that:

FoE local groups in Derbyshire, South Wales and South
Yorkshire are campaigning on opencast. Our aim is to con-
solidate those individual efforts into an opencast network of
campaigners carrying forward the first 'Area Campaign
Priority' This will also involve us working closely with other
community groups already active in this area.[40]

Local groups in South Wales developed these initiatives, producing their own World Wide Web pages as networking entered
the realms of cyberspace. Here Celtic Energy's plans were
attacked and the company identified as 'one of South Wales'
biggest environmental enemies'. They chronicled the activities
of the company and conclude:

our persistence in this matter can and eventually will prevent

[this] short-sighted, selfish agenda from destroying what is still a green and pleasant land.[41]

This resonance of Blake and the past critical traditions was echoed by Simon Jenkins, when he recalled Cobbett's *Rural Rides*. After reflecting that a similar journey today would produce a 'cry of anguish' at the sight of the anarchy and the greed he remembered that:

> Cobbett wrote that 'from a very early age, I imbibed the opinion that it was every man's duty to do all that lay in his power to leave his country as good as he found it.' Today the old growler would survey the landscape, turn in his saddle and spit.[42]

This sentiment is shared by many. Undoubtedly the electoral victory of the Labour Party in May 1997 built on sentiments such as these. Equally clear is the fact that many of the people who have been brought to the edge of these protests over the environment expected a more enlightened policy from the new government. For many it will be seen as the touchstone to its success or failure. In the view of Peter Melchett, executive director of Greenpeace and former junior Labour environment minister:

> The environmental crisis is not going to go away, just because they have not put it in the draft manifesto. Either they will embrace these issues, or events and public opinion will force them upon them.[43]

But the crisis, and its relation to the rest of society, was not likely to be easily resolved.

NEW GOVERNMENT—NEW POLICIES?

On 1 May 1997, the Labour Party under the leadership of Tony Blair gained an overwhelming victory in the General Election. The new Government—under the banner of 'New Labour'—raised the hope for many people that, after the eighteen years of Conservative rule, there would be a real change of perspective. This view was strongly held in the coal districts. Here there was an expectation that the deep-mined industry would be stabilised and that the precipitous decline in its fortunes would be halted. More generally, there was a belief that the new Government had established clear credentials in relation to environmental policy and that this would, of necessity, produce an approach which would further adjust the balance of power away from the opencast operators. In addition, whilst in opposition, the Labour Party had made strong claims in relation to constitutional reform and devolution. Many expressed the hope that this would lead to a further democratisation of the British state with a real and significant impact upon local government freedom of information and the overall planning process. By the end of this century, progress in each of these areas had been ambiguous at best.

THE TROUBLE WITH COAL

Coal was always going to be a problem for the New Labour Government. The only surprising thing is that ministers took so long in spotting it. There were a number of reasons for this. The historical legacy was one thing. Coal and coal mining had left its imprint on Old Labour. The view that the Labour Party would not have survived without the miners and the miners' union is a credible one. In 1997, this memory was a rather unsettling one, made more so by the deep antagonism shown by the Thatcher administration to the industry and its main trade union. In truth it was a memory which the government could happily have suppressed and eventually forgotten. This however, was never going to be a possibility. There were too many links, too many MPs whose constituencies supported the Blair project for government but refused to forget the past. Of course, if the industry, its workers and the people of the coal districts were to carry on as normal, remain placid and accept things as they came, it might have been possible to forget—to build the 'new' in an empty space. But this was not going to happen either. There were too many problems.

The Blair Government inherited the unresolved problems of privatisation. It had no intention of renationalising coal or the electricity supply industry. So it was left with a mess to clear up. To begin with there was the problem of the new coal supply contracts to be negotiated by the electricity generating companies to begin from the end of March 1998. This accompanied the full deregulation of the electricity supply industry with additional generating companies being set up with access to the national grid. The situation was further complicated by the presence of a number of domestic coal producers competing with RJB Mining at a time when the pressure of coal imports—from the EU and beyond—was intensifying with the growing strength of the pound *and* falling international coal prices. The electricity supply coal contracts were vital, and in 1997 it seemed unlikely that RJB Mining would be able to market the tonnage levels it had produced in the protected years that followed privatisation. This was the short-term problem.

There were longer term problems too. Soon after privatisation the electricity supply industry began to invest in Combined Cycle Gas Turbine (CCGT) technology. This emerged as a major investment programme and became known as the 'dash for gas'. Throughout the period of the Major Government the expansion continued, assisted by the generous provision of planning consents (known as Section 36 consents) from the

DTI. Within the UK energy market, the share taken by gas had been increasing for over a decade. However its impact on coal had mainly been through its erosion of the domestic and industrial market by the introduction of gas-fired boilers. CCGT extended the threat to coal by encroaching upon its last major market—electricity generation. Between 1994 and 1997, the amount of gas used for electricity generation more than doubled, and its share of this market increased from 14 per cent to 28 per cent (see Table 5)

TABLE 5
Fuel used in electricity generation 1994–97*

	coal	oil	gas	nuclear	hydro	other	total
1994	37.1	4.1	9.9	21.2	0.4	1.1	73.8
1995	36.1	3.6	12.5	21.3	0.5	1.2	75.2
1996	33.0	3.5	16.4	22.2	0.3	1.2	76.6
1997	28.6	1.9	20.9	23.3	0.4	1.4	76.5

*millions tonnes of oil equivalent
SOURCE: *Energy Trends*, April 1999

In opposition Labour spokesmen had expressed the view that once in Government they would halt this dash. But it was going to be difficult. The coal industry had few friends in the DTI and the new CCGT technology was 'state of the art' with many supporters. It was also 'new' and would seem to fit better with New Labour.

Finally there was the problem of environmental regulation. Conventional coal-fired power stations produce large amounts of sulphur dioxide and carbon dioxide. The former of these is regulable through the use of low-sulphur coals and the installation of FGD equipment. This, however, costs money and in the 1980s and 1990s few substantive capital investments were made. Carbon dioxide emissions can also be reduced, but this involves major research and investments in 'clean-coal technology' such as 'fluidised bed' and gasification-based combustion systems. A major demonstration project for this technology—at Grimethorpe in South Yorkshire—had been closed down, and there was no support for similar develop-ments. The critical implications of these issues for the coal industry became clearer as the decade progressed. These were addressed by the DTI in April 1999. However its energy paper *Cleaner Coal Technologies* delayed any financial support for new demonstration plants until after the next general election.

In December 1996, the UK had ratified the Second United Nations Economic Commission for Europe (UNECE) Sulphur Protocol with its commitment to reduce 1990 levels of emis-sions by up to 80 per cent by 2010. New emission targets, proposed in March 1996, were much tighter and threatened a reduction in the UK coal burn to 30 mt in 2001, and 25mt in 2005. These targets were revised downwards in January 1998 with further proposals from the Environment Agency being issued in March 1999. The coal industry and its allies cam-paigned extensively against these tighter emission limits, but achieved little support

The situation with regard to carbon dioxide raised even greater problems. Under the UN Framework Convention on Climate Change (signed at the Rio Earth Summit in 1992) the UK agreed to reduce its CO_2 and other greenhouse gas (GHG) emissions to their 1990 levels by 2000. This would be achieved only through the reduction of coal-fired generation. In March 1997 the Environment Ministers of the European Union set a new tougher target involving a 15 per cent reduc-tion in GHG emissions below 1990 levels by 2010. In opposition the Labour Party agreed with this, going even fur-ther with a manifesto commitment to a *20 per cent reduction* of CO_2 emissions. Although the scientific basis for this target and its implications for the UK economy and society was unclear, the new Labour Government confirmed its commitment. It was reasserted by Tony Blair in his keynote speech to the UN Environment Conference in New York. He congratulated the previous Tory administration on achieving the earlier target and acknowledged that achievement of the new target would require significant measures: more efficient use of transport; improved energy conservation; and the greater use of renew-able sources of energy.[1]

The implication of this pledge had barely sunk in by the time John Prescott went to the next summit at Kyoto in Japan. Such a reduction (however desirable) would mean that the UK's carbon emissions would need to fall from the estimated 1990 level of 54mt to 43mt in 2010. Such a change would require an enormous and rapid restructuring of the economy in its patterns of energy use and transportation. The easy option involved a further reduction in coal-fired generation. All signs pointed to an extended 'dash for gas'. But what about coal? And how sustainable was gas? How long would it last? And on top of all this there was the problem of opencast coal, the growing problem of local protest and the party's commitment whilst in opposition to sort it all out. It was going to be interesting.

CRISIS IN THE DEEP MINES

The new Energy Minister, Leeds MP John Battle, had many connections with the mining industry. On 5 November 1997 he told the House of Commons that the Government was taking six main actions 'to ensure that there are diverse and secure supplies of energy, including coal'.[2] It intended to complain to the European Commission about the subsidies paid to the German and Spanish coal industries which would affect the volume of coal trade between Germany and the UK. He argued that ways would be found of supporting clean coal technology. In addition a review of the electricity industry and the infamous 'electricity pool' would take place to ensure that a level playing field operated for all fuels. As part of this, the generating companies would be required to offer their unwanted coal-fired stations to other parties, while the regulator (OFFER) would be encouraged to prevent generators from passing on excessive costs under early take-or-pay gas contracts. Provisions would be added to the Fossil Fuel Levy Bill to remove the financial advantages obtained by nuclear power and imported electricity from France.

This announcement produced some cautious optimism within the coal industry. Observers of the energy sector felt that, even if each of the policies was to be successful, it was probably a case of 'too little too late'. As it turned out, the protests to Europe were only partially successful with subsidies to German anthracite exports to the UK being successfully challenged. These worries for the industry were further exacerbated by the continued 'dash for gas'. By the Autumn of 1997 over 17GW of CCGT and large gas-fired CHP plant was either operational or under construction. Furthermore, large numbers of applications for additional CCGT projects were under consideration by the DTI. In addition to this, there were proposals for coal-fired stations like Didcot A (National Power) and Drakelow (Eastern Electric) were converted to dual-firing (coal/gas units).[3] The new Labour Government did not halt these developments. It continued to give planning consents. It seemed that Battle's views on energy did not differ much from those of his predecessor. The environmental advantages of gas, as compared to coal-fired generation, were repeatedly stressed.[4]

Ironically it was opposition spokesman, John Redwood, the arch monetarist who sounded the alarm bells most loudly. In the House of Commons he questioned the wisdom of further planning permissions.

> Is the Government worried that permission for this station could close another coal mine….How many more stations will it licence in the dash for gas? How many more pits does it plan to close as a result?[5]

The situation was both difficult and complex. Coal, in its reduced role, remained firmly in the energy market where it faced two powerful private electricity generation companies keen to take advantage of a highly dynamic and competitive market. The electricity supply contract was critical for all the coal companies. This had been protected under the arrangements for privatisation, but this protection lasted only until March 1998 when the electricity market would be fully deregulated. These circumstances alone (involving greater uncertainty for the generating companies) meant that coal supply contracts would be smaller and there would be no return to the good old days of guaranteed bulk deliveries. It was going to be tough for coal—with lower tonnages and lower prices the likeliest outcome. In this market RJB competed with the other British companies, all of them united in their hope for greater stability.

In Wales, the employee buy-out at Tower Colliery continued to thrive though diversifying its markets and arranging a new supply contact with National Power. This contract related to Aberthaw power station which was designed to burn local coal. Celtic Energy was also successful in obtaining a £100m contract to supply 3.4mt of opencast coal to this power station over a five-year period. This nevertheless involved a decline. To make good the loss, the company planned to enter the generating industry with two of its own power stations. It intended to buy the closed Uskmouth Power Station, recommissioning it along with a new 360MW clean coal technology plant at East Merthyr. Although unsuccessful (Uskmouth was recommissioned, but then taken over by the US company AES) this marked a significant move by a coal company attempting to transform itself into an integrated energy concern. It met with considerable opposition from National Power.

For its part, RJB stuck to what it knew best—persistent lobbying for Government support in the face of an impending disaster. In October, the company began a concerted campaign focusing on its disadvantaged position in the market and the impact of this on coal mining jobs. Speaking on BBC Radio 4's *World at One* programme, Colin Godfrey the company's marketing director argued that the 'dash for gas' meant that:

The coal industry is under severe threat. There is no point in producing coal to go to stockpile.[6]

The appeal, however, seemed to fall on deaf ears. The policies of New Labour ruled out the re-nationalisation of the coal industry. Faced with a private coal owner, whose past political loyalties were clear, the new administration felt no compulsion to help. John Battle put it bluntly:

The power generations are private businesses. I have no say at the negotiating table. I don't know why Mr Budge thinks

6. Scraping the surface, Co. Durham

I have…[further subsidies] it would be grossly unfair to all other companies in negotiations.[7]

Meanwhile, RJB's estimates that ten of its seventeen deep mines were at risk was supported by a number of independent reports.[8] As if to confirm these predictions, the Monktonhall colliery in Scotland, run initially as a workers' buy-out since its closure by BCC, and then Waverley Mining announced the end of its operations. RJB followed this with the announcement of the loss of 100 jobs at the Maltby Colliery in South Yorkshire as a result of 'uncertainty in the market'. The company claimed that it was a necessity and that it would continue to 'make decisions necessary to maintain a robust coal mining industry'.[9] It became all too clear that in the view of the DTI such an industry would be significantly reduced in size. In its submission to the European Commission it estimated that over 5,000 jobs would be lost in the deep-mined sector in 1998. *The Times* noted that:

> The Commission's Report will say that miners directly employed in deep mines will fall from 9,900 this year to a yearly average of 6,700 next year with the end-year work-force predicted at 5,000.

This view was supported by reports that PowerGen had informed RJB that it had satisfied its coal supply needs for the coming year through imports and the smaller suppliers. It would take a small amount of RJB coal if the price was cut by 15 per cent. In response, John Grogan MP for Selby said:

> These official DTI figures will send terrible shock waves through the coal-mining communities. We need an energy policy coordinated at Cabinet level to avoid the crisis in coal we are facing.[10]

Things however got worse for RJB. The contract with National Power was also much reduced and the company concluded that 'a significant segment of the production will have to be taken out'.[11]

Simon Holberton agreed:

> After yesterday's deal between RJB Mining…and National Power…it has become plain that more than half of RJB's employees engaged in deep-coal mining face redundancy…
>
> According to industry sources the coal burn by UK generators in 1998–99 is expected to be about 35 million tonnes…going forward however the outlook worsens so that by 2000–01 it falls to 26 million tonnes. The decline of coal reflects the effects of new gas-fired power stations and tighter environmental controls.[12]

In the face of this onslaught the Government's position began to weaken. On the day the details of the National Power contract were announced, John Battle had written, in clearly unsympathetic terms, of RJB's own responsibilities.

> When coal was privatised, RJB got the best mines and the best reserves. RJB has done well financially with strong profits…£173 million in 1995 and £189 million in 1996. Yet this has not stopped Mr Budge from calling on government money to save the deep-mine industry, while I see that he …wants to start more opencast pits in the UK.[13]

Battle was nevertheless caught in a cleft stick. His lack of sympathy for Budge and RJB Mining did not extend to the workforce. In his view, the publicised

> rundown in capacity…would be a tragedy for the industry and for the company's loyal and committed workforce who stand to be the losers here.

Nevertheless he was clear that 'these problems are for the company itself to resolve…'. In his view 'the ball is in RJB's court' and 'the Government is doing all it can to help'.[14] In the face of 'redundancies before Christmas' however, this position was unsustainable. Kevin Barron spoke out strongly, relating the

1997 crisis to one that had occurred in 1992 while Labour was in opposition:

> it is unacceptable that five years ago we were hammering the Tories and now we are excusing that by saying the industry has moved into the private sector. This is a great natural asset and it would be foolish in the extreme to get rid of it.[15]

Once again the language of 'natural assets' and 'job security' was seen to sit uneasily with that of 'the market'. The new Government, with its Tory legacy, had hoped to ride out future problems of the public/private divide by accepting the status quo and encouraging the market to work. It assumed that this would be accomplished without too great a strain on its commitment to preserving employment, generating growth and encouraging work and effort. It is ironic that coal was to provide the first stumbling block to that view. As the Lex Column in the *Financial Times* put it 'Old King Coal has come back to haunt another British Government'.[16] In commenting on Battle's arm's-length approach, Stephen Fothergill of the CCC described as 'nonsense' the view that the Government was powerless in the face of 'the dash for gas'.

> The government sets the framework, gives approvals for power stations and sets sulphur limits and everything else should follow from these decisions. The situation is not irretrievable, but there's probably no more than two or three months left to act.[17]

The situation produced a clear, if predictable, response from mining MPs like Denis Murphy. In his view the problem faced by the government flowed from the privatisation of the industry.

> Asking RJB to look after your coalmining industry is like asking Imelda Marcos to look after your shoe shop. [18]

Less predictable perhaps were statements from the closest of Blair's supporters. Yvette Cooper, (the wife of Ed Balls, close

advisor to the Chancellor of the Exchequer) found that, as MP
for Pontyfract and Castleford, she too needed to speak out
about the need for a 'level playing field'. Its privately owned
status, she argued, did not absolve the government from
responsibility. 'It is a good competitive industry and we must
look at the future, ten or twenty years down the line'.[19]

Within a week, the press was full of reports of 'strain' in the
Cabinet room.

> Cabinet unity on the crisis facing the coal industry is coming
> under strain, with several government members, including
> John Prescott, the deputy prime minister lobbying for a more
> interventionist approach to save jobs. Tony Blair, the prime
> minister and Gordon Brown, the Chancellor are under pres-
> sure to produce a package to avert the loss of up to 8,000 jobs
> in the deep-mining industry after the failure of RJB
> Mining,…to secure enough orders to keep its staff in work.[20]

An anonymous 'ally' of John Prescott indicated the dilemma
neatly:

> He doesn't want any money to go into the company's pocket,
> but he knows the political and social repercussions of sitting
> by and allowing these jobs to go to the wall.[21]

A spokesman for the Prime Minister agreed that 'in some quarters' it was being suggested that the government should step in
and save a private company. Arthur Scargill made clear his
opposition to privatisation and insisted that the NUM was not
'looking for a subsidy to deep-mine coal'. What it wanted was
for coal (and by implication RJB) to have 'a guaranteed share
of the market'.[22]

The pressure was unsurmountable. John Battle's opposition
was overruled on 3 December 1997 when, twenty-four hours
before the critical meeting of the Trade and Industry Select
Committee, Tony Blair announced a moratorium on Section
36 consents for new gas powered stations. He explained that
'we want to preserve as much of the deep-mined coal industry

as we possibly can'.[23] Budge however was not optimistic. In evidence to the Select Committee he insisted that 'we will not be able to run the business at a loss'. While he expressed gratitude for the halt in the 'dash for gas', this did nothing to affect the short-term situation. On the same day, Pat Carragher, General Secretary of the British Association of Colliery Managers expressed similar sentiments and added that he thought it:

> significant that the timing of the announcement came before the minister appeared at the Committee but after the unions and industrial association had given evidence so they had no opportunity to comment.

This view was shared by many of the financial commentators. Simon Holberton put it tersely:

> There is one thing that John Battle's moratorium on new gas-fired power stations approvals will not do. It will not save the coal industry.[24]

He added that

> Although the long-term outlook for coal is bleak, it is most bleak for RJB Mining...[which] cannot compete against other UK coal producers and cheap imported coal.

The squeeze tightened. Battle's position, already weakened, was further undermined by Tony Blair's announcements in parliament on 10 December of a 'corporatist solution'[25] in which the generating companies were being asked to buy RJB's excess capacity. To this was added the need to keep opencast production under check. This was a new style of 'corporatism' however, which seemingly had not involved the companies. They demurred when questioned about the details. It was left to Geoffrey Robinson, the Paymaster General, to call an emergency meeting with Budge, and the heads of PowerGen and National Power and the smaller Eastern Group. In the view of the *Financial Times* the purpose of the meeting was to:

hammer out an agreement to save the pits and jobs at RJB mines. The government had been stung by the generator's failure to endorse Tony Blair's statement in the Commons...that they had agreed in principle to buy more coal from RJB.[26]

The deal was finally struck, extending RJB's contracts until the middle of 1998. Budge described the settlement as a 'decent stop-gap measure' which would give the company 'breathing space'. So it was more of a holding operation than a settlement. In the view of David Gow, nobody

> believes the deal brought anything but temporary relief...the question hanging over the RJB collieries is this: will 1998 mark the end of the industry after nearly 200 years of painful glory?[27]

In answering this question Tyrone O'Sullivan, ex-NUM lodge secretary and chairman of the Tower Colliery Company, revealed an acute sense of irony. He pointed out that the future of the worker cooperative in Hirwaun was tied inexorably with that of (his once arch antagonist) Richard Budge:

> we're a small firm like a pimple on the camel's back and if they allow Budge to collapse and other firms like Celtic Energy to succumb, Britain will slowly decline to the point where we won't be self-sufficient in energy resources. It is important for coal to get on the base-load for producing energy, say 60 million tonnes a year, so we can plan for the future....[28]

As the energy review proceeded, the likelihood of this forming the basis for a solution for British energy appeared remote. The CCC produced detailed proposals for an energy future based on a strong coal supply. There were few indications that this would be taken up by the New Labour administration.[29] Increasingly the emphasis seemed to be on retraining and adaptation rather than market planning and state support for the industry. This became clear in the publicity given to John Prescott's Coalfields Task Force and its emphasis on new jobs and the role of inward investment.[30] Clear too are the ways in which the UK's 'Know-How Fund' actively developed a view of industrial resurrection in the coalfields of Russia and Eastern Europe. Such was the case in South Eastern Ukraine, visited by international employment minister George Foulkes in late 1987. Foulkes, an MP for a Scottish mining constituency, sympathised with the lot of miners and their families in Myshketovskaya. However, his message was an optimistic one—with the proper resources and training, mining communities could survive mining closures.[31]

But the internal pressures supporting coal were powerful ones. These were co-ordinated by Michael (Mick) Clapham through the newly formed group of MPs from coal mining districts and the Coalfield Communities Campaign. Throughout the early months of 1998, the Select Committee continued its discussions and these filtered through the Parliamentary Labour Party and the Cabinet. Its report was eagerly anticipated. As the publication date neared speculation swayed from ultra pessimism to supreme optimism. One 'senior ministerial source' informed the *Observer* that:

> Britain's deep-mine coal industry faces extinction....The future for pit communities is bleak and the best hope is a ten-year exit strategy to ease the pain.[32]

This contrasted with what another 'senior minister' told its sister newspaper the *Guardian* a week later.

> Tony Blair is preparing to end two decades of Government hostility towards the mining industry and lift the threat to thousands of coalfield jobs by acting to guarantee coal a substantial slice in Britain's energy markets....'It would simply be irrational to let the coal industry go under'.[33]

The Select Committee's report ended the speculation. It seems that the Committee's view was somewhere between the two extremes. It recognised the plight of coal and took seriously the possibility that the next phase of decline could lead to the extinction of the industry. As such it recommended a weakening of the targets on sulphur dioxide emissions. In its view, the proposal by the Environment Agency to bring forward by four years to 2000 plans to cut emissions by 84 per cent should be shelved. However the Committee saw little to be gained from the commercial protection of the coal industry. It felt strongly that the 'dash for gas' should not have been halted and that the moratorium should be lifted. Neither did it think that the government should have intervened in the contract negotiations between RJB Mining and the generator companies. It felt that:

> The commercial judgement and negotiating tactics of RJB Mining are both open to criticism. We have also been left with the firm impression that the company could have been more energetic in driving down costs.[34]

It seemed like going back to square one. On 25 June, however the situation seemed to have been clarified. Margaret Beckett, President of the Board of Trade announced that its independent research had established 'distortions' in the energy markets which needed to be ironed out.

> Without action to address these distortions, prices for consumers will continue to be higher than necessary and diversity and security of supply will suffer.[35]

The strong emphasis in the speech was upon the need for a 'wide reform agenda'. This would require another, more detailed, period of consultation. In the meantime, Mrs Beckett announced that Section 36 consents would 'normally be inconsistent with our energy policy concerns relating to diversity and security'. CHP projects were to be the exceptions. However:

> we do not believe that to identify a defined share of the market (for coal) regardless of other considerations would be the right course to take....I must make it clear, against a background of speculation in the press, that there is no deal with

the generators by which the Government has offered to intro-
duce new policies in return for the generators buying British
coal.[36]

Furthermore:

> Coal purchase decisions are...a matter for the generators.
> But if UK coal...can be competitive on price and other
> terms of supply, I see no reason why it cannot have a very
> positive future in the electricity generation market. Achieving
> that success is a matter for the management and the work-
> force of coal producers. Decisions on any pit closures would
> also be a matter for coal producers. However in the event of
> any closures taking place, this Government is firmly com-
> mitted to taking early action to put effective regeneration
> programmes in place. Consideration will be given to estab-
> lishing a regeneration fund to help affected communities.[37]

It may not quite be square one; but to many people it felt as if
it might as well be. It was left, once again, to Geoffrey Robinson
to come up with a deal between the coal companies and the
generators that would give some stability. In the summer of
1998 few people in the industry considered that this would be
anything other than short term.

In October the Government's deliberations on energy policy were finally published as a White Paper: *The Conclusions of
the Review of Energy Sources for Power Generation*. This consolidated
the policies that had been outlined in June by Maragret
Beckett. There were to be not direct subsidies for coal but a full
review of the Electricity Pool (the market-trading arrangements) would take place with a scheduled completion date in
2000. In the meantime Section 36 consents for CCGTs and
other gas-fired schemes would be restricted. Where CHP
schemes were involved however consents would be granted in
line with policy to expand CHP capacity to 10 GW early in the
new millennium. Further support for coal was provided by the
requirement that all operators of coal-fired generators would
be requested to have at least one plant fitted with FGD equipment. This led to proposals for FGD at West Burton,

Ferrybridge C and Fiddler's Ferry. The two main generating companies (National Power and PowerGen) were to be forced to move ahead with the sale of more of their power stations— allowing new entrants into the sector.

The White Paper was seen to be broadly supportive of coal. It altered the climate and helped to create the conditions whereby RJB was able to conclude coal supply contracts with the two large generating companies as well as with other industrial customers. These contracts removed the immediate threat to RJB's coal mines, but the fact that they involved a greatly reduced coal price (in some cases below the existing costs of production) did little to lift a sense of gloom in the industry. This was confirmed as RJB embarked on a cumulative policy of job reductions involving manual workers in its deep mines and many of its administrative and managerial staff. The company chose this crisis to re-emphasise the importance of opencast mining to its survival and the growing impediment of local protest groups and unsympathetic MPAs (see Table 6)

TABLE 6
UK coal production 1994–98 (million tonnes)

	Deep-mined	Opencast	Other*	Total
1994	31.9	16.8	0.3	49.0
1995	35.1	16.4	0.1	51.6
1996	32.2	16.3	1.7	50.2
1997	30.3	16.7	1.5	48.5
1998	25.1	14.8	1.4	41.3

* coal recovered from tips, etc.
SOURCES: *UK Mineral Statistics* and *UK Digest of Energy Statistics*

Nevertheless, the Government's position seemed clear enough. It was not going to intervene directly but (given the importance of employment and security of energy supplies) it would curtail the expansion of gas turbines and manage the energy markets in a way which shifted the balance more in favour of coal. This was upset in 1999 when it was decided that permission should be given for the construction of a large CCGT at

Baglan Bay in South Wales. This decision, taken on the eve of the elections for the Welsh Assembly, confirmed the view for many that the policy was at best short-term and at worst opportunist. Either way it created an acute sense of uncertainty as 2000 approached and with it the probable ending of the moratorium on CGT applications. It wasn't eased by the statement made by Stephen Byers, the new Secretary of State at the DTI, on a visit to Durham on 6 September 1999. In his view the moratorium would be lifted 'when the time was right'.

NEW POLICIES FOR OPENCAST?

Throughout the crisis months of the late 1997, opencast mining was mentioned only tangentially by the government. Yet in the run-up to the general election opencast coal was seen as a key issue in several marginal constituencies particularly in the English Midlands and Yorkshire. Senior figures in the Labour Party, led by the then environment spokesman Frank Dobson, promised to restrict new site developments. Dobson had produced the revised policy paper in December 1996 entitled *Opencast Coal Mining—Too High a Price* on the eve of the election. The paper promised that Labour would revise *MPG3*. The paper also graphically described the various impacts of opencast mining on the environment and on nearby local communities. The climax of Mr Dobson's critique was a 10-point plan for reducing the impact of opencast. (See Table 7)[38]

This campaign was highly successful and seemed to tap the pent-up hostility and frustration of communities facing new opencast site applications. However, the plan was not universally appreciated. As well as facing hostility from the mining industry, staff in several MPAs commented that it would be extremely difficult to incorporate all the points into a revised *MPG3*. This view was endorsed in the Department of the Environment. The changes, it argued, would certainly put opencast coal mining into a special and highly regulated category of development.

Furthermore, in the run-up to the election, Tony Blair had seemed to take a much softer approach. His inclinations to support new activities, entrepreneurship and innovation had drawn him to some of the activities of the extractive industries in the north east of England. In April 1996 he had supported the expansion of quarrying in Bishop Middleham, opposing the decision of the district and parish councils. The extension would, he argued, create more jobs. In September 1996 he was photographed with Harry Banks on the edge of the restored opencast site at Oakenshaw in Blair's Sedgefield constituency. Banks indicated that his company 'had become more concerned with environmental issues and this site offered the opportunity to turn it into a wildlife reserve'. Tony Blair planted the last tree on the site and said: 'This site shows what can be done'.[39] The newspaper article regarding Blair's views was circulated on the environmental network and drew many comments. Peter Stringer, Clerk to Llanfihangel Community Council and a prominent local campaigner wrote:

> The Council, whilst recognising that you were referring to one specific site, viewed your comment with alarm and instructed me to write to you to urge you to stand by the Labour Party's policy that opencast mining should only be permitted with the consent of local people.
>
> For years now local people have been lobbying all the political parties for policies which protect them from the social, economic and cultural impacts of opencast development. I personally was present in February 1992 when in the Grand Committee Room Labour MPs lined up to condemn opencast development. In July 1995, in the same venue, Frank Dobson confirmed the Labour Party's policy on opencast mining. Since then there has been no indication that there has been a change in Labour's policy towards opencast development.[40]

The letter outlines the costs incurred by the local council in taking Celtic Energy to a public inquiry, asserting that '90 per cent of local people oppose the development' and urging the Party's leader not to forget them. Others wrote in a similar vein. Blair's fellow Northern MP, Bill Etherington was one. He received the following reply:

TABLE 7
Labour's Ten-Point plan for Opencasting

The incoming Labour Government will change the law and practice to:

1. Prohibit opencast working except where it is of benefit to the local community and local environment—for example by clearing up an area of dereliction or contaminated land.
2. Allow the rejection of planning applications for opencasting where they may prejudice efforts to attract other investment in the locality.
3. Restrict repeated applications for the development of broadly similar sites or extensions of existing workings.
4. Treat applications for extensions of existing workings as entirely new applications.
5. Apply environmental assessment procedures to existing as well as future opencast workings.
6. Require future planning consents for opencast workings to set more strict and enforceable environmental standards.
7. Set strict and short time limits whether for starting preparatory work or starting or ending coal extraction.
8. Tighten the rules to secure prompt and full restoration of sites and ensure that funds to do this are available from the operators.
9. Subject proposed and existing opencast workings in areas covered by Interim Development Orders to normal planning and environmental controls.
10. Reduce the reliance on opencast coal as part of overall energy policy.

SOURCE: The Labour Party, *Opencast Coal Mining—Too High A Price?*, 1996

I well understand and agree with the widespread concerns about the impact of opencast mining on the environment. As you know current planning guidelines contain a presumption in favour of opencast development and we would reverse this. New planning guidelines would give greater emphasis to environmental considerations. Where opencast has taken place the proper restoration of the site is essential and underlining that point was the purpose of my visit to Oakenshaw.[41]

It seemed that the policy would stick. Nevertheless once the election was over, a new campaign was initiated by activists and several coalfield MPs. Their aim was to ensure that the new government proceeded quickly with a revision of the *MPG3* in England and Wales and the comparable planning advice note in Scotland. Dobson had been now put in charge of the Department of Health—and John Prescott and a new team inherited the Party's commitments in a new super-ministry of Environment, Transport and the Regions. Prescott had once held the shadow brief on energy and he was familiar with the issues. However when the issue was first discussed in parliament (as the subject of yet another adjournment debate) Richard Caborn the Sheffield MP and Minister of State for the Environment seemed to prevaricate. The government, he indicated, would need to consider carefully (in the light of Labour's Ten-Point Plan for opencast coal) whether any further changes were necessary 'to ensure even stronger protection for the environment'. Furthermore, whilst replying to a question from Mr Michael Clapham (MP for Barnsley West), Caborn commented that:

> the figures show that we need about 9 million tonnes from opencasting in England for the sweetening process....[42]

The government's response to the debate represented a remarkable change of tone. Many activists and campaigning groups were concerned that the promises made by Dobson would be dramatically watered down. The 9 million tonnes figure was quickly adopted by opencast companies who quoted it in the applications for new sites, causing a degree of consternation among local planners and industry analysts. It soon became clear that the source of the figure lay in the House of Commons Trade and Industry Select Committee's report on the coal industry in 1993.[43] Caborn and Clapham were both members of this Committee which had noted that:

> According to British Coal, about 1.5 million tonnes a year of opencast coal is needed for blending on account of low moisture content, low volatile content or high calorific value. At least 7 to 8 million tonnes a year are needed for blending on account of low chlorine content...

These were estimates from BCC of the volumes of opencast coal that it thought were necessary for blending with all of its UK deep-mined coals in 1992. However deep-mine output has fallen from 65.8mt to 32.2mt in 1996 and (accepting the argument to be a valid one) opencast tonnages might have been expected to decline proportionately, a view endorsed by Clapham.[44] For some it confirmed that the government was not on the ball; others smelled a rat. Either way, a large number of letters were posted to Caborn and to local MPs. As a result the minister met a delegation of Labour MPs on 25 June to discuss the future of opencast policy. In this Caborn expressed his support for the party's policy and revealed that he had asked all the relevant departments to examine the practical issues involved in the implementation of the Ten-Point Plan. In spite of years in opposition it seemed that the party did not have a clear policy or a plan to implement it. It needed to take advice and consult.

The DETR published its Consultation Paper reviewing planning guidance on opencast coalmining on 30 July 1997.[45] The Scottish Office published its own Consultation Paper on 18 August 1997[46] following publication of the results of a survey of mining companies and MPAs carried out by consultants RKS Energy Ltd on opencast coalmining in Scotland.[47] The Welsh Office followed with its document on 15 September. The general concern was to seek views on the issues raised by the Ten-Point Plan. Each point was listed, with comments, proposals from the Government and a brief assessment of the possible issues involved. In a statement that accompanied the Paper, Mr Caborn noted that it was intended that 'this should be a short but thorough inquiry to remove any uncertainty'.

Both the Scottish Office and DETR asked that comments on the respective Consultation Papers should be submitted by 31 October 1997. As with previous consultations, many submissions were expected from environmental and community groups, other organisations, MPAs and other interested parties.

Evidence was, of course, forthcoming. Most of it was predicable, already well known and well rehearsed. The Geological Society reaffirmed its position on the issues indicating that, in its view, opencast mining was 'a wide and blatant abuse of the environment'. It was critical of the new government and of its Ten-Point Plan which was described as paying 'feeble lip-service to broader issues'. Insisting on the importance of the 'geological environment', the Society's evidence stressed that applications for opencast mining should no longer be considered by MPAs but by English Nature, the Government environmental body.[48]

In its evidence, RJB Mining took the offensive and claimed to represent 'the wider public interest' which was contrasted with the 'representations of single interest and anti-development pressure groups'. The company claimed that

> in recent years RJB has received unsolicited and spontaneous support for its case for new opencast sites from large groups of people living within the local communities affected.[49]

In this it called upon the experience of the Derbyshire group Bring Opencast Back (BOB) which, in its view, 'raises fundamental questions about local democracy'. More generally, RJB considered that 'there is a danger of opencast coal becoming politicised, and the Ten-Point Plan would reinforce this trend'. RJB had few friends in the government, and environmental ministers had become convinced that most of its arguments in support of opencast mining were, at best, exaggerations. But Celtic Energy was a different proposition. Keen to establish itself as an environmentally sound energy company, it was already complaining bitterly about its treatment by the power generators. And it was a coal company that rested entirely upon opencast methods of production. Its evidence on the need for opencast mining to continue seemed more persuasive.

While evidence was being presented opencast protest continued. On 31 October, the last day of the consultation period, the *No Opencast* group staged an occupation of the H.J. Banks & Co. Doe Hill site in north east Derbyshire. Three hundred people—ex-coalminers, trade unionists and environmental activists— demonstrated on the site, closing it for the day. Later a smaller group occupied Banks's office in Chesterfield and there were 41 arrests. The *No Opencast* policy statement was a clear one:

- the closure of all opencast pits;
- a comprehensive strategy for energy policies rooted in sustainable power generation and use—regionally based;
- where coal is still used it should be from deep mines in the UK;
- the extensive introduction of clean-burn technologies in all coalfield power stations and the introduction of combined heat and power schemes;
- economic and social support for traditional mining communities in transition, particularly those devastated by pit closures and opencast mining.

They complained too about the consultation process itself, claiming that:

> though mining and energy groups were directly invited to contribute to the consultation, only a few anti-opencast community/environmental groups were invited, which calls into question the validity of the exercise.[50]

They complained about the limited nature of the exercise in contrast with the wider Energy Review which the government was undertaking. The opencast issue was, they claimed, getting marginalised.

The opponents of opencast mining were encouraged by Tony Blair's statement in the House of Commons in December which seemed to suggest that opencast mining would be cut back and limited in scope. But there was no clear indication as to how this would be achieved. Certainly there was no talk of a ban. Activists became convinced of the need to 'maintain the pressure' on the government. They did this in many ways; some of them were highly original.

Keiran Lee a Nottinghamshire teacher entered into a competition organised by the *Nottinghamshire Evening Post*. The competition offered the prize of meeting the Prime Minister and quizzing him on one of the 'burning issues of the day'. Keiran had been centrally involved in the campaign to keep opencast mining out of the Erewash Valley. Along with many others he had watched with apprehension as Budge retained BCC's interest in the Cossall-Robinettes site. However they had been reassured by the election victory for Labour in the Broxtowe seat. In his campaign Nick Palmer, the Labour candidate had identified opencast mining as a key issue. An election leaflet declared:

> Almost nobody wants the opencast mining project with its despoliation of the countryside and just a handful of temporary jobs. Even fewer want the additional projects that are expected....You can stop the project dead with your vote on May 1. A change in government will stop the opencast threat—and as Broxtowe's MP I'll make sure they stick to the promise.

This promise was what concerned Kieran Lee. He visited Downing Street with his wife and two children, who took along a copy of a *Thomas the Tank Engine* story *Percy's Promise* which dwells on the importance of keeping promises. The whole family thought that it was ' a good way of emphasising how we hoped he would keep his party's pre-election promise on opencasting'. They left delighted with the response they had received:

> It was marvellous. Mr Blair made us feel completely at ease and listened to what we had to say. I asked him if Labour was going to honour its pre-election pledge to implement a policy presuming against opencast mining. His response was

clear. He said: 'That is our position and we will stick to it.' We will now make sure that that is exactly what he does.[51]

In the local newsletter he explained how they had:

> confronted him with the fact that Labour-controlled Mineral Planning Authorities were still giving planning consents for opencast mines on greenfield sites and this was leading many people to question the integrity of the government on the issue. He promised he would look into the matter.[52]

On 25 June, national opencast action groups in association with Friends of the Earth and the CPRE organised a national lobby of parliament aimed at pressing home the need for the Ten-Point Plan. The activists came to lobby their MPs, to listen to speeches from Tony Benn and others, and to share their local experiences. It was clear that feelings were running high. Dr Nandy from Muirkirk in Ayrshire broke into tears as he described the persistent encroachment of three opencast sites on his local community. The organisers had booked the Grand Committee Room for an hour and as such asked speakers to discipline their contributions to no more than two minutes so as 'to give everyone who wants to speak a chance'. This arrangement worked well. The atmosphere in the meeting altered however when the Planning Minister, Richard Caborn arrived to speak. People were taken aback by his tone which most of them interpreted as authoritarian and patronising. In his address he emphasised that opencast coal was needed by the industry for blending with the coals of the deep mines. When questioned he was less than reassuring on the idea of a clause incorporating a 'presumption against' opencast mining in any new planning guidance. His hectoring manner ('I am telling you...') upset many people who felt that their knowledge of the issues was being belittled. He left amidst catcalls and loud boos. The action groups returned home worried and upset about Labour's strategy for opencast mining.

Part of Caborn's problem at the meeting was his knowledge of the inspector's decision on the Shortwood Farm Appeal. The

Appeal had been granted and had been resting with the DETR for over a year. The ministers had decided against over-turning the decision—the site was to go ahead. The decision was announced on 30 July and the *Nottinghamshire Evening Post* announced it under the banner headline 'SHAFTED'. It summed up the sentiments of many people. Ken Wood the out-going chairman of the Cossall-Robinnettes Action Group told the *Sunday Telegraph* that:

> I'm 78 and I have been a Labour supporter for 60-odd years, but I've written to Tony Blair telling him I've torn up my card and that he has betrayed us.[53]

This was not unusual. Bob Peck who lives close to the bound-ary of the proposed Shilo North site was very upset by the decision. He had been an active member of the Shilo North Forum which had campaigned aggressively against granting permission for the site. He had met with Frank Dobson and been impressed by his manner, his assurances and his promises. He joined the Labour Party, partly as a result of Dobsons's cat-egorical assurances that 'sites like Shilo North and Shortwood Farm would be safe and would not be opencasted if Labour won the general election'. His membership of the Party was to be short-lived. He no longer trusted the government to carry out its policies on opencast mining. He felt that other sites in the Erewash Valley were now extremely vulnerable. He, along with several other local campaigners, was cutting up his Labour Party membership card. Jamie Lee was also disappointed. He wrote a letter to Tony Blair asking for his book back. In due time, he received the book together with a letter from the Prime Minister's private secretary Claire Hawley. The letter explained that the decision on Shortwood Farm was made on the basis of planning rules in place under the previous government. She made clear that:

> Planning guidelines are a bit like the rules that the Fat Controller has to follow when running the railway.

The analogy was maintained when she explained that the case was:

> Like a train which has started its journey before this gov-
> ernment won the election. Railways have to wait until the
> trains have finished their journeys before changing their
> operating rules. It was these rules or guidelines…which the
> government promised to change if it won the election.

The work, she added, 'is nearly finished'.

Six months later, in March 1999, and after a further period
of consultation, and a considerable amount of lobbying the
newly revised version of *MPG3* was finally published. Given the
constitutional changes affecting Scotland and Wales, it was a
guidance document for England alone. It represented the
Labour Government's considered response to the planning
regime that surrounded opencast mining applications. It represented a severe dilution of the ten-point programme it had
developed in opposition. Nevertheless, it marked a tightening
of the environmental controls and a number of important concessions to the critical arguments that had been developed
though the 1980s and 1990s by opponents. In doing so the
English *MPG3* rejected the arguments put forward by the opencast operators on a number of key issues. On blending, for
example, it concluded that:

> The government…does not regard a need for coal blending
> as a significant issue for the land use planning system, nor
> does it see a role for the system in influencing the operation
> of the market for coal (para. 3)

In considering the principles that should underpin the assessment of new sites, it stressed the importance of sustainable
development and argued that 'there should normally be a presumption against development' unless the proposal satisfied a
number of tests. First amongst these was:

> Is the proposal environmentally acceptable, or can it be made

so by planning conditions or obligations (para. 8)

These represented important concessions and many of the opponents of opencast mining felt that a number of their arguments and objections had been vindicated. There was even a dramatic change of fortune over the Shortwood Farm site. Nottingham County Council combined with Broxtowe Borough Council to mount a legal challenge to the Secretary of State's decision in the High Court. The government wisely chose not to defend its decision and the judge found in favour of the councils, overturning the decision. In Nottingham, people were delighted by this news, but firmly anticipated a re-opened public inquiry in 2000.

MORE OPENNESS—MORE DEMOCRACY?

One of the great claims and appeal of the New Labour Government was its emphasis upon 'openness' and a radical reform of the British state. It promised radical constitutional reform involving devolution, the reform of the House of Lords and a Freedom of Information Act. Here, for many people, lay an important dimension of 'newness'—light shining in many a darkened cupboard and the acceptance of democratic principles of political life rather than those that stemmed from tradition or established notions of 'office'. Sentiments such as those were tapped in the 1997 *British Social Attitudes Survey*,[54] which recorded strong support, even amongst Conservative voters, for constitutional reform. The issue of 'open government' scored highest of all—88 per cent of people thought that they had the right to know about future plans for the economy and 90 per cent felt the same about plans to change the law. These sentiments were especially strong amongst young people. It was this group (key members of Tony Blair's 'young country') which most strongly emphasised the value of freedom of speech, and the right to protest. It was they too who had least time for the institutions of traditional authority, like the monarchy. This was supported in a report published by the Industrial Society in late

1997. This found young people to be strikingly lacking in deference. Only 2 per cent of those talked to in the months before the general election felt any attachment to a political party: most were openly scornful of public figures and institutions and the superficiality of the media. Generally they wanted more say in their lives and in the major issues which affected them and the people in their local communities. The survey detected a strengthening of local points of reference in an increasingly insecure world where impersonal, global, forces appeared to predominate. All this confirmed previous survey evidence which indicated that people's political activity was no longer confined to (or even included) political parties.[55]

These surveys confirm many of our experiences in the coal districts over the past fifteen years. They certainly gel with the increasingly irreverent approach taken by opponents of opencast mining to 'the experts' and the logic of 'necessity'. If their sentiments were to be supported a lot rested on the shoulders of the Deputy Prime Minister John Prescott and his new super-ministry. Prescott's instincts favoured a more open approach. He would certainly reject notions of himself as 'closed' or secretive and discussion of the coal crisis was extended by his idea of a Task Force which travelled across England taking evidence from local people and their representatives. The Task Force was chaired by Paula Hay-Plumb, Managing Director of English Partnerships—the organisation concerned with providing public funding for site reclamations and infra-structural support. In its publicity the Task Force, emphasised that it had 13 members who:

> were chosen because of their experience and expertise on issues affecting former coalfield areas and the people who live and work there. They are from a broad spectrum of backgrounds—government departments, local authorities, the Coalfield Communities Campaign, the voluntary sector and the church.

In this respect the Task Force sat easily in the established British tradition of public inquiries. It was exceptional in that its legal and constitutional status was unclear. It was yet another consultation exercise—public inquiry meets focus group. Its aim was stated clearly. It wanted people to have their say. In its view

> nothing has been ruled out. Our intention is to influence those who have money to spend on the coalfields....The Deputy Prime Minister has given the Task Force a wonderful opportunity to focus attention on the former coalfield areas. To maximise this opportunity we need the direct involvement of people in the coalfields.[56]

It was a clear attempt to enter into partnership with 'the people' in order to develop ways of providing more capital investment in the coal districts. In this respect it can be seen as an important and well intentioned initiative. However, it is doubtful whether its form was radical enough to achieve its aim. The meeting places chosen for its 'regional hearings' were centres of administrative power. Places, one suspects, where the Task Force felt at ease and which attracted evidence from 'the people' who were equally used to those civic surroundings. In a way the proceedings (while far less legislative and ordered) were reminiscent of the public inquiries we had attended. In these hearings and through its written evidence, the Task Force tapped expert and informed opinion. It never approached the status of a popular event with the kind of public involvement its newsletter heralded. Nevertheless, the final report seemed to mark a radical departure, both in its understanding of the linked and related problems faced by the coalfield areas, and the need for a cohesive and integrated action plan to deal with them.[57]

For all its populist tone and the radical content of its conclusions, the Task Force was in fact a rather conventional state initiative. If this was to be indicative of its overall policies, expectations for radical changes in (say) the public inquiry system would be forlorn. When John Prescott took over responsibility for environmental issues, he inherited the Department's *Consultation Document on Planning Appeals*. This document was strongly rationalist in tone. It proposed minor changes in procedures allowing for more 'cross examination by correspondence' and patterns of mediation aimed at improving administrative efficiency and speeding up the appeal process. This approach had its attractions from the point of view of administrative efficiency. However, there was a real danger that this concern for cost-cutting could interfere with the other democratic role of the appeal process. For example, there was the danger that mediation between an MPA and a developer could exclude or disadvantage third parties (such as local community groups and individuals). The DoE's view was that third parties could make representations to the inspector on the occasions when mediation narrows, but does not dispose of, an appeal. However, this does not deal with the vexed issue of arrangements made 'behind closed doors'. At a time when there is growing sensitivity by the local public to the question of the local environment, this policy (whilst cost-effective) could affect the legitimacy of the Inspectorate System itself.[58]

The changes suggested by the DoE were entirely motivated by administrative expediency and the need to reduce costs and delays in the appeal system. No attempt was being made to deal with these wider concerns. After attending many inquiries we have concluded that the large majority of the general public had virtually no knowledge of the rules and procedures which govern the operation of public inquiries in England and Wales. This exacerbated a real and deeply felt sense of frustration held by many people with a clear interest in and concern for the issues being discussed.

Guidance in documents, such a *Circular 15/96* as well as other booklets, is of some help, but the problems go much deeper. An invigorated educational programme on political participation supported by video tapes and visual materials would help, as would a more enlightened approach to radio and television coverage. The Inspectorate had most unusually refused to consider such developments, considering that edited highlights of an inquiry would give a misleading impression of the evidence and issues presented. Television cameras, it claimed, would also inhibit witnesses and generally disrupt the orderly running of events. To many this seemed like special pleading, especially at a time when parliament was televised and 'fly on the wall' documentaries revealed people entirely at ease with the cameras. With the expansion of television channels the case is reinforced for opening-up events such as public inquiries to the public in a genuine way, demystifying them, and making the issues and evidence more accessible.[59] On this issue, the new government was silent.

CONCLUSIONS

This book has been about many things, but the main threads that run through it concern the changing nature of the British state and the changing relations between people and the environment. We have considered the period since 1945, but the main changes we have dealt with took place in the 1980s and 1990s. In this we have focused upon a particular industry (coal mining) which in its nature has had a strong historical connection with particular places (the coalfields). This focus has allowed us to examine state policies though the concrete problems and dilemmas associated with industrial and environmental policies formulated in the context of changing sets of economic interests and systems of values. In this approach, state policies emerge as being less the product of abstract forces and more related to contingent (economic, technological, social) aspects of specific problems.[1] In the case of coal, the state once seen as the solution to problems in the industry had become very much a part of the problem itself. For fifty years it had owned both the mineral and the main mining corporation. As coal mining declined and environmental issues become more salient, it has often seemed to us that state policies came more to resemble attempts to fit a carpet to a differently shaped room: no sooner is one corner in place than all the others crumple up. In this conclusion we reflect on this problem and consider its implications for the coal districts.

THE DECLINE OF COAL MINING

Coal mining has been in secular decline since the first decade of this century. Throughout that time it has posed major problems for state policy and governments have reacted in different ways. State ownership was the most dramatic form of intervention and this ordered both the coal industry and the political economy of the coal districts for forty years. In the crisis of the 1960s, the state orchestrated the coal mine closures through direct involvement—moving coal miners to other mines, often in other areas, building new houses as required and enticing new industries to the damaged coal districts via a range of incentives. These changes had the full support of the mining trade unions and the local authorities. As part of this arrangement, deep mines were protected wherever possible from opencast production (which was severely curtailed) and coal imports. A similar policy was attempted in the 1970s, this time in the context of expansion. The 1974 *Plan for Coal* represented a clear attempt to maintain a tripartite approach to coal production, which incorporated the local authorities. Deep mining and opencast mining would be expanded together. The deep mines would receive substantial investments for new technology and new mines would be opened. But it all went horribly wrong. Coal demand did not increase as anticipated (by 2000, the *Plan* envisaged demand for almost 200 million tonnes of coal!) and the encouraged expansion of opencast methods let a genie out of the bottle. Private companies thrived in the coal trade in the 1970s and 1980s and were one of the forces pressing for the privatisation of the whole industry.

The 1980s was a world apart from previous decades. All the 'Plans' had failed. The dramatic (and world-wide) perception that states had become 'too big' and were experiencing a 'fiscal crisis' was orchestrated by Mrs Thatcher into a full scale attack upon public ownership and the involvement of the state in the economy in any direct way. This alone guaranteed severe and complex conflict. This conflict existed within the state itself, with the NCB remaining a powerful institutional force *within* the Department of Energy. It also existed *between* the state and the coal miners' trade union (the NUM) and between the deep-mined and opencast sectors of the industry. The defeat of the NUM in the major strike of 1984–5 settled many of these issues. Under BCC the deep mines would close and opencast output would be encouraged. The state would guarantee redundancy and other benefit payments to the displaced coal miners, but there would be no determined policy aimed at direction of industry to the coal districts. The markets would be allowed to operate freely, and enterprise would be encouraged. To assist this, the BCC would be privatised, along with the CEGB. To assist in the restructuring process British Coal (Enterprise) was established with the aim of encouraging job formation. However, no protection would be given to the industry from cheaper imports. It was a different world.[2]

The implications of these changes for the coal districts *and* for the state have been enormous. In many respects they echo the processes identified by Schumpeter as creative destruction.[3] The destruction has, without doubt, been extensive. Large numbers of productive deep mines have been closed down. Major investments made by the state in new facilities and new mines like Asfordby in Leicestershire needed to be written off. Millions of tonnes of workable reserves were sterilised.[4] The human costs have also been great. There were winners and losers in this process of change. Economically active coal miners were made redundant, many of them embarking upon long periods of unemployment and illness.[5] Established local communities experienced social dislocation. The creative, dynamic side of the couplet was more ambivalent, especially given the distributional issues involved. Yet some positive changes can be seen in the new industries and economic activities which developed in the coal districts, although they provided only a fraction of the jobs lost from coalmining. Within the coal industry itself creative developments were associated with a form of mining that had, for decades, appeared as marginal and deviant. In the opencast sector technical innovations of a startling kind were developed which permitted the mining of coal at depths which previously had required underground techniques. However, this development encountered a problem which few of the classical thinkers in political economy had considered. For Schumpeter, nature and the environment provided a context for economic activity. Toward the end of the twentieth century, this context had become a politicised relationship. Concerns were increasingly expressed about the finite nature of material resources. More generally, a growing awareness of environmental risk and ideas about the human environment placed tighter limits upon the boundaries of (neo-classical) economic behaviour. Opencast mining and the mining corporations were caught in this pincer. This represented a serious problem for the state and its environmental agencies.

THE STATE AS PLANNER

We have recounted the complex route through which planning regulations in relation to the opencast industry have altered and developed since 1945. In this we have drawn attention to the role of Commissions of Inquiry (like CENE) and the Inspectorate in informing the policy context. Burton and Carlen have argued that such government publications and official inquiries play a vital role in retaining stability in society. In their view, it is through such processes that the state and its various agencies incorporate new kinds of argument and discussion, thereby revitalising state policies and reinforcing the capacity for the state to regulate and govern society. In this way public inquiries, along with commissions of inquiry and formalised consultation processes represent a process:

> The effect of which is to replenish official arguments with both established and novel modes of knowing and forms of reasoning.[6]

Were this to be the only purpose of such investigations, it would seem that over the years they had expended considerable time and energy for comparatively little return. Therefore, Ashforth argues that the public inquiry system must achieve more than new forms of discourse. In his view these inquiries can be seen as:

> Symbolic rituals within modern states, theatres of power which do 'make policy' but which do much else besides.[7]

The rituals effectively elevate 'the state' above the rest of society, securing it as an arena in which truth and rationality operate in relation to human interests. Viewed in this way, the public inquiry becomes:

> A theatre in which a central received truth of modern state power is ritually played out before a public audience...subjects can speak freely of their interests and they will be heard, State power is a benign partner with Society in pursuit of the Common Good.[8]

As such, Ashforth sees public inquiries adhering to 'norms of decorum consonant with the majesty of State'. Typically these 'derive from courtroom practice, particularly concerning the asking and answering of questions'. In his view these rituals and procedures work like a spider's web, drawing protest into itself and reconstructing it, for they:

> Allow full and free expression of contrary views...[and] by this means they serve in the transformation of contentious matters of political struggle into discourses of reasoned argument...allowing 'the State' to sit above 'Society' as the embodiment of the 'Common Good'.[9]

These comments were directed at commissions of inquiry in the main, but there are many parallels with public inquiries also. There is much in his account, which resonates powerfully with our own researches in the coalfields. His conclusion that the involvement of protest groups in such inquiries does little more than secure their own subjugation is, however, questionable. In the UK in the late 1980s and early 1990s public involvement in the inquiry process (when allied with political lobbying and other forms of protest) did achieve ends which many people thought to be acceptable ones. Plans to develop opencast sites were shelved when they could easily have gone ahead. There is considerable evidence that these successes caused real difficulties for the coal companies and that this led to a reassessment in the Department of the Environment, followed by major changes of the rules which regulated the opencast decision-making process. These too became contested and changed. As a result of protest, often orchestrated through the inquiry process itself, the boundaries of the practicable and possible were altered.

To present our conclusions in this way is not to deny the processes identified by Ashforth but to emphasise the practical (material) context within which these features of state power are enacted. In the inquiries that we attended, it was clear that local protesters wanted their voices to be heard. In this respect the Inquiry allowed them a forum within which to participate and have their say. We have indicated how they occupied a particular place in the inquiry and how many of them have reflected on this, considering the best ways to 'get our ideas across'. But they wanted more than a discursive intervention. More than anything they wanted to ensure that the land close to where they lived did not become an opencast site. There was a strong aesthetic and instrumental reason for their involvement.

This instrumentality applied in spades to the coal companies. As decisions began to go against them in the late 1980s and early 1990s, they began to put pressure upon the Department of Environment to get the rules changed. They complained that the public inquiry system was too expensive, too time-consuming and too democratic, allowing for too many voices, taking up too much space. They developed tactics aimed at circumventing the rules and wrong-footing 'the opposition'. 'Don't let the locals dig a hole for you' was the message, and with it came a much more strident approach toward protesters. As a result, the coal industry and CoalPro became a central part of a strong anti-environmentalist lobby. On the one hand they attempted to generate scientific research which would 'disprove' the anti-environmental impact of both opencast coal production and general coal use. They disputed the relationship between acid rain and sulphur dioxide emissions from power stations. They argued persistently that the environmental effects of opencast mining were positive ones. They persisted in making exaggerated claims for the quality of coals produced through opencast methods of mining and propagandised these views with considerable effect. At the same time they were involved in an ongoing attack on the credentials and motives of the environmentalist lobby. It became common for environmental activists to be described as 'poofters', and for the whole environmentalist argument to be referred to as something vaguely effeminate and not something that 'real men' should take seriously. Mostly this kind of language was used in committee rooms and in natural conversation in bars and at dinner tables. Publicly, however, the industry kept up a quite relentless attack on what became known as 'the environmental lobby'. Colin Goldfrey, RJB's Director of Market Development used this term when he addressed the Annual Conference of the Coalfield Communities Campaign on 19 September 1996. In his view, this lobby was a threat to the entire industry, and its influence had to be marginalised.[10]

These rhetorical attacks were combined with a concerted attempt to put financial pressures on local authorities. This approach involved the stick as well as the carrot. MPAs were made aware that a rejection would certainly meet with an appeal and the inevitable public inquiry. Such inquiries involved real financial costs to the authorities, which were exacerbated by the risk that, should the appeal be upheld, the appellant would successfully demand a cost settlement from the inspector. The coal companies made it increasingly clear that they would sue for costs; that it would be 'no holds barred' if their request was turned down. These risks were frequently great enough for local authorities to turn a blind eye to the protests of the local people.

This process was complicated by the offer of the carrot. With regularity the coal companies offered some financial benefit to the local authority as payment for a public amenity. This was dressed up as 'planning gain', a benefit which flowed in some direct, if not intended, way from the mining development. This relationship was increasingly interpreted very broadly and often described to us by local planners as 'a bribe'. In many of the coal districts it was the subject of considerable political dispute and public wrangling. This tormented discussion over 'planning gain' made clear the expanded role which money had come to play in planning decisions in areas of increasing economic insecurity. In these places, the coal companies gained in power because amenities were required, and (outside of the Lottery) they seemed to be the only likely source of funds.

In these ways therefore the planning role of the state can be seen as occupying a discursive space through which the uses of land in the coal districts is regulated. However, this regulation relates to real material conflicts of interest, and it became clear that the coal companies were only prepared to go so far with discussion, argument and disagreement. To get planning permission from the state, they were prepared to bend the rules, press to get them changed and pressure the decision makers in a relentless fashion. This was keenly noted by the planners and local state representatives; it didn't escape the attention of the companies' opponents, the local protesters, either.

PATTERNS OF PROTEST AND OPPOSITION

One of the critical dynamics of social change in the coal districts in the last two decades of the century has related to changing patterns of protest and forms of oppositional politics. This has been particularly evident in relation to opencast developments, but it has had a more general resonance as these places adapted to life without deep mining. These changes illustrate well a general tendency within contemporary societies. Increasingly, as the state withdraws and the standing of politicians declines, political action is pursued outside of the main institutional channels. In Paul Byrne's view this has represented a 'revolution in the conduct and practice of British politics'.

> Most people, most of the time, continue to participate only sporadically, and politics remains a relatively low priority in their everyday lives. What has changed, however, is that there are many amongst those who are actively interested for whom politics no longer means just participating in national parties, local politics and conventional interest groups like trade unions.[11]

This has been the experience on the coalfields, and is illustrated

TABLE 8

ORGANISED FORMS OF LOCAL RESPONSE TO OPENCAST MINING

	POLITICAL PARTIES	LOCAL ACTION GROUPS	OPPOSITIONAL GROUPS
ORGANISATION FORM	Formal bureaucracy of local state, coal companies and trade unions	Locally based with informal alliances with MPAs, environmental groups and some local trade unions	Independent action groups, locally based, national network
FORM OF ACTION	Individual complaints and legal action. No formalised opposition — 'nothing can be done'	Lobbying of councillors, union and party branches and MPA committees. Involvement in public inquiries	Direct action through forms of public demonstration: occupation, sit-down, riot
DISCOURSE	Progressive productionist 'we need the coal'; national plans	Sceptical environmentalist 'do we need the coal?'	Militant environmentalist 'we don't need the coal'; local issues
IDEOLOGY	Deferential	Reformist	Radical

on p.249. For decades, issues in relation to opencast mining were dealt with within the bureaucracies of the local authority and the NCB. The NUM was overwhelmingly concerned with production and welfare issues relating to its members in the deep mines. Opencast mining was seen as marginal to the industry and irrelevant to the interests of deep-coal miners.

At this time, the NUM accepted the view of the state-owned company that some opencast coal was necessary to 'sweeten' deep-mined coal (especially coking coal) and isolated protests by individuals were largely ignored. The failure of the *Plan for Coal* and the closure of the deep mines changed this situation dramatically. Local action groups no longer felt that they were threatening the jobs of deep mines; in fact they felt that they were helping to save them. Faced with recalcitrant local bureaucratic organisations and formalised planning regulations these groups learned about planning law. This knowledge increased their capacity to oppose. This was strengthened by contacts with NUM activists and sympathisers who also knew about the coal industry, about coal and about energy markets. It marked a dynamic reformist move in which these local alliances marshalled new kinds of evidence for public inquiries. They were also able to draw upon the political clout associated with the trade union in these districts. It was a powerful new alliance and it made real gains.

Writers on the 'new social movements' have noted an 'incremental militancy' taking place in those groups (like Greenpeace) associated with environmental protection. They have also noted a tendency for this to lead to internal schisms and rifts.[12] Certainly this was a phenomenon associated with protest over opencast mining. The tactics of the companies assisted in this. The successes gained through conventional tactics of lobbying and presenting evidence at inquiries came to be seen as, at best, partial. 'What's the point of arguments when nobody listens'. This was a sentiment which gained ground across the coalfields and which became represented in different kinds of organised action. The contrast between organised evidence presented at a public inquiry and night raids on ministerial homes is a graphic one. It marked a move from the discursive to the demonstrative field. In Pakulski's view the new social movements often:

> Use examples rather than discursive arguments; they aim at moralising politics through action, reforming social life and changing individual orientations, all in the name of values and principles seen as neglected, distorted or corrupted.[13]

On the old coalfields this tendency was a powerful one, the sentiment of which was captured in the publicised and organised activities of groups like No Opencast. In our travels across the coalfields in the 1990s, we were made aware of the increasing support for ideas of direct action. People—mainly the young and the old—made it clear to us that they would be prepared to lie down in front of bull-dozers, trespass, and demonstrate in whatever ways seemed feasible to stop an opencast development. When pressed on issues of legality it has been made plain that the law courts and notions of arrest and punishment carry few of the normative sanctions which once held sway in these districts. Here the sanction of the local community is all-powerful. 'It's all we have left' is a common expression, and when backed with a strong local campaign it has turned into a powerful radicalising force. This raises many questions about the social nature of opencast protest within the context of environmental social movements.

Discussions of these new kinds of political movements have most often linked them with the emergence of a 'new class' made up of educated people, especially those working in the 'humanistic' professions. Through their formal knowledge they have come to understand the nature of environmental problems and the potential for severe damage to local environments and eco-systems. This group, through early socialisation reaffirmed within its professions, was seen to have strongly altruistic values that drew its members into political participation. These people were seen by Offe[14] and others to form the backbone of the new social movements that brought single issues like peace and the environment into the forefront of political life in ways which cut across traditional class boundaries and the lines of demarcation between established political parties.

The protests over opencast mining and its impacts upon the local environment did involve members of this 'new class'. Young lawyers, school-teachers and postgraduate students were involved, but they did not predominate. A key activist like Desmond Napier in the Derwent Valley in West Durham was a self-made businessman. Many planners were drawn into support through notions of rational planning rather than any deep altruistic concern. 'Middle class' involvement therefore extended beyond the 'new class'. On occasions, it also included the aristocracy. In Fife, Andrew Wemyss, a local landowner, was instrumental in fending off opencast developments.

More important perhaps, is the fact that many poorer, working-class people were also involved in these protests. This, of course, reflected the social composition of the old mining districts. A mixture of 'brown ale and claret' is how John Smith typified Tony Blair's Sedgefield constituency in Co. Durham. It serves to bring out, once again, the distinctiveness of these places and their rural industrial history. This past retained a strong hold upon people's loyalties and understandings. It was often invoked as the opencast sites penetrated and reworked coal seams that had previously been partially mined by deep miners. As a result opencast protest groups in these areas drew upon the experiences of unemployed miners and trade unionists. Steve Parry of the No Opencast group made an interesting observation in this regard:

> I don't think there is any other green issue that is so clearly linked in with the traditional demands of trade unionists, both in terms of jobs and wages and health and safety, but also in terms of the culture of the mining communities. Miners who spent their days and nights underground have probably appreciated the natural environment and the fresh air more than anybody else. It's part of the life of the mining community.[15]

The experiences of the 1984–5 miners' strike were important too. Opencast mining had been identified as a trade union issue in this dispute. People who had been involved in local miners' support groups and organisations like Women Against Pit Closures had become aware of the wider arguments associated with this form of mining. In the years that followed, many of them brought this awareness to bear through their involvement in a local protest group. This linkage between elements of the 'new class' with working-class people and more traditional forms of organisation like trade unions may be a particular and unique feature of this form of protest. However, its uniqueness should not be exaggerated. In their 1984 survey of political participation, Geraint Parry and his colleagues found that the peace and environmental movements drew support from two main groupings within British society. First there were:

> Those whose educational resources are high but whose material resources are at an average or low levels—the less well off graduates.

These combined with:

> A strong phalanx of the generally low resourced—with few educational qualifications, poor and working class as well as the unemployed.[16]

This was the situation in the coal districts where, in many instances, this 'strong phalanx' dominated. Supported by the experience and resources of people who had played an active role in trade unionism and other forms of social protest they helped to form a powerful grouping. While men tended to occupy most of the leadership positions in these groups, they attracted a significant number of women who articulated powerful arguments in relation to the local community and its general security.

These qualifications to the 'new class' argument can be extended. Political activism in the coal districts points to ways in which people with little formal education can learn about and come to an understanding of deep social issues. In this respect the trade union branch, with the attendant educational programmes of the union, has been an underestimated source of 'lay knowledge'.[17] So too, we suspect, have been more informal processes. The local protest groups once established became dramatic 'learning zones' as the activists (in a rather 'hit and miss' fashion) learned of others who knew something, and then of others who knew a lot. Pamphlets and documents were distributed in this way, and this knowledge-transfer accelerated with the arrival of the Internet. This knowledge was used in a variety of ways in their attempts to protect the 'local environment'.

Our researches on the coalfields both support and extend these conclusions. Most of the people we talked with were drawn into protest groups as a consequence of a particular initiative associated with a planning application for opencast mining. In assessing their opposition, people called upon a variety of arguments, many of which related to the particular local context. General accounts about the future of the planet were often alluded to but the critical issues were local ones. In this respect our account fits well with Kate Burningham and Martin O'Brien's observations on the views and values of anti-road protesters. Here, they argue, people often deploy notions of 'the environment' instrumentally, adjusting them to the local context. In their view, 'local environmental commitments are regularly translated to *fit into* local conditions'. As such:

> Considerable disagreement exists between people in any given situation about what exactly 'the environment' is. This is clearly illustrated by looking at planning disputes in which individuals and groups ascribe environmental values differently to specific areas of land, claiming that one area is 'the environment' and deserves protection, while another is not. These ascriptions of environmental value are informed by a complex web of personal, social and political commitments and not simply by formal environmental considerations.[18]

This process of 'local transfer' operated on the coalfields, but in a more complex way. Here notions of the local environment and landscape were also interpreted through a humanistic frame. By way of reference to past experience, and also to material issues such as noise, dust and health, notions of the local environment were constructed in ways that pressed forward an oppositional case. There were undoubtedly strong instrumental logics operating here: people did not want an opencast site in the vicinity of their homes. Nevertheless, there were clearly aesthetic and abstract notions at work in the way in which these people constructed 'the local environment'. It wasn't simply a matter of property values and a quiet life. We were often taken aback by the capacity for formally uneducated people to grasp and extend abstract notions of the human environment and sustainable communities as they talked, often evocatively, in pubs and clubs, kitchens, meeting rooms and public inquiries. Here, the historically received physical experience of working with coal in mines played a part. So too did the importance attached by many of the people to walking and the sensuous relationship which they have established with the countryside—its smells, the shape and its silences. In this way, and through notions of 'need' and 'greed', protest groups increasingly argued against opencast mining *per se*, and not simply as it related to their local context.

The processes which saw this mixture of local self interest combining with a general programme of opposition were political ones. In the late 1980s, before the introduction of *MPG3*, local protest groups and Mineral Planning Authorities seemed reasonably content. At that time they felt that reasoned objections could be heard and opencast mining restricted to an acceptable number of sites, mostly involving derelict land on the old coalfields. Subsequently the situation changed. The changes in the rules and the behaviour of the coal companies intensified local opposition. This was further fuelled by the crisis that affected the industry in 1992, leaving many of the old coal districts without deep mines. The subsequent privatisation of the industry exacerbated a sense of betrayal, and it also provided more recruits as many ex-miners and their families were drawn to the cause of opposition and protest. At this time, the sense of 'blocked participation' in the formal machinery of politics which has been noted in relation to other kinds of protest,[19] fostered involvement in opencast protest groups.

These changes in the overall context of mining and the significance of this for the mining trade unions and local Labour Party branches was often decisive in changing the tone of protest especially after the 1992 General Election. Once again, the parallels with anti-road protest are helpful ones. In such a context the:

> meanings and values of the environment which end up informing public attention are as much the result of political pressure and political clout as they are the result of shared understandings and shared values.[20]

On the coalfields, in the 1990s, Frank Dobson's references to the opencast industry (especially the notion of an 'environmental mega-lout') provided the final decisive step in moving protest into outright opposition. In doing so it encouraged the creation of a comprehensive linkage between local opposition and more general environment politics.

A NEW POLITICS OF THE ENVIRONMENT?

One of the most noticeable features of the last two decades or so has been the rise of environmental issues to prominence on the political landscape. It is a development that continues to pose problems for established political parties. The environment does not map easily onto the anatomy of party politics, constructed as it is around ideas of shared class and material interests. The stock response to the major political parties has been to add a green tinge of their current suite of policies in an attempt to dispel environmental criticisms and win some votes from the environmentally concerned. This approach has not been noticeably successful in dispelling fears or allaying environmental concerns.

In his assessment of political life in Britain at the end of the century, Larry Elliot argued that environmental protest had become 'the focal point of grass roots political opposition in Britain'. In his view:

Twyford Down and Newbury have replaced Saltley coke depot and Orgreave as the flashpoint of the struggle between the state and its opponents.[21]

In opposition, the Labour Party attempted to harness this discontent and build it into its strategy for electoral success. Joan Ruddock, as Shadow Minister for Environmental Protection, had issued a *Briefing Note* in relation to opencast mining which pointed out that 'independent investigations invariably conclude that the effect on local communities and the environment can be extremely severe'. It made clear that in government it would give 'greater emphasis to environmental considerations'.[22] For many, this opened up the exciting prospect of a New Labour government committed to resolving many of the tensions between a 'red' and 'green' politics, taking forward a strategy of openness linked with an increasing environmental awareness. But this underestimated the difficulties of reconciling an increasingly complex and sophisticated environmental politics, grounded in the local but globally sensitive, with the national structures of party politics. Certainly the structures of New Labour have been shown to be flexible ones in its quest for a Parliamentary majority. But as this involved appropriating much of a Thatcherite neo-liberal economic agenda, it exacerbated the problems for New Labour in addressing environmental concerns. Embracing the market was always going to sit uneasily with anything other than the palest shade of green politics. A further set of reasons lay in the disjunction between the boundaries of political parties and environmental movements. For environmental groups bring together people from across the divides that provide the organizational parameters of party politics. A stalwart Conservative such as Desmond Napier could work long and closely with Pitch Wilson, a Labour Party member to defend the Derwent Valley from the predatory activities of opencast mining companies precisely because 'their shared attachment to *their* place' was of greater significance to them than other differences between them, including those of party politics. And this was a story that was repeated innumerable times in the emergence of environmental movements.

To achieve a dynamic balance between issues of employment and growth and those of the environment and local sustainability was therefore always going to be a difficult task. It would necessitate finding a new way forward that simultaneously satisfied capital's requirements for profits, respected the environmental limits to production, transportation and consumption, and incorporated a greater distributional equity and concern for social justice. It would also involve hard choices as to the means to pursue these multiple and competing objectives in terms of regulatory limits and standards as opposed to the market as the alternative mechanism. In its first year in office the Government's approach to confronting such issues could best be described as 'cautious'. On all contentious issues, it set up inquiries and consultation exercises; it made no quick decisions but stressed 'the legacy' it had inherited from the Tories. It was not going to be enough.

By the spring of 1999 however, the cracks we had been observing in Labour's heartland increased. In South Wales (the Rhondda), Northumberland (Wansbeck) and Yorkshire (Sheffield) Labour majorities proved vulnerable to radical locally based alliances attached to liberal and nationalist parties. The low turnout in these local and European elections was another indicator of disaffection from the political process by many of Labour's traditional supporters. If it is to win them back, the Party will need to carefully address many of the issues and discontents that had been given voice by the new politics of the environment.

A NOTE ON SOURCES

This is a list of the official publications, periodicals and handbooks which we have refereed to during our research. We have put it together in a way which people, actively involved in one way or another in issues relating to opencast coal mining, will find. We have added a list of the names and addresses which we have called upon from time to time.

All Government/official publications can be purchased from:
The Stationary Office, PO Box 276, London SW8 5DT.
Enquiries—Tel: 020–7873 0011 Orders—Tel: 020–7873 9090

Primary Legislation
Wildlife and Countryside Act (1981)
Town and Country Planning (Minerals) Act (1990)
Town and Country Planning Act (1990)
Environmental Protection Act (1990)
Planning and Compensation Act (1991)
Coal Industry Act (1994)
Environment Act (1995)

Department of the Environment Circulars
15/88—Environmental Assessment
9/95—General Development Order Consolidation 1995
11/95—The use of conditions in planning permissions
15/96—Planning Appeal Procedures

Mineral Planning Guidance (England and Wales)
These are periodically reviewed and updated
MPG1—General conditions and the development plan system
MPG2—Applications, permissions and conditions
MPG3—Coal mining and colliery spoil disposal
MPG4—The review of mineral working sites
MPG7—The reclamation of mineral workings
MPG11—Control of noise at surface mineral workings
MPG14—Environment Act (1995): Review of mineral planning permissions

Planning Policy Guidance Notes
Various PPGs have been published which relate to opencast mining, these include:

PPG1—General Policy and Principles
PPG2—Green Belts
PPG7—The Countryside and Rural Economy
PPG9—Nature Conservation
PPG13—Transport
PPG17—Sport and Recreation
PPG18—Enforcing Planning Control
PPG23—Planning and Pollution Control
PPG24—Planning and Noise

Regional Planning Guidance Notes
Various RPGs have been published which relate to coalfield areas—these include:

RPG1—Strategic Guidance for Tyne and Wear
RPG2—Strategic Guidance for West Yorkshire
RPG4—Strategic Guidance for Greater Manchester
RPG5—Strategic Guidance for South Yorkshire
RPG7—Regional Planning Guidance for the Northern Region
RPG8—Regional Planning Guidance for the East Midlands Region

Other Related Official Publications
Secretary of State for the Environment et al, This Common
   Inheritance, Cmnd 1200, HMSO, 1990. Each year the
   Department of the Environment also publishes This Common
   Inheritance: UK Annual Report, which highlights the achievements
   and progress in meeting the environmental targets and sets out priorities for the next year.
Secretary of State for the Environment et al Sustainable
   Development, Cmnd 2426, HMSO, 1994

Statistical publications
Energy Trends Monthly Statistical bulletin published by the Department
   of Trade & Industry, 1 Victoria Street, London SW1H OET
Digest of UK Energy Statistics HMSO
Digest of Environmental Statistics HMSO
Opencast Coalmining Statistics, Durham County Council (on behalf
   of the County Planning Officers' Society). Available from: Durham
   County Council, Director of Environment, County Hall, Durham
   DH1 5UQ—Tel: 0191–386 4411

Periodicals

Planning Inspectorate Journal (quarterly)
Subscription details: Alison Seward, Planning Inspectorate,
Room 13/01, Tollgate House, Houlton Street, Bristol BS2 9DJ
Tel: 0117–987 8585
This publication aims to inform the public about the internal organisation of the Inspectorate and the appeal process

Mineral Planning (quarterly)
Published by Mineral Planning, 2 The Greenways, Little Fencote,
Northallerton DL7 0TS
Tel/Fax: 01609–748709
Contains comprehensive reports and updates on developments in the various mineral industries (including coal), local mineral plans, site applications, etc. The publishers also produce the annual directory: Mineral & Waste Planning Officers & Authorities in Great Britain

UK Coal Review (monthly)
Published by Energy Intelligence & Marketing Research Ltd,
192 Sandyford Road, Newcastle upon Tyne NE2 1RN.
Tel/Fax: 0191–2615274
Contains regular reports on the UK coal scene and opencast sector

Parliamentary Companion (quarterly)
Published by PMS Publications Ltd, 19 Douglas Street,
London SW1P 4PA
Tel: 020-7233 8283 Fax: 020-7821 9352
Contains key information on the UK Parliament, Government, Departments and Executive Agencies, Local Government, the Media, European Commission and European Parliament

Handbooks and Campaigners' Guides, Countryside Commission, Opencast coal mining: advice on landscape and countryside issues, CCP 434, 1993

Richard Bate, *Campaigners' Guide to Minerals*, CPRE, 1996
Excellent reference handbook and introduction to the complex subject of mineral planning

Roy Speer and Michael Dade, *How To Stop and Influence Planning Permission*, J.M. Dent, 1996. Practical manual that gives guidance to communities and individuals on the planning system and how to influence decisions on development

MPG3 (REVISED)
OPENCAST COAL APPEALS MONITOR

There have been 30 opencast coal planning appeal decisions in England and Wales since the Revised Mineral Planning Guidance Note No.3 (*MPG3*) was published in July 1994.

A list of the appeal decisions issued to date is shown below. Other details shown are:

> Mineral Planning Authority (MPA);
> Estimated tonnage of coal in the appeal sites;
> Total site area (hectares);
> Working period (includes coaling and initial restoration periods—but not any further after-care period);
> Name of the appellant;
> Appeal reference numbers;
> Determination by the Inspector or by the Secretary of State;
> Name and main qualifications of the Inspector at the public inquiry;
> The dates of the inquiry or hearing (including site visits where known) or date of written representation site visit;
> The appeal decision—plus the date the decision/decision letter was issued.

Nine appeals have been allowed (planning permission for the sites was granted and their development could proceed) and 21 appeals have been dismissed (planning permission was refused).

Eleven of the 30 appeals were determined by the relevant inquiry inspector, while 19 appeals were determined by the Secretary of State.

Approximate tonnage in sites allowed: 6,046,000 tonnes
Approximate tonnage in sites refused: 10,288,000 tonnes

Appeal decision details:

1. Barwick Road, Garforth, Leeds

MPA:	Leeds CC
Site tonnage:	100,000 tonnes
Site area:	21 ha
Working period:	13 months
Appellant:	H.J. Banks & Co. Ltd
Reference:	T/APP/N4720/A/94/435504/P7
Determination by Inspector	
Inspector:	Mr W.P. Walker BA (HonsTP) MRTPI
Dates of Inquiry:	1–10 June 1994
Allowed:	8 August 1994

2. Shellbrook and Wood Farms, Willesley, Leicestershire

MPA:	Leicestershire CC
Site tonnage:	210,000 tonnes
Site area:	47 ha
Working period:	2 years
Appellant:	R.J. Budge Mining Ltd
Reference:	T/APP/J2400/A/93/230876/PS
Determination by Inspector	
Inspector:	Mr J. I. Mcpherson JP BSc DMS CEng MICE MIWEM MIMgt
Dates of Inquiry:	27–30 September 1994
Allowed:	1 December 1994

3. Club Room Farm, Smalley Common, Nr Ilkeston, Derbyshire

MPA:	Derbyshire CC
Site tonnage:	180,000 tonnes
Site area:	31 ha
Working period:	2 years
Appellant:	R.J. Budge Mining Ltd
Reference:	T/APP/D1000/A/94/238417/P5
Determination by Inspector	
Inspector:	Mr D.L.J. Robins BA PhD FRTPI
Dates of Inquiry:	8–17 November 1994
Allowed:	3 March 1995

4. Ladywood Farm, Dale Abbey, Ilkeston, Derbyshire

MPA:	Derbyshire CC
Site tonnage:	129,000 tonnes
Site area:	35.7 ha
Working period:	15 months

Appellant: Miller Mining Ltd
Reference: APP/D1000/A/94/238708
Determination by Secretary of State
Inspector: Mr C.S. McDonald MA(Oxon) DMA LMRTPI
                      Solicitor
Dates of Inquiry: 13–16 December 1994
Refused: 10 May 1995

5. Westwood New Road, Howbrook, Wortley, Sheffield

MPA: Barnsley MBC
Site tonnage: 160,000 tonnes
Site area: 43 ha
Working period: 2 years
Appellant: Cobex Ltd
Reference: T/APP/R4408/A/94/243489/P2
Determination by Inspector
Inspector: Mr P.D. Walker BA(HonsTP) MRTPI
Dates of Inquiry: 21–24 March, 20–21 April 1995
Refused: 17 July 1995

6. Arch Lane, Garswood, St Helens

MPA: St Helens MBC
Site tonnage: 90,000 tonnes
Site area: 9.5 ha
Working period: 2.5 years
Appellant: LEMS/Ward Bros Ltd
Reference: T/APP/H4321/A/94/246660/P5
Determination by Inspector
Inspector: Mr K.P. Durrant MA BArch RIBA ARICS MRTPI
                      FRSA
Dates of Inquiry: 27–30 June 1995
Refused: 21 July 1995

7. Lightmoor Colliery, Near Cinderford, Gloucestershire

MPA: Gloucestershire CC
Site tonnage: 400,000 tonnes
Site area: 66 ha
Working period: 5 years
Appellant: Coal Contractors Ltd
Reference: APP/T1600/A/94/244950
Determination by Secretary of State
Inspector: Mr S.J. Pratt BA(Hons) MRTPI
Dates of Inquiry: 28 March–7 April 1995
Refused: 31 July 1995

8. Fenwicks Close, Earsdon, plus land near Holywell and Backworth

MPAs:	Northumberland CC and North Tyneside MBC
Site tonnage:	1,500,000 tonnes
Site area:	121 ha
Working period:	5 years
Appellant:	Coal Contractors Ltd
References:	APP/R2900/A/94/241278 & APP/W4515/A/94/241233

Determination by Secretary of State

Inspector:	Mr A. Mead BSc MRTPI AMIQ
Dates of Inquiry:	21 February–1 March 1995
Refused:	14 August 1995

9. Bretton Lane, West Bretton, Wakefield

MPA:	Wakefield MDC
Site tonnage:	100,000 tonnes
Site area:	8 ha
Working period:	14 months
Appellant:	Cobex Ltd
Reference:	T/APP/X4725/A/94/242732/P6

Determination by Inspector

Inspector:	Mr A.K. Bragg FRICS MRTPI
Dates of Inquiry:	25–28 April and 1–2 May 1995
Refused:	24 August 1995

10. Brierley Road, South Hiendley, Wakefield

MPA:	Wakefield MBC
Site tonnage:	80,000 tonnes
Site area:	20 ha
Working period:	1 year
Appellant:	Cobex Ltd
Reference:	APP/X4725/A/94/243092

Determination by Secretary of State

Inspector:	Mr R.D. Donnison BA(Hons) DipTP ARICS MRTPI
Dates of Inquiry:	10–17 May 1995
Refused:	6 November 1995

11. Leadgate Plantation, Prudhoe, Northumberland

MPA:	Northumberland CC
Site tonnage:	68,000 tonnes
Site area:	14.2 ha
Working period:	17–19 months
Appellant:	Coal Contractors Ltd
Reference:	APP/R2900/A/94/239377

Determination by Secretary of State
Inspector: Mrs V. Harris BA(Hons) DipTP MRTPI
Dates of Inquiry: 28–30 March and 3–5 April 1995
Refused: 12 December 1995

12. Ryders Mere, Ryders Hayes, Pelsall, Walsall

MPA: Walsall MBC
Site tonnage: 199,000 tonnes
Site area: 37.67 ha
Working period: 29 months
Appellant: Parkhill Reclamation Ltd
Reference: APP/V4630/A/94/239377
Determination by Secretary of State
Inspector: Mr R.D. Donnison BA(Hons) DipTP ARICS MRTPI
Dates of Inquiry: 4–11 July 1995
Allowed: 19 March 1996

13. Coggra Fold (land at the former Bury Road Colliery), Radcliffe, Bury

MPA: Bury MBC
Site tonnage: 54,000 tonnes
Site area: 25.4 ha
Working period: 24 months
Appellant: The Earl of Wilton's Estate
Reference: APP/T4210/A/94/233921
Determination by Secretary of State
Inspector: Mr B.H. Smith DipTP MRTPI
Dates of Inquiry: 30 August–7 September 1995
Refused: 19 March 1996

14. Chester House Extension (land located between Acklingon, Amble and Warkworth), Northumberland

MPA: Northumberland CC
Site tonnage: 417,000 tonnes
Site area: 79 ha (extension area)
Working period: 2.5 years
Appellant: RJB Mining (UK) Ltd
Reference: APP/R2900/A/94/243499
Determination by Secretary of State
Inspector: Mr K.P. Durrant MA BArch RIBA ARICS MRTPI
                      FRSA
Dates of Inquiry: 3–6, 10–12 October 1995
Allowed: 24 June 1996

15. Weeland Road, Sharlston, Wakefield
MPA: City of Wakefield MDC
Site tonnage: 196,000 tonnes
Site area: 26.4 ha
Working period: 2.5 years
Appellant: H.J. Banks and Co. Ltd
Reference: APP/X4725/A/95/247548
Determination by Secretary of State
Inspector: Mrs J.Brushfield LLB PhD FRICS FCI Arb
Dates of Inquiry: 25–28 July, 1–3 August, 9–13 October, 28–30
                     November 1995, and 30 January–2 February 1996
Refused: 26 September 1996

16. Stanley Grange Farm, Stanley, Derbyshire
MPA: Derbyshire CC
Site tonnage: 40,000 tonnes
Site area: 10.4 ha
Working period: 5 months
Appellant: R.J. Budge Mining Ltd
Reference: T/APP/D1000/A/95/257212/P5
Determination by Inspector
Inspector: Mr A.Mead BSc MRTPI AMIQ
Dates of Inquiry: 6–8 August 1996
Allowed: 27 September 1996

17. Tir Dafydd, west of Llandybie
(formerly Dyfed—now Carmarthenshire)
MPA: Dyfed County Council (at time of inquiry)
Site tonnage: 800,000 tonnes (anthracite)
Site area: 136.5 ha
Working period: 3 years and 3 months
Appellant: Celtic Energy Ltd
Reference: PP121-98-001 (formerly APPG/6100/A/94/507634)
Determination by Secretary of State (for Wales)
Inspector: Mr D. Sheers BA DipTP MRTPI
Dates of Inquiry: 11 January–14 February 1996
Refused: 7 November 1996

18. Birch Laithe Farm, Bretton Lane, Bretton, Wakefield
MPA: City of Wakefield MDC
Site tonnage: 30,000 tonnes
Site area: 6.5 ha
Working period: 6 months
Appellant: Miller Mining
Reference: T/APP/X4725/A/96/270740/P5

Determination by Inspector
            (Appeal by written representations)
Inspector: Mr D. Ward BSc (Hons) CEng MICE FIHT
Site Visit: 18 November 1996
Refused: 10 December 1996

19. Yewtree Farm, Shire Lane, Sutton Scarsdale, Chesterfield Derbyshire

MPA: Derbyshire CC
Site tonnage: 126,000 tonnes
Site area: 15.8 ha
Working period: 63 weeks
Appellant: Derbyshire Mining Ltd
Reference: T/APP/D1000/A/267055/P4
Determination by Inspector
Inspector: Mr H.R. Stephens BA MPhil DiPTP MRTPI
Date of Hearing: 10 December 1996
Site Visit: 12 December 1996
Refused: 10 February 1997

20. Bleak House Extension, Norton Road, Heath Hayes, Cannock, Staffordshire

MPA: Staffordshire CC
Site tonnage: 2,200,000 tonnes
Site area: 38 ha
Working period of extension: 3 years
Appellant: RJB Mining (UK) Ltd
Reference: APP/N3400/A/95/259160
Determination by Secretary of State
Inspector: Mr E.J. Horton CEng MICE MIHT DiPTE
Dates of Inquiry: 8–18 October 1996
Refused: 3 March 1997

21. Pegwhistle Site, Netherton Moor Farm, Hartford Bridge, Bedlington, Northumberland

MPA: Northumberland CC
Site tonnage: 225,000 tonnes
Site area: 38 ha
Working period: 3.5 years (coal extraction period: 2.5 years)
Appellant: Gordon Harrison Ltd
Reference: T/APP/R2900/A/96/266541/P5
Determination by Inspector
Inspector: Ms Norah Ball BSc(Hons) MRTPI
Dates of Inquiry: 8–11 April 1997
Refused: 14 May 1997

22. Land off Bretton Lane, West Bretton, Wakefield

MPA: City of Wakefield MDC
Site tonnage: 80,000 tonnes
Site area: 19.9 ha
Working period: 12 months
Appellant: Cobex Ltd
Reference: T/APP/X4725/A/96/275717/PS
Determination by Inspector
                    (Appeal by written representations)
Inspector: Mr P.D.Walker BA(HonsTP) MRTPI
Site Visit: 12 June 1997
Refused: 14 August 1997

23. Towers Farm and New House Farm, Poynton, Cheshire

MPA: Cheshire CC
Site tonnage: 250,000 tonnes
Site area: 67 ha
Working period: 3.5 years (coal extraction period: 2.5 years)
Appellent: Coal Contractors Ltd
Reference: APP/N0600/A/95/259707
Determination by Secretary of State
Inspector: Mr R.J. Tamplin BA(Hons) MRTPI Dip Cons Studies
Dates of Inquiry: 1–23 October 1996
Refused: 1 August 1997

24. Land at Hall Road, Burnhope, Co. Durham

MPA: Durham CC ·
Site tonnage: 130,000 tonnes (125,000 tonnes in the planning
                    application)
Site area: 86.6 ha
Working period: 2 years
Appellant: Hutchinson Mining
Reference: APP/Y1300/A/96/262453 & N/P/Y1300/l5l/96/l
Determination by Secretary of State
Inspector: Mr E.A. Simpson BA(Hons) MRTPI
Dates of Inquiry: 6–8, and 12 November 1996
Refused: 7 October 1997

25. Former New Stubbin Colliery, Rawmarsh, Rotherham

MPA: Rotherham MBC
Site tonnage: 270,000 tonnes
Site area: 40 ha
Working period: 4 years (coal extraction period: 36 months)
Appellant: Coal Contractors Ltd
Reference: APP/P4415/A/96/262603

Determination by Secretary of State
Inspector: Mr J.S. Nixon BSc(Hons) DiPTE CEng MICE MRTPI MIHT
Dates of Inquiry: 7–10 and 15–16 January and 4 February 1997
Allowed: by Inspector
Refused: by Secretary of State: 13 October 1997

26. Extension to the Nant Helen Site and land at Mynydd-y-Drum, south of Abercraf, Powys

MPA: Powys CC
Site tonnage: 3,000,000 tonnes
Site area: 320 ha (portion in existing Nant Helen site)
Working period: 10.5 years
Appellant: Celtic Energy Ltd
References: APP T6850L/A/96/510161 & APP T6850/W/97/511220
Determination by the Secretary of State (for Wales)
Inspector: Mr J.J. Parkinson MSc CEng MICE MIHT MRTPI
Dates of Inquiry: 25–28 November 1997 and 3–5, 9–11 December 1997
Allowed: 21 July 1998

27. West Lodge Farm, Shildon, Co. Durham

MPA: Durham CC
Site tonnage: 100,000 tonnes
Site area: 10.5 ha
Working period: 14 months
Appellant: Andrew Golightly Ltd
References: APP/H1345/A/96/26994 & N/P/Y/1300/151/96/3
Determination by Secretary of State
Inspector: Mr P.D. Walker BA(Hons) TP MRTPI
Dates of Inquiry: 8–10 July 1997
Allowed: 28 July 1998

28. White Lea Farm, near Sunniside, Co. Durham, and Castle Farm, Tow Law, Co. Durham

MPA: Durham CC
Site tonnage: 1,900,000 tonnes (White Lea)
Site area: 238 ha (including 56 ha in the Castle Farm site)
Working period: 7.5 years
Appellant: RJB Mining (UK) Ltd/R.J. Budge Mining Ltd
References: APP/H1345/A/96/270125
APP/H1345/A/97/277514 N/P/Y1300/151/96/2
GO-NE/97/5053/1/04

Determination by the Secretary of State
Inspector: Mr A. Mead BSc MRTPI AMIQ
Dates of Inquiry: 10 June–4 July 1997
Refused: 28 July 1998

29. Land at Hathery Lane, Bebside, Blyth, Northumberland
MPA: Northumberland CC
Site tonnage: 1,500,000 tonnes
Site area: 159 ha Working area: 100 ha
Working period: 4.5 years
Appellant: RJB Mining (UK) Ltd
References: N/P/R2900/220/96/1 GO-
              NE/P/R2900/220/97/1 DN5068/35/l/93
              GO-NE/97/5068/35/01
Determination by the Secretary of State
Inspector: Mr C.S.McDonald MA DMA LMRTPI Solicitor
Dates of Inquiry: 8 July–22 August 1998 (11 days)
Refused: 28 July 1998

30. Shortwood Farm, Cossall, Nottinghamshire
MPA: Nottinghamshire CC
Site tonnage: 1,800,000 tonnes
Site area: 151 ha
Working period: 5.5 years
Appellant: RJB Mining (UK) Ltd
References: APP/M3000/A/96/265657
              APP/M3000/A/96/268602 EMP/3000/529/14
Determination by Secretary of State
Inspector: Mr K.G. Smith BSc(Hons) MRTPI
              (assisted by Mr Philip Wilson, Architect Assessor)
Dates of Inquiry: 28 January–19 February 1997
Allowed: 28 July 1998

Andrew W. Cox, *UK Coal Review,*
192 Sandyford Road, Newcastle upon Tyne NE2 1RN
Tel/Fax: 0191-2615274
Email: awcox@eimr.demon.co.uk

USEFUL ADDRESSES

Council for the Protection of Rural England (CPRE)
National HQ, Warwick House, 25–27 Buckingham Palace Road,
London SW1W 0PP
Tel: 020–7976 6433 Fax: 020–7976 6373
Internet Site http://www.greenchannel.com/cpre/

Council for the Protection of Rural Wales (CPRW)
Headquarters: Ty Gwyn, 31 High Street, Welshpool, Powys SY21 8JD
Tel: 01938–552525

Association for the Protection of Rural Scotland (APRS)
3rd Floor, Gladstone's Land, 483 Lawnmarket, Edinburgh EH1 2NT
Tel: 0131–225 7012/3

North East Opencast Action Group
Hon.Secretary, Holme Farm House, Old Quarrington,
Co. Durham DH6 5NN
Tel: 0191–377 2027

Scottish Opencast Action Group
42 Woolfords, Cobbinshaw, By West Calder, West Lothian, EH55 8LH
Tel: 01501 785202

Friends of the Earth (FoE)
26–28 Underwood Street, London N1 7JQ
Tel: 020–7490 1555 Fax: 020–7490 0881
Internet site: http://www.foe.co.uk

Earth First!
Main internet site (with links to local groups):
http://www.hrc.wmin.ac.uk/campaign/ef/earthfirst.html

House of Commons
Westminster, London SW1A 0AA
Exchange Tel: 020–7219 3000
Internet site: http://www.parliament.uk

NOTES

PREFACE

1. H. Beynon, *Masters and Servants: Class and Patronage in the making of a labour organisation* (with Terry Austrin), Rivers Oram, 1994 is the first major publication based on this work
2. See for example R. Hudson, *Wrecking a Region*, Pion, 1989
3. See H. Beynon, R. Hudson and D. Sadler, *A Tale of Two Industries: The Decline of Coal and Steel in North East England*, Open University Press, 1991
4. See A.W. Cox 'Future Strategies for Coal in the UK', PhD Thesis, University of Newcastle upon Tyne, 1987

INTRODUCTION

1. See Ulrich Beck, *Risk Society*, Polity, 1990
2. See, for example, A. Jamison, R. Eyerman and J. Cramer, *The Making of the New Environmental Consciousness*, Edinburgh University Press, 1990 and A. Melucci, *Nomads of the Present*, Hutchinson, Radius, 1989
3. House of Commons Select Committee of Energy, *The Coal Industry*, HMSO, 1987, Para.152
4. Coalfield Communities Campaign, *The Opencast Charter*, Barnsley, 1991

I TWO INDUSTRIES IN ONE

1. There were a few exceptions; 'alienated' coal reserves (such as on Crown Land in the Forest of Dean and in very small pockets around the country) remained in private ownership; these deposits were small and insignificant
2. W. Ashworth, *The History of the British Coal Industry, Vol.5, 1945–1982, The Nationalised Industry*, Oxford University Press, 1986, p.452
3. BCCOE, *Opencast Coal Mining in Great Britain*, 2nd Edition, 1988
4. J.Hancock, *Opencasting in the UK*, McCloskey Coal Information Services Ltd., 1995, p.23
5. J. Hancock, *Opencasting in the UK*, op.cit., p.24
6. BCO, *Opencast Coal Mining in Great Britain*, 2nd Edition, 1988

7. M. Prior and G. McCloskey, *Coal on the Market*, FT International Coal Report, 1988, p.60

8. Opencast Executive, 1989

9. P. G. Cotgrove, 'The Opencast Executive' in H. Beynon, R. Hudson and A. Cox (eds), *Opencast Coal—The Industry*, Conference Proceedings, University of Durham, 20 July 1989

10. House of Commons Select Committee on Energy, First Report, Session 1986–87—*The Coal Industry*, HMSO, 1987 (Para.147)

11. House of Commons Select Committee on Energy, First Report, Session 1986–87—*The Coal Industry, Minutes of Evidence*, Vol.1, HMSO, 1987, p.21

12. BCO, *Opencast Coal—A National Assessment*, BCC, 1986. Also published in: House of Commons Select Committee on Energy, First Report, Session 1986–87—*The Coal Industry, Minutes of Evidence*, Vol.11, HMSO, 1986, pp.268–70

13. W. Ashworth, *The History of the British Coal Industry, Vol.5, 1975–82, The Nationalised Industry*, Oxford University Press, 1986, p.471

14. M. Prior and G. McCloskey, *Coal on the Market: Can BCC Survive Privatisation?*, FT International Coal Report, 1988, p.58

15. P.G. Cotgrove, 'The Opencast Executive' in H. Beynon, R. Hudson and A. Cox (eds), *Opencast Mining—The Industry*, Proceedings of ESRC Conference, University of Durham, 20 July 1989, p.2

16. M. Prior and G. McCloskey, *Coal on the Market: Can BCC Survive Privatisation?*, FT International Coal Report,1988, p.60

17. P.G. Cotgrove, 'The Opencase Executive', op.cit.

18. For an illustration of this see 'Ryan Group obtain finance for expansion', *UK Coal Review*, May 1992, pp.11–12; and for a fuller discussion of the rise of the private companies and their relation to the local state see H. Beynon, R. Hudson and A. Cox, 'Opencast coalmining and the politics of coal production', *Capital and Class*, No.40, Spring 1990, pp.89–114

19. RJB Mining plc, 'Acquisition of UK Businesses of Young Group plc', press release, 16 December 1993

20. RJB Mining plc, Offer of Sale of Ordinary Shares, 1994

21. 'The Outlook for RJB Mining', *UK Coal Review*, March/April 1995, pp.2–5

22. Coal Industry Act (1994), HMSO

23. *Independent on Sunday*, 28 August 1994

24. *Hansard*, 16 May 1995, p.234, Stephen Byers, Wallsend

25. RJB Mining took control of three English mining businesses (the North East, Central North and Central South) plus two other stand-alone mines (Ellington in Northumberland and Thorne in Yorkshire). In Scotland, Mining Scotland took control of one large deep mine (the Longannet complex) and several large opencast sites. In South Wales a management-led buyout team, Celtic Energy, took

over mining assets solely composed of opencast sites. Tower colliery, was sold to a management and employee group—trading as Goitre Tower Anthracite Ltd. Coal Investments acquired the mothballed Annersley-Bentinck colliery in Nottinghamshire.

26. *The Times*, 10 December 1994
27. Ibid.
28. J. Hancock, *Opencasting in the UK*, McCloskey Coal Information Services, 1995, p.vii
29. J. Hancock, *Opencasting in the UK*, op.cit., 1995, p.24
30. 'Edwards Outlines Strategy', *UK Coal Review*, 31 January 1995, pp.2–5
31. R. Budge, Speech to the Coal Society Luncheon, London, 6 March 1995

2 REGULATING OPENCAST

1. Opencast Coal Act (1958), HMSO, Chapter 69
2. Commission on Energy and the Environment (CENE), *Coal and the Environment* (CM) HMSO, 1981
3. White Paper, *Coal and the Environment, The Government's response to the Commission on Energy and the Environment's Report on Coal and the Environment* (CM 8877) HMSO, London, 1983
4. Department of the Environmental *Circular 3/84*, Welsh Office Circular 13/84, *Opencast Coal Mining*, HMSO, 1984
5. See Department of the Environment *Circular 3/84*, HMSO, 1984, Para.16
6. H. Beynon, R. Hudson and D. Sadler, *A Tale of Two Industries*, Open University Press, 1991
7. H.J. Banks evidence, Jobs Hill Public Inquiry, Crook, Co. Durham, 1981
8. Town and Country Planning Association, Evidence to the House of Commons Select Committee on Energy, First Report—Session 1985–86—*The Coal Industry: Minutes of Evidence*—Vol.II, HMSO, 1986, p.195
9. CPRE, Evidence to the House of Commons Select Committee on Energy, First Report—Session 1985–1986—*The Coal Industry: Minutes of Evidence*—Vol.II, HMSO, 1986, p.191
10. British Coal Opencast, 'Opencast Coal—A National Assessment', *Mimeo*, 1986
11. Housing and Planning Act (1986), HMSO, Ch.63
12. House of Commons Select Committee on Energy, First Report—Session 1986–87, *The Coal Industry*, HMSO, London, 1987, Para.149
13. House of Commons Select Committee on Energy, *The Coal Industry*, 1987, Para.156

14. Department of the Environment and the London Office, *Mineral Planning Guidance Note No.3 (MPG3), Opencast Coal Mining*, HMSO, 1988

15. White Paper, *Lifting the Burden* (Cm 9571), HMSO, London. Details also summarised in: DoE Circular 14/85 *Development and Employment*, HMSO, 1985

16. P.N. Grimshaw, 'Sunshine and Success: The First Half-Century of Opencast Coalmining in Britain', *Mine and Quarry*, Jan/Feb. 1992, p.24

17. *MPG3*, Para.41

18. The Town and Country Planning (Inquiries Procedure) *Rules*, HMSO, 1988, SI 1988, No.944; The Town and Country Planning Appeals (Determination by Inspectors) (Inquiries Procedure) *Rules*, HMSO, SI 1988, No.945, HMSO, 1988

19. Coalfield Communities Campaign, *Statistics on Opencast Mining and the Planning System*, 1993

20. Department of Trade and Industry, *The Prospects for Coal—Conclusions of the Government's Coal Review*, HMSO, London (CM 2235) HMSO, 1993

21. Department of the Environment, News Release No.212—*Interim Planning Guidance for Opencast Coal*, 1993

22. Cutsyke Road, North Featherstone, Wakefield MDC, *Opencast Public Inquiry*, January 1994

23. Department of the Environment, Minerals Division, Minerals Planning Guidance—*Coal Mining and Colliery Spoil Disposal—Revision of MPG3—Draft Consultation Document*, HMSO, 1993

24. Department of the Environment and Welsh Office, *Mineral Planning Guidance Note 3 (MPG3): Coal Mining and Colliery Spoil Disposal*, HMSO, 1994

25. R. Bate, 'Revised *MPG3*: Fig-leaf Gone But Coalfield Less Exposed', *UK Coal Review*, July 1994, pp.12–13

26. *Sustainable Development—The UK Strategy* (Cm 2426), HMSO, 1994

27. Durham County Council, 'Comments on draft consultation document *MPG3*', Mimeo, Durham, 1994

28. Wakefield MDC, 'Review of Minerals Planning Guidance Note 3', Mimeo, Wakefield, 1994

29. White Paper, *This Common Inheritance—Britain's Environmental Strategy* (Cm 1200), HMSO, 1990

30. R. Bate, 'Revised *MPG3*: Fig-leaf Gone But Coalfield Less Exposed', op.cit.

31. We awaited the results of this research with interest and were disappointed to wait until 1997 before a research contract was awarded to CRE group, with the final report published in 1999. A.J. Minchener and D.I. Barnes, *Chemical Variation and the End Uses of Coal at the Present and in the Future.*

32. Countryside Commission, *Opencast Coal Mining: Advice on Landscape and Countryside Issues*, Advisory Booklet CCP, 434, 1993
33. House of Commons Select Committee on Trade and Industry, First Report—Session 1992–93, *British Energy Policy and the Market for Coal*, HMSO, 1993
34. House of Commons Welsh Affairs Committee, Second Report—Session 1990–91, *The Future of Opencast Coalmining in Wales*, HMSO, 1991
35. A full list of these appeal decisions is contained in a note at the end of this book

3 OPENCAST MINING: THE CHALLENGE

1. A.J. Pratt, *Opencast—Casting a Shadow: The Social and Environmental Effects of Opencast Coal Mining*, Durham Area Miners' Support Group, 1989, p.48
2. British Coal Opencast Executive, *Opencast Coal Mining in Great Britain*, 2nd Edition, 1988, p.1.
3. W. Ashworth, *The History of the British Coal Industry, Vol.5, 1945–1982, The Nationalised Industry*, Oxford University Press, 1986, p.471
4. W. Ashworth, *The History of the British Coal Industry, Vol.5, 1945–1982, The Nationalised Industry*, Oxford University Press, 1986, p.471
5. House of Commons Select Committee on Energy, First Report, Session 1986–87, *The Coal Industry*, HMSO, 1987
6. J. Hancock, *Opencasting in the UK*, McCloskey Coal Information Services Ltd, 1995, p.14
7. P.G. Cotgrove, 'The Opencast Executive' in H. Beynon, R. Hudson and A. Cox (eds), *Opencast Mining—The Industry*, ESRC Conference Proceedings, University of Durham, 20 July 1989, p.2
8. Coal Information and Consultancy Services Ltd (CICS), *The British Opencast Coal Industry*, London, 1989, p.14
9. P.G. Cotgrove, 'The Opencast Executive' in H. Beynon, R. Hudson and A. Cox (eds), *Opencast Mining—The Industry*, ESRC Conference Proceedings, University of Durham, 20 July 1989, p.2
10. In 1989, British Coal maintained that additional reserves were being proven at a rate of 24mt a year
11. M. Parker, 'UK Fossil-Fuel Reserves: Are We Running Out?' *Oxera*, March 1996, p.25
12. *Opencast Coal Mining in Great Britain*, 2nd Edition, 1988, Preface
13. *Opencast Coal Mining in Great Britain*.
14. See for example, A. Glyn, *The Economic Case Against Pit Closures*, National Union of Mineworkers, 1985; R. Hudson, F. Peck and D. Sadler, *Undermining Easington*, Durham University, 1985; H. Beynon, R. Hudson and D. Sadler, *A Tale of Two Industries*, Open University Press, 1991

15. D. Cooper and T. Hopper (eds), *Debating Coal Closures*, Cambridge University Press, 1986

16. This view was developed most clearly by Malcolm Brocklesby and the Opencast Mining Intelligence Group (OMIG). It was published in its pamphlet *A Reassessment of Opencast Mining*, 1979

17. *UK Coal Review*, 31 January 1995, pp.2–5

18. J. Hancock, *Opencasting in the UK*, McCloskey Coal Information Services Ltd., 1995, pp.vi, vii

19. British Coal Corporation, *Annual Report and Accounts 1993–94*, pp.33–4

20. RJB Mining plc, *Annual Report and Accounts 1996*, p.36

21. British Coal Opencast Executive, *Opencast Coal Mining in Great Britain*, 2nd Edition, 1988, p.1

22. Department of the Environment and Welsh Office, *Mineral Planning Guidance Note 3*, HMSO, 1994 (Para.73)

23. B. Grossling, *World Coal Resources*, Financial Times Ltd., 1979, p.7

24. See for example J. Hodges, W. Ladner and T. Martin, 'Chlorine in Coal: A Review of its Origin and Mode of Occurrence', *Journal of the Institute of Energy*, September 1993, pp.158–69; CRE Group Ltd, *Chlorine Reduction in UK Coals*, DTI Coal R&D Programme Report No: R050, 1995

25. Co-extruded tubes have a corrosion resistant outer layer (up to 50 per cent Cr stainless steel). In 1986 the CEGB reported that over 100,000 metres of co-extruded tube had been installed in 38 boilers at 13 stations. See CEGB, *Achievements in Technology Planning and Research*, 1986, pp.81–5

26. Central West Region sites with high sulphur levels are: Birch Coppice (2.16 per cent), Coalfield West (2.20 per cent), Lounge Remainder (2.10 per cent) and Bannel Bridge (2.65 per cent). Other high sulphur coal is found in sites in other coalfields in England— recent examples being: Coggra Fold, Bury (1.99–2.20 per cent) and Fenwicks Close Farm, North Tyneside/Northumberland (2.13 per cent).

27. A. Clayton, *Evidence*, Berryhill Opencast Public Inquiry, Stoke-on-Trent, 1992

28. M.V. Lovat foundered at sea on 25 January 1975 with the loss of 11 of her crew. Formal Investigation under the Merchant Shipping Act (1894), *Report of Court No.8066*, M. V. Lovat (O.N. 360735), HMSO, 1977

29. W. Ashworth, *The History of the British Coal Industry Vol.5, 1945–82 The Nationalised Industry*, Oxford University Press, 1986, p.471

30. BCO, *Opencast Coal Mining in Great Britain*, 2nd Edition, 1988, p.4

31. 'The Outlook for RJB Mining', *UK Coal Review*—March/April 1995, pp.2–5

32. *The Journal* (Newcastle upon Tyne) 15 November 1991

33. Ibid.
34. Quoted in Rhys George, 'Lay-offs at mine spark controversy', *South Wales Guardian*, 18 June 1998
35. 'The Opencast Executive' in H. Beynon, R. Hudson and A. Cox (eds), *Opencast Mining: The Industry*, Conference Proceedings, University of Durham, 1989
36. David Napier, *Evidence*, Hathery Lane Opencast Public Inquiry, Northumberland, 1987
37. For example, see White Lea Opencast Public Inquiry, Co. Durham, 1997
38. A.B. Trigg and W.R. Dubourg, *Opencast Discussion Papers in Economics No.1/1993*, 'Valuing the Environmental Impacts of Opencast Coalmining—The Case of the Trent Valley in North Staffordshire', The Open University, Faculty of Social Science, 1993
39. K.G. Willis, G.B. Nelson, A.B. Bye and G. Peacock, 'An Application of the Krutilla-Fisher Model to Appraising the Benefits of Green Belt Preservation versus Site Development', *Journal of Environmental Planning and Management*, Vol.36, No.1, 1993, pp.73–90

4 LIVING WITH OPENCAST

1. Weeland Road Opencast Coal Public Inquiry, Wakefield MDC, *Inspector's Report*, 1996, Appendix A
2. CPRE, *Campaigners' Guide to Opencast Coal Mining*, 1991, p.vi
3. Billingside Opencast Public Inquiry, *Inspector's Report*, 1987 (Para.38)
4. See Building Research Establishment, 'Effects of Environmental Noise on People at Home' BRE Information Paper 22/93 and Construction Research Communications Ltd., 'Attitudes to Noise', *Digest of Environmental Statistics*, No.19, HMSO, 1997
5. R. Hudson and A.W. Cox, *British Coal and Opencast Mining*, ESRC Discussion Paper No.9, University of Durham, 1990, p.87
6. Rose Hills Opencast Coal Public Inquiry, Co. Durham, *Inspector's Report*, 1987
7. Hathery Lane Opencast Public Inquiry, Blyth, Northumberland, July 1997
8. See Building Research Establishment, 'Effects of Environmental Noise on People at Home', BRE Information Paper 22/93
9. R. Hudson and A.W. Cox, *British Coal and Opencast Mining*, ESRC Discussion Paper No.9, University of Durham, 1990, p.62
10. R. Hudson and A.W. Cox, *British Coal and Opencast Mining*, ESRC Discussion Paper No.9, University of Durham, 1990, p.83
11. 'Safety alert at mines', *The Journal*, Newcastle upon Tyne, 16 July 1997
12. *Mineral Planning Guidance, 3*, HMSO, 1988, Para.6. It is worth noting that in the Revised 1994 edition of *MPG3* (Para.9) this expression

was revised to: 'mineral working is not a permanent use of land…'

13. A.J. Pratt, *Opencast—Casting a Shadow, The Social and Environmental Effects of Opencast Coal Mining*, Durham Area Miners' Support Group, 1989, p.61

14. In H. Beynon, A. Cox and R. Hudson (eds), *Opencast Mining: Digging Out the Issues*, ESRC Conference Proceedings, Durham, 1988

15. Whiteside Farm Opencast Public Inquiry, Co. Durham, *Inspector's Report*, 1991

16. J.M.F. Temple and A.M. Sykes, 'Asthma and Opencast Mining', *British Medical Journal*, 1992; 305; pp.396–7

17. P. Weaver, 'The Health and Wealth of the Opencast Coal Industry', *Mineral Planning*, No.57, 1993, p.21

18. R.C. Love et al., *A Cross-sectional Epidemiological Study of the Respiratory Health and Exposure to Airborne Dust and Quartz of Current Workers in Opencast Coal Mines*, Institute of Occupational Medicine Report, 1992

19. Weeland Road Opencast Public Inquiry, *Inspector's Report*, 1996

20. As a consequence of these developments, the Departments of the Environment and Health combined with the Medical Research Council in 1994 to issue a joint call for proposals for work on air pollution and respiratory disease. In 1996 details were released of 26 research projects which received funding, worth a total of £3.5m, designed to provide a better understanding of the relationship between air pollution and health. One of these research projects, entitled 'Does living near to opencast mining impair health?' was awarded funding totalling £266,000. It was based at the Department of Epidemiology and Public Health, in the University of Newcastle upon Tyne's Medical School (contact address shown in Appendix 2). It will examine whether there is a relationship between opencast coal mining and ill-health in the surrounding populations.

21. J.H. Atkinson, 'The Living Landscape Opencast Coal Working', in J.D. Peart and L.A. Rutherford (eds), *A Review of Opencast Coal and its Environmental Impact*, Conference Proceedings, Newcastle upon Tyne Polytechnic, 1986, p.28

22. Weeland Road Opencast Coal Public Inquiry, *Inspector's Report*, 1996, Appendix A, Para.35

23. Ellerbeck West Opencast Coal Public Inquiry, Lancashire, *Inspector's Report*, 1987, Para.327, pp.71–2

24. See A.J. Pratt, *Opencast—Casting a Shadow: The Social and Environmental Effects of Opencast Coal Mining*, Durham Area, Miners' Support Group, 1989, p.56

25. Ibid., p.56

26. Billingside Opencast Public Inquiry Co. Durham, *Inspector's Report*, 1987 (Para.38)

27. Linton Lane Opencast Public Inquiry, Northumberland, *Inspector's*

Report, 1988 (Paras.51 and 52)

28. Ibid.
29. J. Stevenson, *Evidence*, Marley Hill Opencast Public Inquiry, Co. Durham (Para.80)
30. Hathery Lane Opencast Public Inquiry, Northumberland, 1997
31. Joanne Bird 'The Accused: £175,000 offered in mining wrangle', *Leicester Mercury*, 10 June 1996
32. Cutsyke Road Opencast Public Inquiry, Wakefield, 1995
33. Committee on Standards in Public Life (Chairman: Lord Nolan), Third Report: *Standards of Conduct in Local Government in England, Scotland and Wales*, HMSO, 1997, pp.77–80. Weeland Road Opencast Coal Public Inquiry, Wakefield MDC, Inspector's Report, 1996, Appendix A

5 THE STATE, THE PUBLIC AND THE INQUIRY

1. J. Hancock, *Opencasting in the UK*, McCloskey Coal Information Services Ltd, 1995, p.13
2. Ibid., p.16
3. Harvey Wood, 'The friendly face of mining', *Planning*, 18 April 1997, p.12
4. See *The Efficiency Unit, Making the Most of Next Steps: The Management of Minister's Departments and their Executive Agencies (The Fraser Report)*, HMSO, 1991. For a discussion of these Agencies, their changed role within the British State and the implications for employment practices, see P. Fairbrother, *Politics and the State as Employer*, Mansell, 1994 and 'In a State of Change: Flexibility in the Civil Service' in A. Pollert (ed.), *Farewell to Flexibility*, Blackwell, 1991, pp.69–83
5. *Planning Inspectorate Journal*, Winter 1996, Issue 6, p.22
6. Michael Howard MP, Speech to the Planning Inspectorate Annual Meeting, 28 April 1989
7. These procedures are prescribed in primary legislation and regulations. A comprehensive guide is set out in the Department of the Environment, PPG 12, 1992 and its booklet *Development Plans—What You Need to Know*
8. 'Co. Durham Minerals Local Plan Progress Report', Durham County Council, Environment Committee, 1 July 1996; see also Mel Mason, 'Unacceptable Face of Mining', *The Northern Echo*, 2 July 1996, p.5
9. Steve Leddy, 'Planning Applications: Talking them through', *Mine and Quarry*, Vol.20, No.11, November 1991, pp.10–11
10. The wide range of qualifications held by Inspectors can be judged by reference to those listed in *MPG3 (Revised) Opencast Coal Appeals Monitor*, pp.262–72. The careers of two Inspectors (who have recently conducted opencast appeals) were briefly outlined in the

Planning Inspectorate Journal, Winter 1996, Issue 6, pp.10–12. Mrs Jean Brushfield worked in private practice as a Chartered Surveyor, and then in local government, before joining the Planning Inspectorate in 1977. She has been conducting major planning inquiries since 1979. David Sheers qualified as a chartered town planner. He joined the Planning Inspectorate in 1981 from the DoE, following a career in local government in the West Midlands, South Wales and London, and for the Government of Fiji

11. The Planning Inspectorate, *Business and Corporate Plan,* 1995/96—1998/99, HMSO, 1995, p.14

12. In some circumstances this can be made after the expiry of the decision period of the application. A checklist for appellants, as well as general guidance on appeals, is provided in the Planning Inspectorate's booklet, *A Guide to Planning Appeals*

13. They are based upon the Town and Country Planning Appeals (Written Representation) Regulations, 1987

14. A Code of Practice for Hearings is included as Annex 2 *Circular 15/96*

15. Town and Country Planning Act (1990), HMSO, Schedule 6, Para.3

16. Public Inquiry Rules SI 1992/2038 or SI 1992/2039

17. Examples include: the Rose Hills Inquiry (Beamish and West Pelton Working Men's Club, Co. Durham, 1986); the Fenwicks Close Inquiry (Seaton Deleval Working Men's Club, North Tyneside, 1995); the Howbrook Inquiry (Staindrop Lodge Hotel, Chapeltown, near Sheffield, 1995), Tir Dafydd Inquiry (Llandybie Methodist Hall, Dyfed, 1996); and the Bretton Lane Inquiry (Wakefield Town Hall, 1995).

18. Local authorities are charged with the responsibility for selecting and providing suitable accommodation for inquiries, though it is the Inspector's task to make sure that the accommodation is fit for the purpose. Suitable venues are sometimes difficult to find—local buildings may not be of sufficient size, have adequate facilities, or be available for long enough to hold what is often a complex event. There have been, for example, complaints that the selected venue ignored the needs of disabled people. In the late 1990s, local authorities and the Planning Inspectorate had become more sensitive to this issue. In order to rectify these problems the Inspectorate is revising its Public Inquiry Facility Note (initially sent by the Chief Planning Inspector to all local planning authorities in March 1996).

19. The general procedures for the PIM are outlined in Para.5 of the Inquiry Rules. The absence of any party or interested persons from the PIM does not prejudice or affect their right to appear at the inquiry and/or make representations on the appeal.

20. These draft conditions are completed before the end of each inquiry

and are solely for use in the event of the appeal being successful (and planning permission being granted).

21. Some Inspectors have asked for proofs of evidence on diskette to assist them prepare their final report (an example being the Inspector at the Weeland Road Opencast Inquiry, at Sharlston in Wakefield MBC). Asking for proofs of evidence on diskette has sometimes caused consternation amongst some local authority staff who have limited knowledge of computing

22. See A. Ashforth, 'Reckoning Schemes of Legitimation: On Commissions of Inquiries as Power Knowledge Forms', *Journal of Historical Sociology*, Vol.3, No.1, 1980, pp.1–20

23. Department of the Environment, *Circular 15/96*, HMSO, Annex 5 (Para.40)

24. The issue of costs in most normally a matter between the *MPA* and the appellants. As such *Circular 15/96* notes that: Awards of costs either in favour of or against third parties are only made in exceptional circumstances. This comment should allay the fears of members of the general public and local groups taking part in an appeal.

25. The report can be written with the Secretary of State Rules (SI 1992 No.2038) or, alternatively, the Inspector can prepare his/her decision letter within the Inspector's Rules (SI 1992 No.2039). With both sets of Rules the parties entitled to appear at the Inquiry have a right to be consulted if it is intended to take account of new evidence or new matters of fact (excluding changes in government planning policy).

    The rules are not meant to be exhaustive on referrals and there is discretion to refer back to the parties in other circumstances where not to do so could result in a breach of natural justice. In such circumstances the parties may request the re-opening of the Inquiry, and indeed the Secretary of State or the Inspector can cause the appeal to be re-opened 'on such matters as he may specify'.

26. Under the provisions of Section 288 of the Town and Country Planning Act (1990), a person who is aggrieved by the decision given in the accompanying decision letter may seek to have it quashed by an application made to the High Court within 6 weeks from the date of the decision letter.

    The grounds upon which such an application may be made to the Court are: that the decision is not within the powers of the Act (that is, the relevant Secretary of State has exceeded his powers); or that any of the relevant requirements have not been complied with, and the applicant's interests have been substantially prejudiced by the failure to comply. The Department of the Environment advises that legal advice should be taken before an appeal is challenged. There is also provision under rule 17(3) of the Town and Country Planning (Inquiry Procedure) Rules 1992 for persons who received the

Inspector's report to apply (within 6 weeks) for an opportunity to inspect any document appended to the report.

27. J. Hancock, *Opencasting in the UK*, McCloskey Coal Information Services, 1995, p.17

28. Such has been the growth in demand for expert witnesses in recent years that specialist directories are now published to assist barristers, solicitors, local authorities and companies in locating competent witnesses—both for public inquiries and for court cases. The Society of Expert Witnesses has also been formed to 'promote excellence in all aspects of the service provided by expert witnesses' and to provide a general helpline, training courses, advice on contractual matters and on fees, *UK Register of Expert Witnesses*, J.S. Publications. This publication is updated annually and available in hard copy format and on diskette. The company also publishes an occasional newsletter *Your Witness* and has held conferences and training courses for expert witnesses. The Society of Expert Witnesses can be contacted through the company. The interim report by Lord Woolf, *Access to Justice* (Ion River Design, 1995) contained sections on the use of expert witnesses. While this report was primarily intended for assistance in litigation some of the findings may also be of relevance to public inquiries.

29. G.C. Warren, Letter, *Planning Inspectorate Journal*, No.6, Winter 1996, p.5

30. For a helpful discussion of the nature of 'expert' knowledge in inquiries see M. Richardson, J. Sherman and M. Gismoldi, *Winning Back the Words: Confronting Experts in an Environmental Public Hearing*, Garamond Press, Toronto, 1993

31. There are several barristers' chambers and firms of solicitors in London and in the provinces which have staff who concentrate on planning issues. A few barristers have even become well-known after their appearances at opencast coal inquiries

32. See Annex 5 of Department of the Environment *Circular 15/96* especially Paras.28–32

33. Weeland Road Opencast Coal Appeal, Wakefield MDC, Inspector's Report, 1996 (Paras.13.12.3–13.12.5)

34. M. Richardson, J. Sherman and M. Gismoldi; *Winning Back the Words*, op.cit.

35. K. Burningham and M. O'Brien, 'Environmental Values and Local Contexts of Action', *Sociology*, Vol.28, No.4, 1994, p.926

36. Shilo North (Nottinghamshire CC/Derbyshire CC, 1989); Marley Hill (Gateshead MBC/Durham CC, 1989/90); Berryhill, Stoke-on-Trent (Staffordshire CC, 1992); Coalburns Farm (Gateshead MBC, 1992); Fenwicks Close Farm (North Tyneside MBC/Northumberland CC, 1995); the Howbrook site (Barnsley MBC, 1995); and Weeland Road (Wakefield MDC, 1995/96).

Strong community action groups were established for each of these localities, presenting themselves with forceful evidence at the inquiry. Some organisations have published background notes and handbooks to assist local groups and individuals in presenting their evidence at opencast and minerals public inquiries. Recent examples are CPRE (1991, 1996 and 1997), the North East Opencast Action Group (1992) and the Scottish Opencast Action Group (1995). Other more general texts have been published on fighting public inquiries and organising campaigns (see Appendix 1).

37. Eric Lee, 'Effective Evidence at Public Inquiries', Mimeo, 1992
38. See P. Bourdieu, *Distinctions*, Polity Press, 1990
39. For a discussion of the effective use of dramatology in social science see E. Goffman, *Where the Action Is*, Allen Lane, 1970

6 DEMOCRACY! WHAT DEMOCRACY?

1. This is discussed in R.Hudson and D. Sadler, 1987 'Manufactured in the UK? Special steels, motor vehicles and the politics of industrial decline', *Capital and Class*, 32, pp.55–83.
2. *Hansard*, 16 May 1995, p.226
3. *Financial Times*, 19 May 1990
4. Sheffield Development Corporation, 'Go-Ahead for £100 million International Airport Complex', press release, 18 May 1990
5. Ibid.
6. See also, Sheffield Development Corporation 'News from Sheffield's Lower Don Valley', press release, 13 July 1989
7. *Star*, 20 January 1989
8. Sheffield Development Corporation, 'News from Sheffield's Lower Don Valley, press release, 13 July 1989
9. *Financial Times*, 19 May 1990
10. Sheffield Development Corporation, 'Go-Ahead for £100 million International Airport Complex', press release, 18 May 1990
11. Ibid.
12. Ibid.
13. Letter to Clive Betts MP, cited in *Hansard*, 16 May 1995, p.226
14. *Hansard*, 16 May 1995, p.242
15. Ibid., p.228
16. Ibid., p.229
17. *Yorkshire Post*, 11 December 1992
18. Ibid.
19. Ibid.
20. Ibid., 20 April 1995
21. Ibid.
22. Ibid.
23. Ibid

23. *Financial Times*, 28 February 1997
24. Ibid.

7 CHANGING PATTERNS OF PROTEST

1. See for example, Huw Beynon, 'Material and symbolic relations in the UK coal mining industry', in Birgit Muller (ed.), *A La Recherche des Certitudes Perdues*, Centre Marc Bloch, 1996 and Dennis Warwick and Gary Littlejohn, *Coal, Capital and Culture*, Routledge, 1992
2. Quoted in Ray Hudson, *Wrecking a Region*, Pion, 1989, pp.132–3
3. See for example, V. Allen, *The Militancy of British Miners*, The Moor Press, 1982; David Powell, *The Power Game: The Struggle for Coal*, Duckworth, 1993
4. See J. Winterton and R. Winterton, *Coal, Crisis and Conflict: The 1984–85 Miners' Strike in Yorkshire*, Manchester University Press, 1989
5. See, for example, Huw Beynon, 'Regulating Research', in Alan Bryman (ed.), *Doing Research in Organisations*, Routledge, 1988, pp.21–33
6. House of Commons Select Committee on Energy First Report, Session 1985–6, *The Coal Industry—Minutes of Evidence*, HMSO, 1986, p.181
7. George Hardy, 'Opencast Mining: the Durham Background', in H. Beynon, R. Hudson and A. Cox (eds), *Opencast Mining—The Industry*, ESRC Conference Proceedings, University of Durham, 1989
8. For more details of this period see H. Beynon, R.Hudson and D. Sadler, *A Tale of Two Industries: the Decline of Coal and Steel in North East England*, Open University Press, 1991
9. *Evidence*, Billingside Opencast Public Inquiry, Co. Durham, 1987
10. *Evidence*, Billingside Opencast Public Inquiry, 1987
11. National Union Of Mineworkers, 'Opencast Coal Mining 'The Threat to the NUM', *mimeo*, 1985
12. *Hansard*, 20 January 1986
13. Quoted in Roger Milne, 'King coal tries to scuttle county opencast figures', *Planning*, 20 May 1988, p.14
14. Appeal by British Coal on Shilo North Site, *Report*, Department of the Environment, 1990
15. *Nottingham Evening Post*, 16 May 1990, p.3
16. Ibid.
17. Ibid., 21 May 1990, p.4
18. Ibid., 29 March 1989, p.5
19. Ibid., 13 March 1991, p.3
20. See for example, Huw Beynon (ed.) *Digging Deeper: Issues in the 1984–85 Miners' Strike*, Verso, 1985
21. *Observer*, 22 January 1995, p.3

22. Peter Lazenby, 'Siege Town', *Yorkshire Evening Post*, 16 January 1995

23. *Yorkshire Evening Post*, 18 January 1995

24. Quoted in *Nottingham Evening Post*, 13 January 1993

25. *Observer*, 22 January 1995

26. *The Economist*, 25 January 1997

27. Geoffrey Lean, 'The Green Giant Will Not Sleep Forever', *Independent on Sunday*, 14 July 1996, p.21

28. Quoted in *UK Opencast Network*, Issue 1, August 1995

29. Mel Manson, 'Unacceptable face of mining', *Northern Echo*, 2 July 1996, p.5

30. Quoted in Mark Summers, 'Open up to Jobs, Don't cast us Out, Cry Miners', *Northern Echo*, 18 March 1997

31. Quoted in Dave Black, 'Miners Battle for their Jobs', *The Journal*, 15 March 1997

32. *Guardian*, 11 November 1995

33. *The Times*, 10 May 1997

34. Andrew Norfolk, 'Protesters Dump Coal on Duke's Doorstep', *Yorkshire Post*, 8 July 1996

35. John Vidal, 'No Welcome in the Valleys', *Guardian*, 5 August 1995

36. Ibid.

37. Quoted in 'Cwmgwrach—Valley of the Witch' Channel 4 Teletext, 7 August 1995

38. Quoted in Richard Sharpe, 'Tax Cut "Proof of Opencast Blight"', *South Wales Guardian*, 6 February 1997

39. Earth First, *Action Update*, No.37, March 1997

40. Robin Maynard, 'Opencast Mining', *Change Your World: The Newsletter of Friends of the Earth's Local Groups*, January/February 1997, p.19

41. Earth First, *Action Update*, No.37, March 1997

42. *The Times*, 8 March 1997

43. Quoted in Geoffrey Lean 'The Green Giant will Not Sleep Forever', *Independent on Sunday*, 14 July 1996, p.21

8 NEW GOVERNMENT—NEW POLICIES?

1. Tony Blair, Speech, UN General Assembly Special Session on the Environment and Sustainable Development, New York, 23 June 1997

2. *Hansard*, 5 November 1997, Col.345

3. Both PowerGen and National Power have evaluated burning other fuels most notably Orimulsion (a high sulphur bitumen-based liquid fuel from Venezuela). National Power abandoned its planning application to convert the large Pembroke oil-fired station to Orimulsion, only after strong local opposition. Other proposals included the trial combustion of petroleum coke at Drax power station (in a blend with locally-mined coals).

4. Department of Trade and Industry, press release, 'John Battle looks at the shape of energy markets to come', 16 September 1997
5. *Hansard*, 17 November 1997
6. *The World at One*, BBC Radio 4, 17 October 1997
7. *Guardian*, 22 October 1997
8. See for example, Mike Parker, *Privatised Coal—Facing the End of the Contracts*, Oxford Economic Research Associates, 1997 which anticipated the market for RJB's coal being reduced by a half in 1998–9
9. *Financial Times*, 13 November 1997
10. *The Times*, 21 November 1997
11. *Financial Times*, 27 November 1997
12. Simon Holberton 'Miners put new jobs on their Christmas list', *Financial Times*, 27 November 1997
13. John Battle 'Coal Industry must dig itself out of its own problems' *The Times*, 26 November 1997
14. Ibid.
15. *Guardian*, 27 November 1997
16. *Financial Times*, 4 December 1997
17. *Guardian*, 27 November 1997
18. *The Times*, 27 November 1997
19. Ibid.
20. *Financial Times*, 1 December 1997
21. Ibid.
22. See the *Financial Times* and the *Guardian*, 2 December 1997
23. *Guardian*, 4 December 1997
24. Simon Holberton 'Coal's cut appears too deep to heal', *Financial Times*, 5 December 1997
25. *Financial Times*, 13 December 1997
26. Ibid., 13/14 December 1997
27. David Gow, 'Painful Glory is not Enough', *Guardian*, 3 July 1997
28. Quoted in David Gow, *Guardian*, 3 January 1998
29. See Coalfield Communities Campaign, *A Market for Coal: How to avoid pit closures and secure Britain's energy supplies*, Barnsley, 1998
30. Coalfield Task Force Report, 1998, *Making the Difference: A new start for England's coalfield communities*, DETR
31. Charles Clover, 'Ukraine Miners Face a Bleak Future: Britain is encouraging workers to readjust in the face of pit closures', *Financial Times*, 9 December 1997
32. Anthony Barnett 'Labour ready to 'let pits die' as Germans reap subsidies', *Observer Business*, 22 March 1998
33. Seamus Milne, 'Blair Acts to Save Mines', *Guardian*, 6 April 1998
34. Trade and Industry Committee, *Coal: Volume 1*, HMSO, 1998
35. 'Parliamentary Statement on Fuels Review by President of the Board of Trade, Margaret Beckett', *press notice*, DTI, 25 June 1998
36. Ibid., op.cit., Paras.5 and 6

37. Ibid., Paras.23 and 24
38. Frank Dobson, *Opencast Coal Mining—Too High A Price?*, The Labour Party, 1996, p.11
39. Quoted in Tony Henderson, 'Opencast site reborn as haven for man and nature', *The Journal*, 7 September 1996
40. Peter Stringer, letter, 3 October 1996
41. Tony Blair, letter, 19 November 1996
42. *Hansard*, 19 May 1997, Vol.294, No.8 (Col.486)
43. House of Commons Select Committee on Trade and Industry, First Report, *British Energy Policy and the Market for Coal*, HMSO, 1993, p.74
44. He made this clear verbally and in a letter to Mr G.D. Halliday, Northumberland CC (10 July 1997), a document submitted to the Hathery Lane, Blyth, Northumberland, Opencast Coal Public Inquiry, August 1997
45. Department of the Environment, Transport and the Regions Consultation Paper: *Opencast Coal—Review of Planning Policy*, HMSO, 1997
46. Planning Division, Development Department, The Scottish Office, Consultation Paper: *Opencast Coal—Review of Planning Policy in Scotland*, 1997
47. Planning Division, Development Department, The Scottish Office, *Review of Opencast Coal Mining Operations in Scotland*, RSK Environmental Ltd. 1997
48. Reported in *Financial Times*, 4 November 1997
49. RJB Mining (UK) Ltd. Evidence to Department of the Environment Transport and the Regions, Consultation on Opencast Mining, October 1997
50. 'No Opencast', leaflet, Mimeo, 1997
51. Jane Abbott, 'PM makes pledge', *Nottingham Evening Post*, 2 May 1998
52. Kieran Lee, 'Taking it to the top', *CPRE Nottinghamshire Branch Newsletter*, May 1998
53. Greg Neale, 'Labour breaks pledge to block coal mine in Lawrence beauty spot', *Sunday Telegraph*, 1 August 1998.
54. *British Social Attitudes, the 1997 Report*, Gower, 1987
55. See for example, A. Marsh, *Protest and Political Consciousness*, Sage, 1977 which found that 55 per cent of people in the survey agreed that 'it is justified to break the law to protest about something you feel may be very unjust or harmful'.
56. Coalfields Task Force *Newsletter*, Issue 1.
57. *Making the Difference: A New Start For England's Coalfield Communities*, The Coalfields Task Force, June 1988.
58. These issues have been actively considered by the Inspectorate. See Chris Shepley (Chief Planning Inspector), 'Mediation in the Planning System', *Planning Inspectorate Journal*, No.7, Spring 1997, pp.9–14.

59. Some inquiries have already been televised. During the public examination of Wakefield MBC's Unitary Development Plan (1993) and later at the Cutsyke Road Opencast Inquiry (January 1994) (both held at Wakefield's Town Hall) a static closed-circuit television camera was placed at the back of the inquiry room. It allowed Council officers, councillors and members of the public who were in other rooms in the building to follow the inquiry's proceedings. No-one complained about the camera at either Public Inquiry—in fact few people even noticed it was there. At these events, as at other inquiries, one or two small remotely controlled cameras could easily have fed pictures and sound to the local television or radio stations, so allowing greater coverage of the proceedings.

CONCLUSIONS

1. For a fuller discussion of the issues involved here see Huw Beynon and Mark Harvey, *The Problem of the State: Taking the Long View*, ICLS Working Paper, University of Manchester, 2000
2. These differences are explored in detail in H. Beynon and R. Hudson, 'The End of Old Certainties: Flexible labour market adaptation or social exclusion in the former coal districts of the UK?', *forthcoming*, 2000
3. See J. Schumpeter, *The Theory of Economic Development*, Harvard University Press, 1934
4. For a full discussion of the scale of these losses see Huw Beynon, *The Case for Houghton Main*, ICLS Working Paper, University of Manchester, 1993
5. For details see K. Coates and M. Barrett-Brown, *Coalfield Communities Under Threat*, Spokesman Books, 1998
6. F. Burton and P. Carlen, *Official Discourse: On Discourse Analysis, Government Publications, Ideology and the State*, Routledge, 1979, p.8
7. A. Ashforth, 'Reckoning Schemes of Legitimation: On Commissions of Inquiry as Power/Knowledge Forms', *Journal of Historical Sociology*, Vol.3, No.1, 1980, p.3
8. Ibid., p.9
9. Ibid., p.12
10. These developments in the UK coal mining industry can be seen as part of a more general pattern in which business groups have 'fought back' against the environmentalist movements in the USA and Europe. See for example, Andrew Rowell, *Green Backlash: Global Subversion of the Environmental Movement*, Routledge, 1996
11. P. Byrne, *Social Movements in Britain*, Routledge, 1997, p.6
12. See for example P. Byrne, *Social Movements in Britain*, Routledge, 1997. In noting this tendency, Byrne observes that: 'Virtually all the political parties formed out of environmental movements have

experienced serious internal rifts over the tactics and directions they should pursue', p.22

13. J. Pakulski, *Social Movements: The Politics of Moral Protest*, Longman, 1991, p.42

14. See for example, C. Offe, 'New Social Movements: challenging the boundaries of institutional politics', *Social Research*, 1985, pp.817–68

15. Quoted in D. Newnham, 'Shallow Grave', *Guardian: Weekend*, 6 September 1997

16. G. Parry, G. Moyser and D. Day, *Political Participation and Democracy in Britain*, Cambridge University Press, 1992, p.215

17. See for example John McIlroy and Sallie Westwood, *Border Country: Raymond Williams in Adult Education*, National Institute of Adult and Continuing Education, 1993

18. K. Burningham and M. O'Brien, 'Global Environmental Values and Local Contexts of Action', *Sociology*, Vol.28, No.4, pp.919–20

19. For a discussion see A. Scott, *Ideology and the New Social Movements*, Unwin Hyman, 1990

20. K. Burningham and M. O'Brien, 'Global Environmental Values and Local Contexts of Action', op.cit., p.921

21. *Guardian*, 20 January 1997

22. Joan Ruddock MP, *Environmental Protection Briefing: Opencast Mining*, 13 August 1995

BIBLIOGRAPHY

Allen, V., 1982, *The Militancy of British Miners*, The Moor Press

Ashforth, A., 1980, 'Reckoning Schemes of Legitimation: On Commissions of Inquiries as Power Knowledge Forms', *Journal of Historical Sociology*, Vol.3, No.1

Ashworth, W., 1986, *The History of the British Coal Industry, Vol.5, 1945–82, The Nationalised Industry*, Oxford University Press

Atkinson, J.H., 1996, 'The Living Landscape Opencast Coal Working', in J. D. Peart and L.A. Rutherford (eds), *A Review of Opencast Coal and its Environmental Impact*, Conference Proceedings, Newcastle upon Tyne Polytechnic

Banks, H.J., 1981, Evidence, *Jobs Hill Public Inquiry*, Crook, Co. Durham

Beck, U., 1990, *Risk Society*, Polity Press

Beynon, H., *The Case for Houghton Main*, ICLS Working Paper, University of Manchester, 1993

Beynon, H. (ed.), 1985, *Digging Deeper: Issues in the 1984–5 Miners' Strike*, Verso

Beynon, H., 1988, 'Regulating Research', in Alan Bryman (ed.), *Doing Research in Organisations*, Routledge

Beynon, H., 1996, 'Material and symbolic relations in the UK coal mining industry', in Birgit Muller (ed.), *A La Recherche des Certitudes Perdues…*, Centre Marc Bloch

Beynon, H. and Austrin, T., 1991, *Masters and Servants: Class and Patronage in the Making of a Labour Organisation*, Rivers Oram Press

Beynon, H. and Hudson, R., 'The End of Old Certainties: Flexible labour market adaptation or social exclusion in the former coal districts of the UK?', *forthcoming*, 2000

Beynon, H., Hudson, R. and Sadler, D.,1994, *A Tale of Two Industries: The Decline of Coal and Steel in North East England*, Open University Press

Bourdieu, P., 1990, *Distinctions*, Polity Press

British Coal Corporation Opencast Executive, 1986, *Opencast Coal—A National Assessment*, BCC, 1986. House of Commons Select Committee on Energy, *First Report*, Session 1986–87—The Coal Industry, Minutes of Evidence, Vol.11, HMSO, British Social Attitudes, 1987, *The 1997 Report*, Gower

Building Research Establishment, 1997, Building Research Establishment, 'Attitudes to Noise', *Digest of Environmental Statistics*,

No.19, HMSO

Burningham, K. and O'Brien, M., 'Global Environmental Values and Local Contexts of Action', *Sociology*, Vol.28, No.4

Burton, F., and P. Carlen, 1979, *Official Discourse: On Discourse Analysis, Government Publications, Ideology and the State*, Routledge

Byrne, P., 1997, *Social Movements in Britain*, Routledge

Coal Information and Consultancy Services Ltd (CICS), 1989, *The British Opencast Coal Industry*

Coates, J. K. and M. Barrett-Brown, 1998, *Coalfield Communities Under Threat*, Spokesman Books Commission on Energy and the Environment (CENE), 1981, *Coal and the Environment*, (Cm) HMSO

Committee on Standards in Public Life, 1997 (Chairman: Lord Nolan), *Third Report: Standards of Conduct in Local Government in England, Scotland and Wales*, HMSO

Countryside Commission, 1993, *Opencast Coal Mining: Advice on Landscape and Countryside Issues*, Advisory Booklet CCP, 434

Cox, A.W., 1987, 'Future Strategies for Coal in the UK', PhD Thesis, University of Newcastle upon Tyne

CPRE, Evidence to the House of Commons Select Committee on Energy,1986, *First Report—Session 1985–6—The Coal Industry: Minutes of Evidence*—Vol.II, HMSO

Department of the Environment and the London Office,1988, *Mineral Planning Guidance Note No.3 (MPG3), Opencast Coal Mining*, HMSO

Department of the Environment and Welsh Office, 1994, *Mineral Planning Guidance Note 3 (MPG3): Coal Mining and Colliery Spoil Disposal*, HMSO

Department of the Environment, 1984, *Circular 3/84, Opencast Coal Mining*, HMSO

Department of the Environment, 1992, PPG 12, *Development Plans—What You Need to Know*

Department of the Environment, 1993, News Release No.212—Interim Planning Guidance for Opencast Coal,

Department of the Environment, *Circular 15/96*, HMSO, London, Annex 5

Department of the Environment, Minerals Division, 1993, *Minerals Planning Guidance—Coal Mining and Colliery Spoil Disposal—Revision of MPG3*—Draft Consultation Document, HMSO

Department of the Environment, Transport and the Regions, 1997, *Consultation Paper: Opencast Coal—Review of Planning Policy*, HMSO

Department of Trade and Industry, 1993, *The Prospects for Coal—Conclusions of the Government's Coal Review*, HMSO, London (CM 2235) HMSO

Dobson, F., 1996, *Opencast Coal Mining—Too High A Price?*, The Labour Party

Fairbrother, P., 1991, *Politics and the State as Employer*, Mansell, 1994

Fairbrother, P., 'In a State of Change: Flexibility in the Civil Service' in A. Pollert (ed.), *Farewell to Flexibility*, Blackwell, Oxford

Formal Investigation under the Merchant Shipping Act (1894), 1997, *Report of Court No.8066*, M.V. Lovat (O.N. 360735), HMSO, London

Glyn, A., 1985, *The Economic Case Against Pit Closures*, National Union of Mineworkers

Goffman, E., 1970, *Where the Action Is*, Allen Lane

Grimshaw, P.N., 1992, 'Sunshine and Success: The First Half-Century of Opencast Coalmining in Britain', *Mine and Quarry*, Jan/Feb

Hancock, J., 1995, *Opencasting in the UK*, McCloskey Coal Information Services Ltd

Hardy, G., 1989, 'Opencast Mining: the Durham Background', in H. Beynon, R. Hudson and A. Cox (eds), *Opencast Mining—The Industry, ESRC Conference Proceedings*, University of Durham

Harvey, Mark, 2000, *The Problem of the State: Taking the Long View*, ICLS Working Paper, University of Manchester

Harvey Wood, 1997, 'The friendly face of mining', *Planning*, 18 April, p.12

Henderson, T., 1996, 'Opencast site reborn as haven for man and nature', *The Journal*, 7 September

Hodges, J., Ladner, W. and Martin, T, 1993, 'Chlorine in Coal: A Review of its Origin and Mode of Occurrence', *Journal of the Institute of Energy*, September

House of Commons Select Committee on Energy, 1986, First Report, Session 1985–6, *The Coal Industry*, Minutes of Evidence, HMSO

House of Commons Select Committee on Energy, 1987, First Report, Session 1986–7, *The Coal Industry*, HMSO

House of Commons Select Committee on Trade and Industry, 1993, First Report—Session 1992–3, *British Energy Policy and the Market for Coal*, HMSO

House of Commons Welsh Affairs Committee, 1991, Second Report—Session 1990–1, *The Future of Opencast Coalmining in Wales*, HMSO

Hudson, R., 1989, *Wrecking a Region*, Pion

Hudson, R., and Cox, A.W., 1990, *British Coal and Opencast Mining*, ESRC Discussion Paper No.9, University of Durham

Hudson, R., Peck, F. and Sadler, D., 1985, *Undermining Easington*, Durham University

Hudson, R. and Sadler, D., 1987, 'Manufactured in the UK? Special steels, motor vehicles and the politics of industrial decline', *Capital and Class*, 32

Jamison, A., Eyerman, R. and Cramer, J.,1990, *The Making of the New Environmental Consciousness*, Edinburgh University Press

Leddy, S., 1991, 'Planning Applications: Talking them through', *Mine & Quarry*, Vol.20, No.11

McIlroy, John and Sallie Westwood, 1993, *Border Country: Raymond Williams in Adult Education*, National Institute of Adult and Continuing

Education
Marsh, A., 1977, *Protest and Political Consciousness*, Sage
Melucci, A., 1989, *Nomads of the Present*, Hutchinson, Radius
Offe, C., 1985, 'New Social Movements: Challenging the boundaries of institutional politics', *Social Research 817–868*
Pakulski, J., 1991, *Social Movements: The Politics of Moral Protest*, Longman
Parker, M., 1996, 'UK Fossil-Fuel Reserves: Are We Running Out?', *Oxera*
Parker, M.,1997, *Privatised Goal—Facing the End of the Contracts*, Oxford Economic Research Associates
Parry, G., Moyser, G. and Day, D., 1992, *Political Participation and Democracy in Britain*, Cambridge University Press
Powell, D., 1993, *The Power Game: The Struggle for Coal*, Duckworth
PRATT, A.J., 1989, *Opencast—Casting a Shadow: The Social and Environmental Effects of Opencast Coal Mining*, Durham Area Miners' Support Group
Richardson, M., Sherman, J. and Gismondi, M., 1993, *Winning Back the Words; Confronting Experts in an Environmental Public Hearing*, Garamond Press, Toronto
Rowell, Andrew, 1996, *Green Backlash: Global Subversion of the Environmental Movement*, Routledge
Sustainable Development—The UK Strategy, 1994 (Cm 2426), HMSO
Schumpeter, J. (1934), *The Theory of Economic Development*, Harvard University Press
Scott, A., 1990, *Ideology and the New Social Movements*, Unwin Hyman
The Efficiency Unit, 1991, *Making the Most of Next Steps: The Management of Minister's Departments and their Executive Agencies* (The Fraser Report), HMSO
The Planning Inspectorate, 1995, *Business and Corporate Plan, 1995/96—1998/99*, HMSO
The Scottish Office, Planning Division, Development Department, 1997, *Review of Opencast Coal Mining Operations in Scotland*, RSK Environmental Ltd
The Town and Country Planning, 1988 (Inquiries Procedure) *Rules*, HMSO, SI, 1988, No.944
The Town and Country Planning Appeals, 1988 (Determination by Inspectors) (Inquiries Procedure) *Rules*, HMSO, SI 1988, No.945, HMSO
Town and Country Planning Association, Evidence to the House of Commons Select Committee on Energy, 1986, First Report—Session 1985–86—*The Coal Industry: Minutes of Evidence*—Volume II, HMSO,
Trade and Industry Committee, 1998, *Coal: Volume 1*, HMSO
Trigg, A.B. and Dubourg, W.R., 1993, Opencast Discussion Papers in Economics No.1/1993, 'Valuing the Environmental Impacts of Opencast Coalmining—The Case of the Trent Valley in North Staffordshire', The Open University, Faculty of Social Science

Weeland Road Opencast Coal Public Inquiry, 1996, *Inspector's Report*

Welsh Office Circular 13/84, 1983, *Opencast Coal Mining*, HMSO

White Paper, 1983, *Coal and the Environment*, The Government's response to the Commission on Energy and the Environment's Report on Coal and the Environment (Cmnd 8877), HMSO, London

White Paper, 1985, *Lifting the Burden* (Cmnd 9571), HMSO, London

White Paper, 1990, *This Common Inheritance—Britain's Environmental Strategy* (Cmnd 1200), HMSO

Willis, K. G., Nelson, G. B., Bye, A. B. and Peacock, G., 1993, 'An Application of the Krutilla-Fisher Model to Appraising the Benefits of Green Belt Preservation versus Site Development', *Journal of Environmental Planning and Management*, Vol.36, No.1

Winterton, J. and Winterton, R., 1989, *Coal, Crisis and Conflict: The 1984–85 Miners' strike in Yorkshire*, Manchester University Press

INDEX